anglistik & englischunterricht

Rhetoric and Representation

Rhetoric and Representation

The British at War

Verantwortliche Herausgeber
für den thematischen Teil des Bandes:
Gabriele Linke und Holger Rossow

UNIVERSITÄTSVERLAG WINTER
HEIDELBERG

Gabriele Linke · Erwin Otto · Holger Rossow
Gerd Stratmann · Merle Tönnies (Hg.)

anglistik & englischunterricht

Band 70

Rhetoric and Representation

The British at War

UNIVERSITÄTSVERLAG WINTER
HEIDELBERG

Bibliografische Information der Deutschen Nationalbibliothek
Die Deutsche Nationalibliothek verzeichnet diese Publikation
in der Deutschen Nationalbibliografie;
detaillierte bibliografische Daten sind im Internet
über *http://dnb.ddb.de* abrufbar.

Herausgeber:
Prof. Dr. Gabriele Linke
Dr. Erwin Otto · Dr. Holger Rossow · Prof. Dr. Gerd Stratmann
Prof. Dr. Merle Tönnies

ISBN 978-3-8253-5390-2
ISSN 0344-8266

Anschrift der Redaktion:
Universität Rostock, Institut für Anglistik und Amerikanistik
18051 Rostock

© 2007. Universitätsverlag Winter GmbH Heidelberg
Imprimé en Allemagne · Printed in Germany
Druck: Memminger Medienzentrum AG, 87700 Memmingen
Gedruckt auf umweltfreundlichem, chlorfrei gebleichtem und alterungsbeständigem Papier
Den Verlag erreichen Sie im Internet unter: www.winter-verlag-hd.de

Contents

Gabriele Linke and Holger Rossow (Rostock)

Introduction

1. The Context

A common European boast claims that since the Second World War, Europe has been enjoying the longest period of peace in the last four hundred years, which has had it prosper like never before. But has Europe been at peace while vicious wars raged on other continents? And what about the United Kingdom with its past as a colonial power and its special relationship with the United States? The wars in the Balkans in the 1990s and currently in Afghanistan and Iraq are only the most recent and most publicly debated cases of British involvement in military actions world-wide. Although the British, like the rest of the European Union, seem to live in times of peace, they have in practice been at war somewhere else in the world most of the time, besides their armed struggles for a solution of the Irish question within the UK. Military actions of British troops have always left their marks on British society and culture; some were formative, such as the Second World War, others were fought in passing with rather indirect effects on Britain, and others again ignited flaming controversies among the British public.

Very quickly, battles and wars pass into memory, become either forgotten or memorialised, and new wars, political and ideological wars, break out on the control over memory and meaning. Memories of past wars keep recurring, images and ideas keep being revived and recycled, serving diverse political and cultural purposes. Quite often, memories of past wars have been utilised as part of complex identity politics as, for example, the English wars against Scotland and Ireland and the British colonial wars, which served to unify Britain through, and in, confrontation with the colonial Other.

British society has always been concerned with questions of war and peace in the past as much as today. These concerns range from foreign policy decisions like the one about Britain joining the United States in their war in Iraq to war as a popular theme in entertainment, such as war films. Furthermore, wars have an essential commercial aspect. But not only the wars themselves are driven by business interests – representations of wars can also be sold profitably. Even just a superficial look reveals how much wars have become part of the marketplace, have been made into popular media products, wrapped in exciting leisure activities and fitted into easy-to-remember story formats. The British-produced documentary series *Colour of War/In Colour*, for example, turned into a "huge global money spinner", whose cumulative export sales from 1999 exceeded 11 million dollar in 2004, and its best-selling part, *D-Day in Colour*, was sold to 75 countries.[1] To pick another random example, in September 2005, the Imperial War Museum offered a "Drop-in art activity" under the motto "Turn tanks into dinosaurs and aircraft into insects", passing on to children knowledge about war machinery embedded in playful creative activities.[2] In the hands-on exhibition "Great Escapes", visitors can look at some of the "ingenious and audacious escape attempts made by Allied prisoners of war during the Second World War" and get a chance to win an original prop from the award-winning film *Chicken Run*.[3] The exhibitions and activities of the high-culture Imperial War Museum deliberately cross over to popular culture, media and, through oral history, folk culture. The Museum makes a strong effort to stabilise a national consensus on Britain's past wars, especially supporting the ideological claim that the Second World War was a people's war.[4] The Museum's *What's On* booklet buzzes with phrases such as "remarkable time", "fascinating reality", "first-hand experience", British "ingenuity", "past", "present", "future" and "the whole nation".[5] These phrases indicate current attitudes towards the representation of the British at war. Past wars are presented as accessible and relevant experiences and as great facilitators of the unity of that "imagined political community" of Great Britain. Such representations also express the dominant culture's interest in employing memories and other aspects of war in their effort to maintain consensus and stability. Images of war pervade all media, not only TV programmes and newspapers but also children's books, video and computer games and the Internet. Discourses and themes of war can be found in all spheres of British culture. This situation prompted the selection of "war" as the topic for the 16th British Cultural Studies Conference, which was held in Rostock from 17 to 19 November 2005.

2. War Studies – Peace Studies – Cultural Studies

Traditionally, wars have been the subject of military and political science. War Studies are taught at the Royal Military Academy Sandhurst, where the academic syllabus comprises military logistics, military – media relations, the history of military doctrine, current issues such as the modern Iraqi army and many other themes.[6]

Nevertheless, War Studies in Britain today are not at all confined to the military academy but have also become institutionalised at a number of British universities. King's College in London has a strong Department of War Studies, which is a multi-disciplinary institution with a leaning towards Politics and International Studies. The University of Glasgow possesses a Scottish Centre for War Studies, established in 1996, which claims to offer an opportunity "to study war in all its aspects".[7] A Scottish perspective is also provided when, for example, the need for an Independent Scottish Defence Force is considered.[8] Other universities such as the University of Kent at Canterbury[9] as well as the Universities of Aberdeen[10] and Wolverhampton offer degrees in War Studies, emphasising their broad interdisciplinary approach and including the effects of war on society and culture in their programmes.[11] War Studies in this context are no longer the study of warfare alone but of propaganda material, films and literature.[12] The website of the University of Kent that advertises their War Studies Degree emphasises, i.e. puts in bold face, the idea that "[w]ar is often thought to be the engine of change in human activity from political structures to society, economics, technology and science".[13] This programmatic statement suggests that there, War Studies take a wide but not necessarily critical approach. Although warfare and its history still play an important role, the teaching and research done in these departments go beyond the purely military aspects and aim primarily at "appreciation and comprehension" of the complex nature of war, humankind's attitude to it and its effects on society and literature.[14]

9

Much later than War Studies and from a different direction, Peace Studies have developed as a response to the wars of the 20th century.[15] The *Journal of Conflict Resolution* first appeared in the 1950s, and the Richardson Institute at the University of Lancaster was established as the first peace research centre in Britain in 1959. It aims to promote a better understanding of the conditions of peaceful change, not only through research into peace-building and conflict resolution but also through teaching practical skills of conflict analysis and peace-making.[16] The Desmond Tutu Centre for War and Peace Studies at Liverpool Hope University was founded as late as 2004; it is an ecumenical Christian foundation[17] while the Richardson Institute was initiated by Quakers.

Peace Studies as a modern academic field have not reached the same degree of institutionalisation and popularity as War Studies, which look back on a long tradition, if under different names and with different, i.e. mainly military, contents and objectives. The University of Bradford features in its School of Social and International Studies a Department of Peace Studies that runs degree courses. Like the Christian institutes, the programme offers practical training besides research and teaching, reaches out across borders and works with NGOs. Like War Studies, Peace Studies are multidisciplinary, employ a wide range of methods and have no homogeneous theory, but there has been some agreement, for example, on elements of peace such as a balance of power, minimal welfare, national sovereignty, international justice and human rights.[18] They also address wars as a form of violent intergroup conflict[19] and analyse the causes and consequences of war and conflicts. In this context, research on war, through a better comprehension of its complex nature, serves the development of strategies that help resolve conflicts before, while and after they turn violent. Peace Studies tend to adopt a global perspective but take local conflicts equally seriously. The study of representations of war plays a rather minor role in a field that values social practice most highly. The *International Journal of Peace Studies*[20] reflects this profile. Articles cover a wide range of different conflicts such as ethnic conflicts and the 'war on terror' as well as theoretical issues such as the usefulness of neo-Marxist approaches.

The question now is how studies on war within the framework of Cultural Studies relate to War Studies and Peace Studies. The field of Cultural Studies has developed in Britain since the 1950s and been taken up by German scholars of English since the late 1980s. It was established as an academic field in its own right in Britain in the 1960s[21] and in Germany in the late 1990s. It draws strongly on the methods and theories of Sociology, Ethnography/Anthropology, Media Studies, History and Literary Studies, and it has been characterised by (and criticised for) its heterogeneous set of approaches.[22] It shares this methodological and theoretical heterogeneity with War Studies and Peace Studies, but its subject area is much broader and war is just one, and a rather marginal, field. The Cultural Studies approach is furthermore marked by a wide concept of culture that includes everyday, popular and folk cultures and an emphasis on representation. It questions the line between high and low literature and values the texts and images of mass media and new media as representations of power structures and carriers of social meaning and ideology.

With regard to Cultural Studies, the lack of methodological homogeneity and of a unifying theory has been seen as both strength and weakness. It is a weakness if one expects Cultural Studies to be a clearly defined academic discipline with distinctive methods and theories because such expectations are not fulfilled. Its strength is that it allows scholars from different fields to come together and investigate an aspect of culture from numerous different perspectives, thus revealing the complexity and the underlying power structures of any field of culture. Central categories in such cultural analyses are, for example, gender, race and ethnicity, class, identity and difference, ideology and hegemony. On the one hand, textual analysis and a focus on the discursive construction of meaning especially in the mass media have played a central role in Cultural Studies; on the other hand, eminent Cultural Studies scholars like, for example, Stuart Hall, understood themselves as agents of social change and emphasised that their research should have an impact on society, taking side with the repressed, advocating social justice, laying bare the mechanisms of domination and criticising the media's struggle to maintain a pro-capitalist consensus and, to use Gramsci's preferred term, bourgeois hegemony. This sets Cultural Studies apart from War Studies, where such practical and critical goals and ideological leanings are rather rare. Rather, Cultural Studies researchers share their interest in social justice and the revelation of power structures with Peace Studies although the interest in questions of representation and ideology is more characteristic of Cultural Studies.

Thus a Cultural Studies conference produces its very own treatment of a socio-cultural issue and a mixture of approaches which is quite different from what can be heard at traditional conferences of historians or literary scholars. For the student of British culture, present and past wars hold innumerable issues worth exploring. Several contributions in this volume turn to representations of war in popular culture and mass media (Dornhofer, Paris, Schneider, Starck, Summerfield). The approaches vary greatly: some employ sociological and ethnographic methods and theories (Starck, Summerfield) and address questions of gender (Paris, Summerfield). Others concentrate on the realm of representation and analyse texts on wars as symbolic negotiations of power (Dornhofer, Paris, Rossow, Starck). Political discourses on war, past and present, are another area well-covered (Berg, Rossow, Schmidt-Kilb). Issues of memory and how past human experience is passed on to successive generations in textbooks and museums is also a subject of critical analysis (Teske), as is how representation – of war and peace – and the construction of meaning work in the field of music (Möller). It becomes obvious that the exciting new insights typically come from the analyses of representations and discourses and not so much from new documentary sources that would be explored to add details to the history of events.

Having said this, it must be emphasised again that there are areas in which War Studies, Peace Studies, History and Cultural Studies overlap when they investigate Britain at war. In the German context, recent publications such as *Der Krieg im Bild – Bilder vom Krieg*[23] defy any attempts at their straightforward classification in that, although primarily historical publications, they include popular culture and mass media and also draw on semiotics, which suggests a closeness to Cultural Studies.

3. The Contributions

Michael Paris, in his article on the pleasures of war, 1850-1914, discusses how popular culture, especially popular literature, shaped British attitudes towards war up to the eve of the First World War.

His starting point is the contradiction between the British self-image as a great peacemaker and creator of the 19th century Pax Britannica and the sudden enthusiasm for war at the outbreak of the First World War. Paris traces the roots of the enthusiasm of 1914 back to the popular literature, especially that for boys, of the early 19th century and the increasingly explicit depiction of violence in literature such as colonial war stories and boys' military adventure stories. Paris' study is based on substantial research on images of war in British popular culture through time, which enables him to trace lines of ideological continuity between the mid-19th century and 1914.

Daniel Dornhofer establishes connections between academic historical debates in the 1970s and 80s and political strands of popular music, especially punk music. On the example of the appropriation of the Levellers' tradition by left, Marxist-influenced punk bands such as The Clash, he shows how the Civil War and the ideals as well as the defeat of the radical democratic wing of the Revolution serve as a historical allegory for the defeat of socialist ideals in the 1970s and the Thatcher years. The article illustrates how different spheres of discourse such as academic history and rock lyrics are intertwined thematically and how both reinterpret and make use of the past in the light of current political interest.

Penny Summerfield writes about the role of women in the Second World War. This issue has been described and discussed in various places but often received superficial and simplifying treatment, often one-sidedly emphasising the liberating effect new wartime roles had on many women.[24] Summerfield, nevertheless, takes an approach that looks not so much at gender differences or mechanisms of oppression but rather at the heterogeneity of the social group of women. She points out the contradictions and complexity of the process of women's integration in war work and the auxiliary armed forces. She emphasises the diversity of women's responses, which include not only a widely shared pleasure in the new autonomy but also show many women clinging to traditional symbols of femininity. But Summerfield finds diversity also in another field, that is, in the different forms and degrees of women's integration. She establishes differences not only between war work and the auxiliary armed forces but also between different industries and between the different branches of the military forces, from the Royal Navy to the Home Army.

Doris Teske approaches the issue of war from a rather practical perspective as she looks at the teaching of the two World Wars in British schools and the didactic principles that have guided the authors of recent British textbooks on the subject. She inspects three textbooks, two museum exhibitions (Imperial War Museum and IWM North) and several institutional web sites that provide material on the World Wars for educational purposes. Her starting points are commonly established paths of teaching and learning about the wars, especially the traditional teaching of facts and figures. She emphasises that recently textbooks and educational exhibitions have sought to find ways of allowing the younger generation access to the experience of past wars rather than providing factual information. Such paths of access are mainly narratives and material objects, plus a new trend towards the virtualisation of access to objects and experience.

Compared with the two World Wars, the Suez Crisis of 1954 does not count as a major war of the 20th century. Nevertheless, it has been widely acknowledged that it was a landmark event on Britain's road towards the loss of its Empire and its influence as a global player. Christian Schmidt-Kilb re-evaluates the event from two discursive fields. Firstly, he inspects critically how Prime Minister Eden tried, with the help of the British press, to make this war another 'people's war'. With excerpts from Eden's correspondence with Eisenhower, he highlights how Eden's imperial aspirations get turned down by the U.S. and how Eden and the press opportunistically change their position under the pressure of the circumstances. Thereby he confirms historians' view that the Suez Crisis sealed Britain's loss of its role as the greatest world power to the United States. Schmidt-Kilb further supports his argument that the Suez Crisis can be read as a turning point in British mentality by reference to a literary work that is set at the time of the Crisis. He argues that Kazuo Ishiguro's *Remains of the Day* constructs that time as one when the feeling grew that the Old England with its values was waning and Americans were appropriating the traditional symbols of power.

The question under which conditions international military interference in another sovereign country is justified, which was strongly raised in the Suez Crisis, remains a central theme into the 21st century. The wars in the Balkans in the 1990s were a historical moment in which this question was raised again with urgency. The two contributions that deal with the Balkan wars do so with the help of very different textual bases, but both come to some very similar conclusions. While Thomas Schneider analyses the British TV Programme *Warriors* with regard to its representation of the British role in the Bosnian war, Holger Rossow inspects New Labour's political rhetoric in the Kosovo conflict. Both analyses conclude with the finding that the simplistic pattern of a clearly defined dichotomy of 'good' and 'evil' (politicians/militias/ethno-religious groups, etc.) still dominates the public discourse with regard to the military conflicts Britain has become involved in. They show how this rhetorical device has been employed in different media and genres but has always served to justify military action. It becomes clear that this pattern of good/evil is not an American predilection but proves equally common – and potent – in British politics and media. The second point of agreement is that the question when military interference in another sovereign state is justified has been raised again by the Balkan wars and demanded new, or modified, answers. Both studies show that the ethical implications of interference came to play a central role in British political and TV discourses.

Nevertheless, the two studies vary in their assessment of these rhetorical moves. While Schneider, in the TV programme he analyses and in other films, finds that the application of the schema of good and evil and the emphasis on the ethical dilemmas faced by the peacekeeping forces combine into an implicit argument for full-scale military interference. Rossow, on the other hand, points out that the altruistic, ethical motives for military interference do not exclude, and are not devalued by, an additional motive of self-interest.

The next contribution to this volume deals with an internal British conflict. The conflict between Britain and Ireland has assumed qualities of a war again and again throughout the last five centuries, and the situation in Northern Ireland can only be understood in the context of the ongoing conflict between republican and unionist forces. Kathleen Starck turns to the sphere of representation to shed light on recent history and the current situation. She chooses the famous Belfast murals as a key to a better understanding of the state of mind of the two sides in the conflict, unionist Protestants and republican Catholics, and of the community structure in a divided city such as Belfast. Although murals can be found in almost every modern city, the ones in Belfast and other Northern Irish cities have acquired unusual fame as symbols of the Northern Ireland conflict, as weapons in the struggle over space and boundaries and as elements of popular culture, the culture of the streets and of popular music through their role in the Cranberries' music video "Zombie".

Starck starts with an overview on the history of the murals and goes on to discuss the differences between loyalist and republican murals, especially with regard to symbols, conventions and change. In the ensuing argumentation, she combines the analysis of representations with an ethnographic approach that looks at the social context of these representations and their place in social practices. She describes in detail the functions the murals have in their respective communities and the Northern Ireland conflict, emphasising their potential for creating unity, identity and community. She illustrates the connection between murals, the symbolic construction of social spaces and questions of power. Employing aspects of theories of rituals, she argues that murals can be read as rituals since they embody ritual qualities on the levels of production, object and reception. The most convincing parts of her argument concern the function of the murals on both sides as sites of the construction of identity, social boundaries and community and, secondly, the differences between loyalist murals, which appear to be conservative, stagnant, backward-looking, and their republican counterparts, which are much more creative, evolving and forward-looking. This study interprets murals as product and cultural process in a wider framework of the Northern Irish struggles for power, resources and territory.

Sebastian Berg's contribution does not deal with military conflict as such but with the effects the British involvement in the post-9/11 'war on terror' has had on official British attitudes towards multiculturalism and the integration of Muslim ethnic groups. Through analysing statements from both Britain's white mainstream society and British Muslims, Berg shows convincingly that 9/11 and its aftermath have suggested a logic of homogenisation and dichotomies on both sides. He argues that in the atmosphere the 'war on terror' created, Islamophobia and 'Westophobia' have blossomed and the belief in the compatibility of different cultures has been shattered for many people on both sides. Since the 'war against terror' turned into a war against states, a war in which Muslims were killed by, among others, British soldiers, the political climate in Britain has deteriorated and multiculturalism has fallen from grace with many people in Britain. This study, which turns to the most recent wars and their effects on British society, concludes the volume. Although dominant themes of the British academic discourses on war such as the two World Wars and the Northern Irish conflict are amply represented among the topics of this issue, the papers dealing with these topics provide new perspectives, and several contributions turn to less well-researched wars, aspects of wars and texts.

4. Representations of War and Peace in the EFL Classroom

Since the series *a & e* pursues the goal of linking current issues in British and American Studies with the teaching of English, our concluding remarks will point out ways in which this volume can inspire teachers who want to address the issue of Britain at war in the English language classroom. Wars have often been watersheds in history and triggered social change, and 20th century wars have been extremely well documented with large amounts of diverse visual and textual materials. Therefore, they lend themselves readily as starting points for the teaching of British culture and for raising questions about war and society that have to be addressed by every generation anew. The two World Wars have also shaped the stereotypes that the older generation in Britain hold with regard to Germans and that many Germans have been confronted with on their visits to Britain. The potential of this kind of cultural material for the EFL classroom has already received some attention.[25]

Especially Doris Teske's article offers a wealth of ideas to the English teacher, not just through the textbooks, museums and web sites she discusses but also through her general reflections on access to historical experience and on authenticity. Nevertheless, other articles may equally inspire the teacher. Dornhofer's choice of punk lyrics sets an example as to how rock lyrics can be related to their historical political context and interpreted with regard to the political messages they convey. Furthermore, some of the wartime films that Summerfield refers to in her argument on women's integration are available on video cassette or DVD. They provide excellent material for teaching the historical specificity of gender images and the tremendous changes that gender images have undergone since the Second World War.

Schneider's discussion of TV programmes on the Bosnian war can very well inform critical classroom interpretations of TV programmes on wars. Since many of Tony Blair's speeches are available on the Internet, they offer themselves for rhetorical analysis. They are readily accessible and may, as Rossow shows in his article, provide material for controversial discussions and simultaneously highlight certain aspects of British politics.

The theme of war is generally well-suited for cultural comparison with regard to, for example, German and British experiences in times of war, gender images, TV programmes on war, history books and museum exhibitions. If this volume can inspire some critical thinking on wars and their representations, the project of Cultural Studies has proved useful once more.

Notes

1 Cf. a note in *Broadcast,* 1 April 2005.

2 Imperial War Museum: *What's On, July – September 2005*, 4.

3 *Ibid.*, 6.

4 The myth of the Second World War as the people's war has its roots in the mobilisation of vast sections of the British population and was later reinforced by some historians, e.g. Angus Calder: *The Myth of the Blitz*, London, 1991, and criticised by others, e.g. Philip Ziegler: *London at War, 1939-1945*. London, 2002, pp. 163-78.

5 *Ibid.*, 3-10.

6 Royal Military Academy Sandhurst: "The Department of War Studies" <http://www.sandhurst.mod.uk/academic/ws.htm, 2007 – 23 March 2007>.

7 Scottish Centre for War Studies: "About the Scottish Centre for War Studies." <http://www2.arts.gla.ac.uk/History/Warstud/html/about.htm, 2007 – 23 March 2007>.

8 In its section "Publications", the Scottish Centre for War Studies advertises an *Occasional Paper* by Jack Hawthorn under the title *Some Thoughts on an Independent Scottish Defence Force*. Cf. <http://www2.arts.gla.ac.uk/History/Warstud/html/publications.htm, last updated 3 May 2005 – 23 March 2007>.

9 At the University of Kent, War Studies are taught at the History Department; cf. University of Kent: "War Studies Degree",

<http://www.kent.ac.uk/history/prosp-undergrad/War/Index.htm, last updated 8 March 2007 – 23 March 2007>.

10 "Conflict and Security Studies Programme: War Studies", <http:abdn.ac.uk/pir/css/warstud.hti, last updated 1 March 2004 – 23 March 2007).

11 Cf. *ibid.* and the University of Kent: "War Studies Degree".

12 This applies, for example, to the programmes in Aberdeen, Canterbury and Kings College, London.

13 Cf. University of Kent: "War Studies Degree".

14 Cf. "Conflict and Security Studies Programme: War Studies".

15 The roots of Peace Studies reach back into the early 19th century when the unavoidability of wars was first questioned. Especially in the USA, pacifism grew in the Progressive Era and around the First World War, of which the Carnegie Endowment for International Peace, established in New York in 1919, is an example. Nevertheless, Peace Studies as an academic field took its shape mainly after the Second World War.

16 The Richardson Institute: "Home" <http://wwwq.lancs.ec.uk/depts/richinst/ – 23 March 2007>.

17 Cf. Desmond Tutu Centre for War and Peace Studies: "Mission Statement" <http://www.hope.ac.uk/research/warandpeace/statement.htm – 23 March 2007>.

18 For the connection between peace and international justice, see, for example, Johan Galtung: *Peace by Peaceful Means: Peace and Conflict, Development and Civilization*, London, 1996.

19 *Ibid.*

20 The *International Journal of Peace Studies* permits free online access under <http://www.gmu.edu/academic/ijps/>.

21 The seminal Birmingham Centre for Cultural Studies, which did seminal work, was established in 1964; cf. Graeme Turner: *British Cultural Studies. An Introduction,* 2nd ed., London, 1996, pp. 70-4.

22 For a brief introduction to Cultural Studies, see, for example, Kathryn Woodward (Ed.): *Identity and Difference,* London, 1997 and Graeme Turner. For a critique of Cultural Studies, see Ansgar Nünning: "Literatur, Mentalitäten und kulturelles Gedächtnis: Grundriss, Leitbegriffe und Perspektiven einer anglistischen Kulturwissenschaft". – In Ansgar Nünning (Ed.): *Literatur-wissenschaftliche Theorien, Methoden und Modelle: Eine Einführung,* Trier, 1995, pp. 173-5.

23 Arbeitskreis Historische Bildforschung (Ed.): *Der Krieg im Bild – Bilder vom Krieg*, Frankfurt a.M. *et al.*, 2003.

24 A typical example is Diana Souhami: *A Woman's Place: The Changing Picture of Women in Britain*, Harmondsworth, 1986, pp. 34–50.

25 Christoph Ehland & Thomas Leuerer: "'Don't mention the war': Fawlty Towers, the 'Funny Walk' and the Anglo-German Relationship in the EFL-

Classroom". – In Walter Delanoy & Laurenz Volkmann (Eds.): *Cultural Studies in the EFL Classroom*, Heidelberg, 2006, pp. 155-69.

Michael Paris (Preston, Lancashire)

Deeds of Pluck and Daring.
The Pleasures of War and British Popular Culture, 1850-1914

When Britain's ultimatum to Germany expired on 4 August 1914, the government's subsequent declaration of war was greeted with enormous public enthusiasm; almost everyone was caught up in the excitement of the moment. There were spontaneous demonstrations of patriotism across the nation, and in the first year alone, some two-and-a-half million men volunteered for the armed forces. Those who were too young solemnly told the recruiting sergeants they were over eighteen, and those who were too old put a spring in their step and equally lied about their age. Reading the letters and memoirs of those men now, one is struck by just how desperate they were to get into the fight. Their greatest anxiety was not that they might be killed or maimed, but that the war would be over before they got to France and into battle. For a liberal society that had long professed its pacifist intent or shown little sympathy for military affairs, this enthusiasm for war clearly requires explanation.

In a seminal essay, published in 1971, Olive Anderson identified a curious phenomenon in mid-Victorian Britain that she called 'Christian Militarism'. This first emerged within the Evangelical movement and gradually permeated the Anglican Church. Essentially Anderson argued that militant Christian zealots sought to turn the British army into an instrument to assist the spread of Christianity, and which in the process began to militarize British society. In 1978, Anne Summers took this further and, by examining popular youth movements, the Rifle Volunteers and the manner in which military heroes were valorized, argued that late Victorian society was actually rife with a "popular militarism".[1] Since then, it has gradually been accepted by most scholars that beneath a veneer of liberal progressivism, Victorian Britain was in fact a highly militarized society, which actively promoted the martial spirit and used war as a deliberate policy for the expansion of empire and the extension of trade. This paper explores one dimension of this popular militarism; it examines how war was made acceptable to the general public and how the martial spirit was promoted among young males through popular culture.

The Victorians were fascinated by war. Throughout the period, and particularly after the 1850s, war became an important theme in popular culture as sanitized representations of battle and the brutality of the imperial warrior were turned into romantic and exciting copy for those at home. The 'war story' was manifested in so many guises that it might well be best described as a 'pleasure culture of war' – heroic representations of war which provided enthralling entertainment for many Victorians.[2] From mid-century, these 'pleasures' were disseminated through virtually every channel of popular culture in forms that were appropriate for diverse audiences, and especially through literary narratives. There was, for example, the poetry of Sir Francis Doyle which proclaimed the gallant exploits of Britain's red-coated heroes in their little wars of empire, and which almost certainly inspired the young Rudyard Kipling to focus similar attention on the common soldier. The poetry of war, perhaps, reached its zenith in the popular anthologies glorifying the romance of past wars like W. E. Henley's *Lyra Heroica* (1897), or *The Imperial Reciter*, edited by Sir Alfred Miles (1900), and which became almost mandatory reading for young middle-class males. Readers might equally immerse themselves in a fantasy world of chivalric medieval warriors powerfully evoked in the historical novels of Sir Walter Scott, particularly in *Ivanhoe* (1820) and *Quentin Durwood* (1823). Or perhaps in Charles Kingsley's immensely popular novel *Westward Ho!* – a tale of the bloody adventures of Elizabethan seamen, or the Peninsula War novels of "Harry Lorrequer" (Charles Lever). For the more serious minded, there was a seemingly endless stream of soldier's memoirs published throughout the century and which detailed virtually every one of the nation's conflicts. And for the ever increasing number of readers lower down the social scale, there were cheaply-produced anonymous war stories with their garish images of battle published as penny-part novels, such as *For Valour: or, How I won the Victoria Cross* (1880) and *The King's Hussars* (1879).

Throughout the period, military displays and parades held considerable fascination for a public anxious to be entertained by martial display. Even routine army manoeuvres were often conducted under the gaze of civilians looking for vicarious thrills from these 'war games'. As one commentator noted of the large-scale exercises at Chobam Camp, in 1853, the spectacle proved "as popular [with the public] as the Great Exhibition".[3] The army itself was very much a 'theatrical' institution: uniforms, parades, displays, flags and stirring music were all part of a spectacle designed to arouse the soldier to courageous acts and intimidate the enemy, but at home such activities were regarded by the public as entertainment and were enormously popular. It was but a short step, then, from the people's enjoyment of this kind of military spectacle to that of enjoying the entertainment of war – it was, after all, just another spectacle and vitally important to the continued prosperity of the nation. Nor was this enjoyment completely passive for after 1859, adult males were not simply limited to watching these exciting pageants but could actually take part and act out their martial fantasies as part-time soldiers in the Rifle Volunteers. Men from all social classes eagerly donned the often outlandishly flamboyant uniforms (usually purchased at the individual's own expense) of the Riflemen and basked in the reflected glory of Victoria's martial heroes with none of the discomfort or danger of the professional soldier. The Volunteers, of course, were initially created because of the fear of a French invasion, but while that crisis soon passed, the Volunteers, never mustering less than 200,000 men annually, remained active until the force was absorbed into the Territorial Army in 1908.[4] Clearly, then, while few men were anxious to serve in the Regular Army, playing at war during their leisure hours was a pleasurable pastime for a significant number of Victorian males. The satisfaction gained from play-acting such a vigorous, more atavistic role, may well have been a reaction to routine domesticity.

Theatrical producers, anxious to exploit the public appetite for war-based entertainment, were quick to stage dramas that reconstructed the latest wars or campaigns. In the 1850s, for example, productions based on the contemporary events of the Crimean War and the Indian Mutiny such as *The Storming of the Malakoff and the Redan* (Manchester Belle Vue, 1855) or *The Capture of Delhi* (Astley's Theatre in Birmingham, 1858) proved highly successful with audiences, who cheered as plucky Britons defeated their Russian foes and ladies screamed in alarm, as the barbarous sepoy mutineers were hurled from the battlements of a cardboard Delhi to meet their just deserts on the rocks below. Throughout the later part of the century, public entertainments, including dioramas and the spectacular open-air pyrodramas, which took contemporary wars as their subject matter, attracted large enthusiastic audiences. By the beginning of the twentieth century, cinematography began to gradually usurp the place of theatre as the main purveyor of the 'theatre of war', and by 1900, audiences were being entertained by short narrative films set against the backdrop of the South African war like *The Sneaky Boer* or *The Attack on the Red Cross Tent*, while music hall audiences happily joined in the chorus of songs that paid tribute to the nation's military heroes such as Colonel Fred Burnaby, killed at Abu Klea in 1885,

> Burnaby the valiant
> Who made a right good stand
> And died a British warrior
> With his good sword in his hand.[5]

From the mid-nineteenth century, newspapers and illustrated magazines featured a new style of reporting war, the work of a new breed of reporters, the war correspondents. The public, eager for news of the latest imperial campaigns, scanned these dramatic reports and battlefield illustrations for exciting deeds of daring. And while readers and correspondents alike appeared to agree that war was indeed a 'dreadful thing', in column after column battle was always described in the most exciting and romantic terms. Bennett Burleigh's dispatch from the battlefield at Colenso in 1899 was typical of such reports:

> It seemed impossible that anything could face and live in that fire [...]. Our indomitable soldiers walked erect and straight onward. Not Rome in her palmiest days ever possessed more devoted sons. As the gladiators marched proud and beaming to meet death, so the British soldiers doomed to die saluted, and then, and with alacrity, stepped forward to do their duty – glory or the grave.[6]

At home, such reports made thrilling reading over the morning marmalade, and prompted the young and unusually cynical

Rudyard Kipling to claim of the campaign to save General Gordon, in his 1902 novel *The Light That Failed*, that correspondents "sweated and toiled" along with the soldiers for, "[i]t was above all things necessary that England at breakfast should be amused and thrilled and interested, whether Gordon lived or died, or half the British army went to pieces in the sand."[7] The people "have no arenas now", he noted, likening imperial Britain to her Roman predecessor, but imperial warfare provided an exciting and often equally gory substitute, and it was the war correspondent that ministered to this "blind, brutal, bestial thirst for blood".[8] Throughout the period, then, war and the exploits of the nation's warrior heroes provided exciting entertainment for the Victorians: a pleasure culture of war, which offered romantic, escapist fictions through which ordinary citizens might temporarily forget the mundane routine of everyday life and indulge in heroic male fantasies.

The pleasure culture of war was not, however, a Victorian creation but a legacy of the past. In the eighteenth century, war, as Linda Colley has pointed out, was the midwife of national unity. The hundred years of warfare that ended with Waterloo was the period that witnessed the creation of the modern nation. Great Britain, she has explained,

> was an invention forged above all by war. Time and time again, war with France brought Britons, whether they hailed from Wales or Scotland or England, into confrontation with an obviously hostile Other and encouraged them to define themselves collectively against it. They defined themselves as Protestants struggling for survival against the world's foremost Catholic powers.[9]

And because for over a hundred years the 'Island Race' had successfully withstood the challenge of powerful Catholic enemies, there developed an almost mystic belief among many Britons that in some way they had become the Chosen People; a widely-shared belief that they had inherited the special relationship with God first experienced by Old Testament Israel.[10] The apparent proof for this view was in the seemingly endless succession of victorious wars where the sailor and the soldier, the agents of deliverance, had not only saved the nation from alien domination but had also been responsible for enormous territorial gains, including Canada, the West Indies, Southern Africa and substantial parts of the Indian

25

sub-continent, and in the process created unrivalled opportunities for the commercial exploitation of these new lands. Yet, as Colley has noted, this was not an homogeneous empire comprised of British emigrants, nor was it predominantly Protestant or even Christian, but included diverse heathen races, most of whom had little liking for their new masters.[11] If the commercial exploitation of this empire was the lifeblood of the British nation, and many believed that it was, then it was essential to hold that empire together, and only military force could ensure its survival. Inevitably the future would increasingly demand that what had been won by the sword would need to be held by the sword as well. By the beginning of the nineteenth century, then, the army, previously ignored and largely despised, was beginning to find a degree of public acceptance, for it was beginning to be seen as the guardian of the nation's prestige and commercial prosperity. In the same way, war, however brutal, bloody and cruel, was essential to the continued well-being of the nation, and to further the perceived divinely sanctioned civilizing mission.

It has often been suggested that the British public had little interest in war or the soldier until late in the nineteenth century when the nation, in common with the rest of Europe, was infected with the virus of militarism. But, as Gillian Russell and others have shown, even the conflicts of the late eighteenth century were far from irrelevant to the common people; rather they were a focus of public interest.[12] The wars against France were a source of national pride and victories were celebrated in songs, paintings, prints, poetry, celebratory monuments and theatrical spectacle. This recurring imagery helped to sustain interest in war and created a more positive view of the army, as Geoffrey Best has noted.[13] Waterloo Day was an annual celebration, and Wellington, Sir John Moore and others were acclaimed as national heroes, joining a succession of popular military icons that reached back to Marlborough, Clive and Wolfe. Memories of the war and of the soldier's role were maintained through a steady stream of veterans' diaries, memoirs, and autobiographies, many written by the rank and file, which found a ready market and which testify to a degree of public interest in the wars. Paintings that commemorated the war and numerous battle sketches, costume studies and cheap woodblock prints indicate the popularity of heroic images glorifying the experience of battle. Theatrical productions, pageants and spectacles also reflected this public interest in battle and pride in the exploits of Wellington's Army. Even as late as 1824, Astley's Amphitheatre in Birmingham was playing J. H. Amherst's spectacular production *The Battle of Waterloo*, boasting a cast of over two hundred and elaborate and 'novel' effects. The century of warfare that ended with Waterloo thus created great interest in war and the exploits of military heroes; and even the rise of radicalism had little consequence on the public appetite for the pleasures of war. As one officer noted in the early 1830s,

> [t]he radical and leveling press [...] has for years directed [its] fiercest attacks against the British army, but has not yet been able to destroy, or even weaken its popularity: the failure may seem strange to some but [...] there is an honest manliness of feeling about the people of Britain that makes them delight in even the contemplation of deeds of hardihood and danger; and makes them proud of the unrivaled achievements of their sons, brothers and countrymen, as well as of the country that produced, and of the institutions that fostered such men.[14]

But while the pleasure culture of war had its roots in the wars of the late-eighteenth century, it was in mid-Victorian Britain that it became a really significant element in popular culture.

The Victorians' fascination with war and admiration for the warrior had, in large measure, been made possible because after 1745 the nation's wars were fought on foreign fields; even the upheavals of the Revolutionary and Napoleonic wars were played out on a stage far removed from native shores. The population of Britain was thus spared the horrors visited upon the inhabitants of France, Spain and the other warring states, and this distancing from the reality of battle enabled the people to enjoy the vicarious excitements of war without any of the hardships or dangers. Real, but distant, wars were thus little different from the exciting stories reconstructed on the stage or in the words of storytellers and balladmongers. For most Victorians, then, war was simply 'theatre', exciting deeds enacted upon a distant stage. Bolstered during the later nineteenth century by a developing racist ideology and an appeal to the biological necessity of war, it became increasingly easy to morally justify virtually any act of aggression on such grounds. And the acceptance of war was undoubtedly made easier by the re-discovery of chivalry early in the century.

Chivalry, the code of conduct evolved for medieval warriors, softened the barbarity of war by putting it into the hands of men committed to high standards of behaviour and noble ideals. Such a code removed the most brutal elements of war by creating a strict moral code for the warrior – the generally accepted 'rules of war'. The nineteenth century interest in chivalry was, in large measure, due to the popular historical novels of Sir Walter Scott – particularly *Ivanhoe* and *Quentin Durwood*, which helped shape the heroic chivalric stereotype. At a time of rapid change and social instability, it is not difficult to see the nostalgic appeal for a more ordered period, a time when kingship and the church were unquestioned and when all knew and accepted their place in the scheme of things. The chivalric code was adopted by Charles Kingsley (a self-proclaimed "joyous knight-errant of God") and Thomas Hughes and provided the underpinning for the cult of 'Muscular Christianity' – the cornerstone of reformed public school education – and it appealed to a diverse audience from Prince Albert to the radical William Morris and the pre-Raphaelite Brotherhood; and to churchmen, teachers and the aspiring middle classes. Scott and the other exponents of chivalry created, as Martin Green has perceptively argued, romantic daydreams and illusions, an alternative to the "banks, counting houses and trading companies most readers saw as contemporary reality".[15] But what is relevant here is that above all chivalry was the way of the warrior – a para-military code of conquest, inherently aggressive and appropriate for a nation with a growing empire. As Jeffrey Richards has explained, the "chivalric ideal was deliberately promoted by key figures of the age in order to produce a ruling elite for the nation and for the expanding empire who would be inspired by noble and selfless values",[16] including, we might add, the martial spirit. Most Victorian males, of course, saw little attraction in a military career, but heroic images of chivalric warriors offered a pleasing and exciting fantasy, an antidote to the tedium of everyday life – an idealised image of masculinity. And by disguising the realities of battle with the chivalric mask, war, the means through which the empire was extended and defended, appeared less brutal and so more acceptable to the public at large.

Thus, while Britain's martial heroes were hailed as chivalric in conduct and purpose, the written accounts and popular illustrations of their wars of empire constantly emphasised the ferocious and outlandish nature of the enemy and continually reinforced ideas of racial inferiority when compared with their civilized British conquerors, who brought to the Other not only the sword of justice, but all the benefits of civilization. Victorian governments never really subscribed to their oft-repeated pacifist policies; to believe that they did, as David French has pointed out, is to mistake the rhetoric of a handful of politicians like Cobden and the Manchester School for the reality of government.[17] Thus for all their much vaunted humanitarian aims and peaceful commercial objectives, the Victorians inherited, accepted and considerably extended, an empire held together by force of arms. War, the legitimate use of state violence, was simply one means by which the British maintained their position in the world. The pleasure culture of war reflected this national interest in war and, by representing conflict as romantic spectacle and the warrior as a chivalric and noble hero, distanced the public from its brutality and provided a forum through which the moral uncertainties over the use of violence could be partially resolved. But some perceptive commentators saw through the charade. In 1845, for example, the radical journalist Douglas Jerrold pointed to the dangers of portraying the brutality of war as theatre:

> When nations [...] cut each others throats [...] we must have red coats and muskets and sabres; but seeing how the duty of their bearers squares neither with our innate good sense, nor our notions of what ought to be – we are fain to gild the matter over – to try to conceal, from ourselves, the butchering nature of the business we are sometimes forced to undertake, and so spring up military spectacle-military finery-military music [...] Clothe war therefore in gayer colours than peace [...] let the steel which cuts glitter like valued gems; the evolutions which destroy, be graceful as the motions of dancing girls.[18]

In part, the pleasure culture of war was a spontaneous celebration of the nation's military prowess but, more importantly, it reflected the nation's commitment to the expansion of empire. After mid-century it was widely disseminated by the new technical processes that made word and image easily accessible to all. While the pleasures of war offered exciting entertainments for all classes, much of this material was aimed at the youth of the nation, and ensured that future generations would be inculcated with the martial spirit and the desire to emulate the heroic deeds of their forefathers and thus ensured that future generations would be prepared to safeguard their heritage – the greatest empire the world had ever seen. The major channel of persuasion through which the young were imbued with these warlike attitudes was the war story – the novel, serial, or short story that extolled the romanticism, excitement and honour of battle. More than that of any other writer, the war story for young males was the creation of the ex-soldier and war correspondent, George Alfred Henty.

Adventure fiction, written for the nation's young emerged at mid-century, and the youth market, with gender specific books and magazines, grew rapidly through the 1860s. The Education Act of 1870 provided further impetus for the development of such fictions and convinced some publishers to increase the material intended for the ten to eighteen-year-old-reader. By the 1880s, over 900 juvenile titles were being published annually and the market was well covered by magazines carrying both fiction and factual articles. The growth of this market encouraged some authors to write almost exclusively for the young, and initially juvenile adventure fiction was dominated by W. H. G. Kingston and R. M. Ballantyne, with a second generation of writers emerging in the period 1870-1880 (George Manville-Fenn, Gordon Stables and G. A. Henty). Publishers, however, did not only rely on sales to juvenile readers and their parents, for substantial numbers of books were also bought by education authorities and Sunday schools to be distributed as prizes and rewards. In order to appeal to this market, the books had, of course, to promote the dominant values of society and, in the guise of exciting adventures, teach moral lessons. Such fictions, then, clearly provide a valuable insight into the attitudes and values the Victorians wanted to instil in their children.

Kingston and Ballantyne did not glorify war – it could only be justified in self-defence – yet there is no lack of violence in their stories; the 'turbulent' are disciplined be they pirates or savages, and force is sometimes a necessary first step in civilizing the 'heathen'. The authors, then, take the ambiguous position of true Evangelicals: a belief in a divinely sanctioned mission of empire, but a dislike of force and only a grudging acceptance that it is sometimes justified as part of God's plan. In their work, war and violence are incidental to the main themes – exploring, hunting, and trapping. But while Kingston and Ballantyne virtually established the adventure mode as the pre-eminently popular reading for juveniles, it was Charles

Kingsley who contributed the idea of war as adventure to the form and established a pattern that would be followed by many later writers. In Kingsley's writings, particularly in his successful novel *Westward Ho!* we can clearly see how many of the central ideas of the nineteenth century came together to form the model of aggressive masculinity that became so prominent later in the century. Steeped in Scott's romances and deeply influenced by the chivalric ideal, he saw himself as a knight-errant fighting to right the social evils of his day. From Evangelicalism, he drew upon notions of the imperial destiny of the British race and their manifest right to predominate overseas. Through his friendship with Thomas Hughes, he became interested in physical toughness and endurance, delighting in strenuous walking tours and swimming in icy pools. This obsession with physical prowess developed into a fascination with war as the ultimate test of manliness. In 1854, he became intensely excited by the Crimean War which he saw as an opportunity for the nation to demonstrate its manliness. In awe of the bravery of the British rank and file, he was inspired to write his epic tale of the war with Spain, *Westward Ho!* Written for an adult readership, it nevertheless proved immensely popular with boys.

Kingsley directed his readers to the continuities between the heroic past and the heroic present, between the new apostles of empire and their Elizabethan forebears, the adventurers who had broken the Catholic challenge to Britain's overseas expansion. The novel deals with the adventures of Amyas Leigh in Ireland and the Caribbean and climaxes in the battle with the Armada – a battle to determine whether "Popery and despotism, or Protestantism and freedom were to dominate half of Europe and the whole future of America". Amyas and his Devon men represent "brave young England longing to wing its way out of its island prison", and blazing the trail for future generations who will realise the destiny of the race. *Westward Ho!* is a novel that revels in the excitement of battle. It was enormously popular with boys and young men and was even distributed to troops in the Crimea. But perhaps its real significance was that here Kingsley has transformed war into acceptable subject matter for the adventure story and introduced the nation's youth to the pleasure culture of war – a model of juvenile fiction that would be developed by Henty.

Henty, in large measure, was a seminal figure in war fiction for boys, a model that was slavishly followed by other writers until well into the twentieth century. He inherited much from earlier writers, ideas about manliness and the nation's imperial destiny, for example, but he added to them his own romanticised view of war and of the soldier. Henty was continually short of money and wrote prolifically in order to solve his financial problems, but he also wrote with another purpose in mind – he was determined to "teach patriotism", to inspire faith in the destiny of the Anglo-Saxon race and to offer bright personal examples of morality. He wanted to show boys how to behave; his friend and biographer George Manville Fenn recalled that he wanted his boys to be bold, "straightforward and ready to play a young man's part, not to be milksops. He had a horror of a lad who displayed any weak emotion and shrank from shedding blood". In *Through the Sikh War*, Henty himself wrote:

> Give me a lad with pluck and spirit, and I don't care a snap of the fingers whether he can construe Euripides or solve a problem in higher mathematics. What we want for India are men who can ride and shoot [...] What do the natives care for our learning? It is our pluck and fighting powers that have made us their masters.[19]

Henty, then, an advocate of imperialism and chivalric manliness, bound these qualities into an idealised portrait of the imperial warrior, the instrument through which the empire would be safeguarded and extended. Influenced by contemporary historical views, he saw British history as a series of inevitable wars that had created the empire, and he believed that future generations must stand ready to wage unceasing war to maintain that heritage. In 1885, he clearly articulated these views in the preface to his novel *St. George for England: A Tale of Crecy and Poitiers*:

> It is sometimes said that there is no good to be obtained from tales of fighting and bloodshed – that there is no moral to be drawn from such histories. Believe it not, war has its lessons as well as peace. You will learn from tales like this that determination and enthusiasm can accomplish marvels, that true courage is generally accompanied by magnanimity and gentleness, and that if not itself the very highest of virtues, it is the parent of almost all the others, since few of them can be practised without it. The courage of our forefathers has created the greatest empire in the world around a small and in itself insignificant island; if this empire is ever lost, it will be by the cowardice of their descendents.[20]

Henty's main subject was the little wars of empire, but here, at least according to this gospel, the British were not just conquerors but liberators as well; bringing good government, justice and improvement to native people who suffered under local tyrants. And once under British rule, he was at pains to point out, most native races were quick to see the benefits. The instrument of liberation and enlightenment, of course, was the British soldier for whom the author had nothing but praise.

Martial prowess and love of fighting had, according to Henty, always been a characteristic of the British race. When Nita, the heroine of *The Soldier's Daughter*, suggests that it is peculiar that men should be so fond of fighting, her companion, Lieutenant Charlie Carter explains:

> It is; I have often wondered over it many a time. All savage races love fighting, and certainly our own people do. If there were a great war, hundreds and thousands of men would volunteer at once. I am afraid this instinct brings us very near the savage. I think no other nation possesses it to anything like the same extent as the British race.[21]

The British, then, are born warriors with an inherent love of fighting. But Nita, the daughter of a soldier stationed on the North-West, is no mean fighter herself and when the British fort is attacked by Afridis, she picks up a rifle and shoots back; she has no "sense of fear [and] was proud of doing her share of the work. That she was doing a share she knew, for scarcely one of her shots missed the mark".[22]

Many of his stories make use of the great imperial warlords around which to construct the novel, Clive, Wellington, Kitchener or Roberts. But the key factor is that it is only through battle that the youthful hero achieves his rewards. Henty's boy heroes are sometimes from public schools, sometimes of low birth but all are manly, resourceful, chivalric and patriotic. In an age when imperial security depended upon a small voluntary army, Henty romanticised war and turned it into an adventure that most boys found enormously appealing in order to inculcate a commitment to defend the empire. Through war a young man could show what he was made of and gain fame and fortune; and every Briton's birthright was an inherent talent for fighting; thus battle posed little danger for the true Briton – little more dangerous than a game of rugby. Many writers disguised the brutality of war with sporting metaphors. Henry Newbolt, for example, that malevolent apostle of imperial violence, transformed a bloody battle in the Sudan into little more than a hard-fought match between the School and a rather unruly visitors' eleven:

> The sand of the Desert is sodden red,
> Red with the wreck of a square that broke:
> The Gatling's jammed and the Colonel dead,
> And the regiment blind with dust and smoke.
> The river of death has brimmed its banks,
> And England's far, and Honour a name,
> But the voice of a schoolboy rallies the ranks,
> Play up! Play up! And play the game.[23]

For boys, such fictions created an exciting world where battle provided the route to fame and fortune and played to their more primitive emotions and fantasies. But these books were also widely approved by both parents and teachers, who passed them on to their children as presents and prizes because they reflected the spirit of the age, mirrored many of the enshrined attitudes of late Victorians and powerfully reinforced those beliefs. Certainly, they had an educational content, blending fact and fiction, for the usual practice was to place the fictitious hero's adventures against the background of some great episode of British history. But they served a more important purpose for they successfully re-directed the uncontrolled violence of the young into approved channels – imperial expansion and a belief in martial prowess, glossed with notions of chivalric behaviour, and ideas about the 'sporting' nature of warfare. These were appropriate qualities for boys for the world of the late Victorians was far less secure than at mid-century. The rapid expansion of the empire after the 1870s, especially in Africa, created even greater demands upon an already stretched British Army while at the same time other European powers were developing imperial ambitions that threatened British interests. German expansion in Africa and the Russian threat to northern India were seen as particularly dangerous to imperial security. The British Army's poor performance against the Transvaal Boers at Majuba in February 1881 compared unfavourably with German military prowess demonstrated during the Franco-Prussian War. This, combined with increasing economic competition from rapidly industrialising nations like the USA, conspired to create a sense of unease for many Britons. Part of the adult approval for the pleasure culture of war, then, was because it promoted a sense of duty and the martial spirit among British boys upon whom the security of their world would ultimately depend. Henty died in 1902, but the style of juvenile war fiction that he had popularised was inherited by a new generation of writers who dealt with combat in a far more graphic manner and exploited the atavistic nature of their readers. The most popular of these younger writers included Frederick Sadlier Brereton, Percy Westerman, Captain Charles Gilson and Herbert Strang. Captain Brereton, Henty's cousin and an RAMC doctor who had served in South Africa, began his writing career in 1900. What is perhaps surprising is the violence in these stories. In Brereton's novel *With Shield and Assegai*, set during the Zulu War, Donald Stewart, a settler's son, is forever shooting Zulus "between the eyes" or putting bullets in their brains, while at the Battle of Ulundi British fire swept the Zulus away, "shattered, broken, and bleeding, and the guns, loaded with canister, completed the awful work".[24] *Tom Graham V.C.*, by William Johnson, has the hero enlist in the army and take part in the Second Afghan War. At the storming of Peiwar Kotal, the young Tom, protecting his fallen captain, finds himself struggling with a huge Pathan, but "with a fierce lunge the young borderer drove his bayonet up to the nozzle in the Afghan's chest". But the native still fights on and only a "terrific blow" from a rifle butt to his head finishes him.[25] In Westerman's *Building the Empire*, set on the North West Frontier, British soldiers are sometimes "hacked to pieces" while loyal Ghurkas wreak havoc on the Afridis with their "razor sharp kukris". However, none of this is quite as unpleasant as A. J. Chalmers' *Fighting the Matabele* – allegedly based upon the author's own experiences in that campaign. Chalmers takes an obvious delight in recalling how, when attacked by a Matabele warrior, "I caught him by the wrist, wrenched the weapon from his hand, and cracked his crown with it; I shall never forget the sickening thud with which the club descended on his skull".[26] Meanwhile, Chalmers' companion dispatches the rest of the war party "more neatly" with his revolver. The author exemplifies the imperialist at his most brutal: at one point threatening to throw native women off a cliff for refusing to reveal where their men are hiding, and later taking great pleasure when an artillery shell bursts among a group of Matabele.

Interestingly, Chalmers concludes his book by claiming that there will be more trouble with the Matabele if the administration continues to treat them in such a "mild manner". The "iron hand" must not be lifted, he argues, for "at best, the Matabele, like the Indians in the States, will most likely be a source of periodical trouble and disturbance, and the country ought to be so controlled as to reduce [...] the risk of outrages [...] All outrages should be visited with instant and severe retribution".[27] *The Liverpool Echo's* reviewer curiously suggested that *Fighting the Matabele* described the recent campaign "with such piquantness" it would become a great favourite with boys.[28]

Such fictions which extolled the virtues of war were reinforced by military-based training provided by youth organisations like the Cadet Corps, the Lads Rifle Brigade, and after 1908, the Boy Scouts; through the speeches made to public schoolboys by imperial warlords like Field Marshall Lord Roberts and Sir Ian Hamilton, and through all manner of toys and games. By the early twentieth century, then, the pleasure culture of war had imbued the youth of Britain with the martial spirit, had convinced them that war was natural, honourable and romantic; that on the battlefield, fighting to further the nation's cause, they would achieve their destiny. Writing in later life, William Earl Johns (b. 1893), the creator of the enduring "Biggles" stories, provides us with the flavour of this turn of the century martial fervour:

> It is difficult for a boy of today to realise the enthusiasm the boys of 1900 had for anything military. Soldiers were gods [...] When troops went overseas they did not creep away furtively, for security reasons, in the middle of the night. They marched through cheering crowds in broad daylight, bands playing, colours flying, flowers in their caps. We boys, decorated with as much red, white and blue ribbon as we could afford to buy, marched with them to the railway station and yelled our heads off as the train steamed out [...].[29]

However, wars of empire were not the only subject for the pleasure culture of war, for beginning in the 1870s authors began to speculate on wars to come – especially the next great European war which many believed to be inevitable given the increasing tension between the Great Powers. Beginning with George Chesney's story, *The Battle of Dorking,* dealing with an imaginary invasion of Britain by the Prussians, the nation's appetite for such dire fictions continually expanded and by the 1890s had even invaded boys' story papers like *Pluck* and *Boy's Friend*.[30] Young Britons, constantly exposed to such tales, could hardly fail to absorb the idea that the nation was poised on the brink of disaster; that a major war was inevitable. Such a belief, combined with constant exposure to a pleasure culture that taught them that war was little more than a romantic escapade, proved a lethal combination in 1914. As Robert Roberts has explained:

> For nearly half a century before 1914 the newly literate millions were provided with an increasing flow of fiction based on war and the idea of its imminence [...] Popular fiction and mass journalism now combined to condition the minds of the nation's new readers to a degree never possible before the advent of general literacy. In France and Germany, too, writings in the genre were equally successful in stimulating romantic conceptions about the carnage to come. When the final cataclysm did arrive, response to such ideas set the masses cheering wildly through the capitals of Europe. 'Der Tag'! – 'The Day – was here at last'![31]

August 1914, then, was simply the fulfilment of that expectation of war; it was what young men had been prepared for, and they rejoiced in the opportunity to take part in the 'great adventure'. The martial fervour that had been so carefully fostered among young males was to have devastating consequences as young men, who had grown up in the shadow of the pleasure culture of war, flocked to the recruiting stations. Even such an intelligent young man as Roland Leighton could write to his friend Vera Brittain in September 1914:

> I feel [...] I am meant to take some active part in this war. It is to me a very fascinating thing – something, if often horrible – yet very ennobling and very beautiful, something whose elemental reality raises it above the reach of cold theorising. You will call me a militarist. You may be right.[32]

He was to realise the extent of this 'old lie' about the romance of war when he reached the trenches.

Notes

1 Olive Anderson: "The Growth of Christian Militarism in Mid-Victorian Britain", *English Historical Review* 86, 1971, 46-72; Anne Summers: "Militarism in Britain before the Great War", *History Workshop Journal* 2, 1976, 104-123.

2 The idea of the 'pleasure culture of war' was suggested by the work of Graham Dawson, see, *Soldier Heroes: British Adventure, Empire and the Imagining of Masculinity*, London, 1994. See also Michael Paris: *Warrior Nation: Images of War in British Popular Culture, 1850-2000*, London, 1999.

3 General Sir Henry Hardinge to Lord Seaton, 16 June 1853, quoted in Scott Hughes Myerly: *British Military Spectacle*, Cambridge, Mass. 1996, p. 151.

4 On the Volunteer Movement see, Ian F. W. Beckett: *Riflemen Form: A Study of the Rifle Volunteer Movement, 1859-1908*, Aldershot, 1980.

5 *Burnaby the Valiant*, music hall song, c. 1885.

6 Quoted in Roger T. Stearn: "War Correspondents and Colonial War, c. 1870-1900". – In John M. Mackenzie (Ed.): *Popular Imperialism and the Military, 1850-1950*, Manchester, 1992, p. 148.

7 Rudyard Kipling: *The Light That Failed*, London, 1891, p. 19.

8 *Ibid.*, 48.

9 Linda Colley: *Britons: Forging the Nation, 1707-1837*, London, 1996, p. 5.

10 See John Wolffe: "Evangelicalism in Mid-Nineteenth Century England". – In Raphael Samuel (Ed.): *Patriotism: The Making and Unmaking of British National Identity* Vol. 1, London, 1989, p. 189.

11 Colley (1996: 109).

12 See Gillian Russell: *Theatres of War: Performances, Politics and Society, 1793-1815*, Oxford, 1995; and Myerly (1996).

13 Geoffrey Best: *War and Society in Revolutionary Europe, 1770-1870*, Leicester, 1982, p. 199.

14 "JM", *Fragments from the Portfolio of a Field Officer* (1831), quoted in Myerly (1996: 151).

15 Martin Green: *Dreams of Adventure, Deeds of Empire*, London, 1979, p. 98.

16 Jeffrey Richards: "Popular Imperialism and the Image of the Army in Juvenile Literature". – In John M. Mackenzie (Ed.): *Popular Imperialism and the Military, 1850-1950*, Manchester, 1992, p. 87.

17 David French: *The British Way in Warfare, 1688-2000*, London, 1990, p. 121.

18 Douglas Jerrold: *The Shilling Magazine* (1845), quoted in Myerly (1996: 151).

19 George Manville Fenn, quoted in Jeffrey Richards: "With Henty in Africa". – In J. R. (Ed.): *Imperialism and Juvenile Literature*, Manchester, 1989, p. 75; George Alfred Henty: *Through the Sikh War*, London, 1894, p. 9.

20 Quoted in Richards (1992: 89).
21 George Alfred Henty: *A Soldier's Daughter*, London, 1906, p. 24.
22 *Ibid.*, 35.
23 Henry Newbolt: "Vitai Lampada". – In H.N.: *Collected Poems, 1897-1907*, London, 1908, pp. 131-133.
24 Captain Frederick Sadlier Brereton: *With Shield and Assegai: A Tale of the Zulu War*, London, 1900, p. 151.
25 William Johnston: *Tom Graham VC*, London, 1906, p. 217.
26 Arthur John Chalmers: *Fighting the Matabele*, London, 1898, pp. 200, 286.
27 *Ibid.*
28 Review in *Liverpool Echo*, quoted in Blackie's catalogue, c. 1900.
29 Quoted in Peter Berrisford Ellis & Piers Williams: *By Jove, Biggles! The Life of Captain W. E. Johns*, London, 1981, p. 11.
30 On the fictions of future war see, Ignatius Frederick Clarke: *Voices Prophesy-ing War: Future Wars, 1763-3749*, Oxford, 1992.
31 Robert Roberts: *The Classic Slum: Salford Life in the First Quarter of the Century*, London, 1990, pp. 179-180.
32 Quoted in Alan Bishop (Ed.): *Chronicles of Youth: Vera Brittain's War Diary, 1913-1917*, London, 1981, p. 114.

Bibliography

Primary Sources

Bishop, Alan (Ed.): *Chronicles of Youth: Vera Brittain's War Diary, 1913-1917*, London, 1981.

Brereton, Captain Frederick Sadlier: *With Shield and Assegai: A Tale of the Zulu War*, London, 1900.

Chalmers, Arthur John: *Fighting the Matabele*, London, 1898.

Henty, George Alfred: *Through the Sikh War*, London, 1894.

---: *A Soldier's Daughter*, London, 1906.

Johnston, William: *Tom Graham VC*, London, 1906.

Kipling, Rudyard: *The Light That Failed*, London, 1891.

Newbolt, Henry: "Vitai Lampada". – In H. N.: *Collected Poems, 1897-1907*, London, 1908.

Roberts, Robert: *The Classic Slum: Salford Life in the First Quarter of the Century*, London, 1990.

Secondary Works

Anderson, Olive: "The Growth of Christian Militarism in Mid-Victorian Britain", *English Historical Review* 86, 1971, 46-72.

Beckett, Ian F.W.: *Riflemen Form: A Study of the Rifle Volunteer Movement, 1859–1908*, Aldershot, 1980.

Best, Geoffrey: *War and Society in Revolutionary Europe, 1770-1870*, Leicester, 1982.

Clark, Ignatius Frederick: *Voices Prophesying War: Future Wars, 1763-3749*, Oxford, 1992.

Colley, Linda: *Britons: Forging the Nation, 1707–1837*, London, 1996.

Dawson, Graham: *Soldier Heroes: British Adventure, Empire and the Imagining of Masculinity*, London, 1994.

Ellis, Peter Berrisford & Williams, Piers: *By Jove, Biggles! The Life of Captain W. E. Johns*, London, 1981.

French, David: *The British Way in Warfare, 1688-2000*, London, 1990.

Green, Martin: *Dreams of Adventure, Deeds of Empire*, London, 1979.

Myerly, Scott Hughes: *British Military Spectacle*, Cambridge, Mass., 1996.

Paris, Michael: *Warrior Nation: Images of War in British Popular Culture, 1850-2000*, London, 1999.

Richards, Jeffrey: "With Henty in Africa". – In J. R. (Ed.): *Imperialism and Juvenile Literature*, Manchester, 1989, pp. 72-106.

Richards, Jeffrey: "Popular Imperialism and the Image of the Army in Juvenile Literature". – In John M. Mackenzie (Ed.): *Popular Imperialism and the Military, 1850-1950*, Manchester, 1992.

Russell, Gillian: *Theatres of War: Performances, Politics and Society, 1793-1815*, Oxford, 1995.

Stearn, Roger T: "War Correspondents and Colonial War, c. 1870–1900". – In John M. Mackenzie (Ed.): *Popular Imperialism and the Military, 1850–1950*, Manchester, 1992.

Summers, Anne: "Militarism in Britain before the Great War", *History Workshop Journal* 2, 1976, 104-123.

Wolffe, John: "Evangelicalism in Mid-Nineteenth Century England". – In Raphael Samuel (Ed.): *Patriotism: The Making and Unmaking of British National Identity* Vol.1, London, 1989.

Daniel Dornhofer (Frankfurt am Main)

It's Just Around the Corner / In the English Civil War. The English Revolution and Popular Music, 1978-1997

1. History

The Civil War has remained the most controversial episode in English history to this day and this controversy is by no means confined to the history departments. The events of the 1640s have provided ammunition for countless political debates and direct action ever since. As Blair Worden puts it in his latest book *Roundhead Reputations*:

> The wars, which tore the nation apart, have been fought again in the heart of posterity. The clash of Cavalier and Roundhead has never gone away. [...] The experiences and images on which it has thrived derive from the wars themselves.[1]

In this article I am going to trace some of those experiences and images in a number of popular songs inspired by the social and political upheavals and protest movements of another highly controversial period: the eighteen years of Conservative rule in the nineteen-eighties and nineties.

Many artists of the Thatcher era found their heroes in seventeenth-century radicals. And they applied the language and traditions they found there to their own stance against a government perceived as just as corrupt and tyrannical as that of King Charles I. The sense of history inviting such identifications relied on a Marxist interpretation that had come to dominate academic discussions in the late nineteen-sixties and found a wide reading public in the seventies. Historians of the thirties and forties had already highlighted movements such as the Levellers and the Diggers as forerunners or even inventors of modern communist ideals. Thus, they had been able to construct a specifically English tradition of resistance and home-grown socialism.[2] Drawing upon those writings, the members of the History Workshop were able to elaborate an alternative and much more radical strand of dissent outside Parliament in a Revolution which was increasingly seen as a bourgeois enterprise. For my purpose, the most important aspect of the books by Christopher Hill, David Wootton, Austin Woolrych and others is the focus on radical groups in revolutionary England and their eventual suppression. The Civil War was understood (I oversimplify) to have been the consequence of long-term socio-economic changes, mainly the rise of a mercantile middle class. The zeal of the ordinary people had won this conflict much more decisively than Parliament could have wished and the bourgeoisie were eager to do away with the radical forces recently sprung up in City and army alike. The discussions among these radicals on issues such as manhood suffrage, annual parliaments, economic and legal reforms, and even the abolition of private property posed a clear threat to the interests of the rising bourgeoisie. So the Cromwellian Protectorate restored order with an iron fist, much to the delight of the profiteering middle classes. Studies like Hill's *The World Turned Upside Down*[3] impressively illustrated the wide range of radical ideas held by Levellers, Diggers, Ranters, Quakers or Fifth Monarchists as well as their experience of revolution and defeat.

However, in the late seventies this account came under fire from historians who saw no long-term causes or socio-economic transformations at work which led to the Civil War. They presented a far more spontaneous and personalised chain of events. This new trend of historiography came to be known as 'revisionism'. It also showed the radical element of the English 'Revolution' (a term they dismissed) to have been much less homogenous and significant than claimed by the Marxists. The result of this criticism was a sometimes bitter feud waged for much of the eighties. To a certain extent the rise of revisionism was linked with the agenda of Thatcherism and the New Right. Academic Marxist interpretations had to adapt to these new and often well-founded challenges and, although in retreat for nearly a decade, had the strength and flexibility to re-group and present some crucial answers. This, however, infuriated a number of left-wing intellectuals associated with the Socialist Workers Party (SWP) and its journal *International Socialism* who were still vilifying the Levellers as liberals and Cromwell as the English Revolution's Stalin.[4]

As I am going to show, much of the Marxist interpretation of the seventies has kept its validity in the material under consideration here. Many artists shifted their emphasis as a result of academic debates but also, and more decisively, of their own experience in a decade of struggle. Still, they kept expressing these in a language and in images reminiscent of mid-seventeenth-century radicalism. By referring to a crucial moment in British history, left-wing bands have been able to voice calls for political action and teach their audiences about an English tradition of dissent, but also to reflect disillusionment and make sense of their political agendas' failure.

2. Songs

When analysing rock music one has to be aware of a number of quite specific factors. First of all, music criticism suffers badly from the implicit demand for authenticity: critics and audiences alike judge songs by the alleged sincerity of the views or emotions expressed. This is more strictly applied to political songs than to love songs, which goes back to the high ethos of folk and protest singers of the sixties. To transfer their standards to popular music with a much more complex structure and an intention to entertain is of course highly problematic, yet wide-spread. Secondly, in sharp contrast to folksongs it is never enough to study merely the lyrics of a political rock song. There are many other means of expression that must be considered, as well as rules of genre, performance, socio-economic background, ideology and audience (or rather audiences).[5] Textual analysis of a rock song has to take all formal qualities into account when trying to describe how ideas and emotions are expressed through the music.[6] Volume, rhythm, beat, voice and instrumentation are often as important as the 'message' of the lyrics. This also means being aware of the fact that different audiences can find very different meanings in the same song. So when discussing political music's didactic impact it is important to keep the sceptical remarks by folksinger Leon Rosselson in mind: "Songs never converted anyone. That is not what they are for. They are for sharing ideas, hopes, feelings about what is sad, funny, ridiculous, horrifying. They are for making a community out of the already converted."[7] Therefore, it is vital to focus on the community which a song addressed at a specific moment in history; in other words, on its social and historical background.

Songs always have to be open to interpretation – by the performers themselves and the audience. Love songs, for instance, do not so much reflect feelings as they provide the listener with the vocabulary to express his or her own experience and emotions.[8] Political songs work pretty much along the same lines. They offer a way of expressing political sentiments in a language of resistance and dissent and also the vocabulary to make sense of defeat.

3. Seasons of Discontent

The first of my examples is "English Civil War" by London punk rockers The Clash. It was taken from their second album *Give 'Em Enough Rope* and released as a 45 in summer 1978 peaking at number 25 in the UK charts. There have not been many years in recent British history which can be labelled 'civil war' with equal justification as the late nineteen-seventies. Soaring unemployment, strikes and the collapse of the post-war social-democratic consensus plunged the nation into crisis and insecurity, compounded by the ongoing very real civil war in Northern Ireland and continuing IRA bombing campaigns in mainland-Britain. The same years saw an alarming increase in popularity of the fascist National Front which took to the streets more and more often and made substantial gains in local elections. Clashes with counter-demonstrators were frequent and often extremely violent (the worst in Lewisham, August 1977). Race riots like those at the Notting Hill Carnival of 1976, provoked by an oppressive police presence, were common in England's inner cities throughout the period. Violence was very much a part of working-class youths' everyday experience, too – be it politically motivated or just fighting in dance halls and pubs. Many bands in the new punk and Oi! scenes took the spread of violence, police brutality and class struggle as their subject (among others Angelic Upstarts, Sham 69, Stiff Little Fingers or The Specials). But The Clash, who had adopted a provocative left-extremist stance, were the first to label what was going on around them: another "English Civil War".

The song is modelled on the anti-war traditional "Johnny I Hardly Knew You" which makes it unusually melodic for a punk track. Guitars dominate from the very beginning and from the first chorus on, there is the typical level of noise. It is a fine dance tune, and you can scream along without even knowing the words. The sheer volume of the music against the voice, compounded by Joe Strummer's mumbling and strong accent, make it very hard to understand what he is singing. Thus, it is a good example of punk's tendency to sabotage its own message by not allowing the audience to hear it properly. However, if you manage to do so, the first two lines already tell you that the English Civil War is here and now, despite the title and pseudo-traditional setting:

> When Johnny comes marching home again
> He's coming by bus or underground
> The world no doubt will shed a tear
> To see his face so beaten in fear
> And it's just around the corner
> In the English Civil War (ll. 1-6)[9]

This song's Johnny is not the crippled soldier of the folksong, but a beaten-up youth, a casualty in the ordinary civil war around the corner. The speaker goes on to point out that this war is "*still* at the stage of clubs and fists" (l. 7, my emphasis), but what has happened to Johnny could happen again at any time and to anyone of the predominantly male working-class audience (l. 20). It remains quite unclear who is meant by "the new party army" (ll. 11 and 16), although the Metropolitan Police's much-hated Special Patrol Group (SPG) would seem an obvious candidate. The speaker's identity is not revealed either (it is most certainly not the lover from the folksong). However, he can see clearly what is going on and cautions against the spread of this civil war. So the song is not actually a call to arms, but tries to make listeners aware of the fact that a war is already being waged around them and that they are not very likely to be spared.

A more systematic, yet radically different and dismissive approach to British history was presented by influential Leeds post-punk outfit Gang Of Four. They put a contemporary coloured woodcut showing the execution of Charles I on the back cover of the band's second album *Solid Gold* (1981) with the words "I hope they keep down the price of gas" written beneath. The graphic picture was used again as the cover for their "What We All Want"-

45 later that year. The B-side "History's Bunk!" spelled out their bleak view of history in a cold, noisy and inaccessible song:

> History's bunk, I've got no past
> In the future we'll invent more junk
> What I'd like to hear: tales of people's history
> Fighting it out for some other's causes
> They're invincible, they didn't exist!
> There are no lessons in the past (ll. 7-12)[10]

This roundly denies any significance history might have for today's political problems even more clearly than the ironic combination of Charles' beheading with the gas price. The notion of having no past is highlighted by the song's bleak and unnerving music that seems to defy tradition. In sharp contrast to other left-wing artists, Gang Of Four's call for a history from below does not suggest that there were alternative messages in British history to be revealed. The "tales of people's history" (ll. 1 and 9) would only highlight the century-long exploitation of the masses by leaders who honoured their own causes with references to the imagined community's past. The band's sense of history is quite typical for the beginning of the new decade. It also responded to new revisionist studies which seemed to shake the very foundations of the seventies' Marxist-oriented interpretation of history. Thus, a number of political activists tried to turn away from now apparently unsafe historical models completely. Yet, only a few years later British artists were much more eager to discover lessons in the past again to admonish them in the struggle against the Conservative government.

4. Miners & Diggers: Billy Bragg

The image of England being at civil war again seemed tailor-made to describe the showdown between government and unions during the miners' strike of 1984/85. It lasted for 358 days and claimed fourteen lives, thousands were injured and more than 10,000 arrested. The tremendous security operation throughout the affected areas cost a fortune and turned Britain into something very much alike a civil war zone. The Labour Party was rather embarrassed by the strike since it had not yet recovered from the 1983 election disaster. Hence political support for the miners was thin with a government determined to crush their union, hostile media and an irresolute opposition. Yet, a lot of musicians rallied to their side. In interviews, benefit performances and compilations, bands (as diverse as Elvis Costello, The Redskins, Style Council and The Flying Pickets) managed to create media coverage of and solidarity with the miners' cause. The broad range of pop bands united in a political struggle led to an unprecedented politicisation among British artists and foreshadowed the Red Wedge campaign that took off not long after the collapse of the strike to help Labour's new leader Neil Kinnock to win the next elections.

At the centre of both campaigns was Billy Bragg. When he brought out the *Between The Wars*-EP in 1985 the strike was nearly over, but the pro-unions title track became quite successful. At the time, a feud was being waged between folk musicians and socialist advocates of political rock music who accused each other of "vulnerability to the whims of the market place" and of failing to attract today's urban youth respectively.[11] To prove both sides wrong, Bragg included a recent song by folksinger Leon Rosselson (in the front line of the debate) on his EP. The song tells the story of the radical Diggers who had occupied common land around St. George's Hill, Surrey, in 1649 to set up a utopian community before being driven away by Cromwell's troops in the following year. Short-lived as this experiment might have been, it proved to be great inspiration to the twentieth-century English left. Especially, their rejection of private property made them very attractive to modern socialists who increasingly regarded Cromwell as the English Revolution's Judas, as he had betrayed the people's victory for a brave new world of the capitalist middle class.

Hence, the topicality of the seventeenth-century Diggers' example for the twentieth-century miners' resistance to privatisation. The song creates an English tradition of socialist protest going back to the crucial years of the seventeenth-century revolution. Eventually, the "men of property" (l. 41) had won the day, but they could not break the spirit and vision of an alternative society. The title also harks back to Christopher Hill's seminal book from 1972. By covering Rosselson's song, Billy Bragg made this story available to a much wider audience, many of whom might have heard about the Diggers for the first time. The song itself is a typical example for his so-called urban folk with highly amplified guitar and voice, loudness, echoing sound and strong working-class accent. It is unusually fast and Bragg's loud singing conveys a sense of authenticity and anger. It is utterly un-danceable, has no chorus to sing along and so the lyrics take centre stage. The lyrics are narrative, with the storyteller arriving at a clear and simple moral at the end:

> You poor take courage
> You rich take care
> The earth was made a common treasury
> For everyone to share
> All things in common
> All people one
> We come in peace
> The order came to cut them down (ll. 49-56)

Bragg hammers his point home quite literally by highlighting certain phrases with a bang from his guitar, especially the quotation from the well-known seventeenth-century "Diggers' Song" ("You Diggers all stand up for glory / Stand up now", ll. 39f.). By including other phrases from Gerrard Winstanley's writings (e.g. "This earth was made a common treasury / For everyone to share", ll. 51f.), avoiding modern socialist vocabulary and narrating in the first person plural, the song creates an impression of Diggers speaking directly to Bragg's contemporaries and admonishing them in their struggle against the same foe: not "the hired men and troopers" (l. 43), but landlords and the apostles of private property:

> The sin of property
> We do disdain
> No one has any right to buy and sell
> The earth for private gain
> By theft and murder
> They took the land
> Now everywhere the walls
> Rise up at their command. (ll. 17-24)

5. Know Thy History

A clear sense of history is of even greater importance to Bradford post-punk band New Model Army. Their name deliberately draws upon the original army's reputation as a fiercely radical political force. In 1947, Christopher Hill had written in the *Communist Review*:

> Three hundred years ago England had a democratic army, really democratic, so democratic that it would give our Whitehall brass-hats the creeps if anything like it existed today. This army produced ideas about politics which are still of interest today.[12]

The original New Model Army was seen as more representative than Parliament and much more progressive. In the tolerant atmosphere of this well-disciplined army, political issues could be discussed freely. For some time, it had even seemed as if the rank and file representatives of the army council (known as agitators) could take it over and transform the country along the radical democratic principles so heatedly debated at Putney church.[13] And their twentieth-century namesakes display a comparable mixture of puritanical fervour and patriotic romanticism. Many of their songs are informed by a strong vision of English history at a time when left-wing intellectuals, as a consequence of the impact of revisionism, were increasingly turning away from the English Revolution and looking once more to Russia for inspiration. In an interview with the *New Musical Express*, singer Justin Sullivan (aka "Slade the Leveller") laid out his sense of history:

> If we're products of anything, it's our own history. [...] we have a great history in this country. We are responsible for the start of all socialist thought [...] look at the Levellers. [...] As far as I can say, the historical references are totally valid. Thatcher comes out and says that it is against the British character to strike and to have mass demonstrations [...] and especially for women to be involved. That's a load of crap. [...] You have to understand history, our history, to undermine ignorant peasants like Thatcher.[14]

They had released a controversial debut album in 1983 and also contributed to the miners' cause. "1984", the B-side of their single "The Price", describes the siege of mining communities by the security forces in claustrophobic images of civil war waged by a government against the weaker part of society:

> Nobody wanted to see the blood
> As the blue lights flash through the night
> But all the words fell on deaf ears

And now the blind frustration bites
Two nations under one crown divided more and more
In our own sweet green and pleasant land in 1984 (ll. 28-33) [15]

Fighting against national division is also at the heart of "My Country" from the album *No Rest For The Wicked* (1985). The song, driven by the band's typical bass, makes a fine dance tune, but the voice is always clearly audible and central to the whole piece. The speaker boldly takes the role of a preacher here, who admonishes his faithful congregation with his beliefs and sends them out to spread the word to those "who believe what they read in the press" (l. 1). So the speaker aims at unifying his audience, making a community of them and calling them to action. "Fight" is by far the word used most frequently, hammering the necessity for action into the listener:

So yes, I will fight for my country
The land that I love so well
Yes, for justice,
A land fit for all our futures. (chorus, ll. 5-8)

Vocabulary and imagery are deliberately archaic, and the slogans are traditional English rather than socialist ones, especially when it comes to the things worth fighting for. Perhaps, this echoes Sir Thomas Fairfax's statement that his soldiers loved what they knew and fought for what they loved. Not many left-wing bands of the eighties would have sung un-ironically about fighting for one's country or "fight all the powers who abuse our common laws" (l. 28). And yet, it is exactly this creed that highlights the sense of an English tradition of resistance to tyranny alluded to in the chorus ("Hear the voices of our history echo all around", l. 11) and specified in the bridge before verse three:

No rights were ever given to us by the grace of God
No rights were ever given by some United Nations clause
No rights were ever given by some nice guy at the top
Our rights they were bought by all the blood
And all the tears of all our
Grandmothers, grandfathers before. (ll. 18-23)

It is worth noting that the voice of the singer is multiplying during the song, from a slight echo in the second chorus to a distinguishable second voice and clear echo towards the end which is to imply the spread of the word. Also the song has no real ending, but fades out while the creed of the chorus is repeated over and over again. So the battle continues. As *No Rest For The Wicked* was the band's first album released on EMI, it was certainly aiming at a broad audience who was not only to be preached at, but also to be entertained (just as The Clash had done when they signed with CBS and Billy Bragg was about to do with the reissue of his EPs on *Back To Basics* with WEA in 1987).

This is perhaps the stance most clearly informed by the sense of being part of a long-standing English tradition of dissent and continuing strife. Its archaic imagery harks back to radical voices of the English past as for example the fiery Quaker preacher Edward Burrough (1634-1663) to whose memory the band dedicated their highly successful album *Thunder And Consolation* in 1989.

7. Alternative Lifestyles: The Levellers

In the early nineties, with the Conservatives' grip on the country as tight as ever, even without Margaret Thatcher, bands like New Model Army began writing songs about their own sentiment of defeat (e.g. the 1993 B-side "Modern Times") and turned to more personal subjects and micro-political strategies. To a certain extent this echoed recent trends in Marxist academic discourse where historians were turning away from the major narrative of the revolution towards multiple stories and experiences of those involved. Critics and disciples alike read books like Christopher Hill's *The Experience of Defeat* (1984) as representations of Marxists intellectuals' reaction to revisionism and Thatcherism.[16]

At the same time, a new interpretation of seventeenth-century radicals took root among a different set of dissenters. The late eighties had seen a boom in alternative lifestyles and neo-hippie movements such as new age travellers, a lively free festival scene or land squatters. Many of them held neo-pagan beliefs and longed to return to a primitive, communitarian way of life. Small wonder that Winstanley's Diggers enjoyed tremendous popularity in these quarters. Yet, here they were not understood as forerunners of modern communism, but as radical individualists and pacifists who had rejected private ownership of land and wanted a just society, based on respect for each other and Mother Earth (not exactly a reading to be found in many history textbooks). Among the anarcho-folk punk bands that sprang up in this scene, The Levellers have been by far the most successful. Like New Model Army, they have attracted a devoted following on their extensive tours (live performance is seen as the main way of communication) and become something like alternative pop stars. The band's name is slightly misleading as it is reminiscent of the Diggers, otherwise termed True Levellers, rather than of the London-based Leveller party. One song from their second album *Levelling The Land* (1992) gives an account of "The Battle Of The Beanfield" in summer 1985 when police broke up a free festival at newly enclosed Stonehenge by excessive force. The well-structured song evokes a number of feelings from helplessness to outrage, oscillating between calm passages with sinister sirens in the distant background and angry shouting by the eye-witness narrator in the chorus, which invites the audience to rant along:

> Hey, hey, now can't you see
> There's nothing here that you can call free
> They're getting their kicks
> Laughing at you and me (chorus, ll. 13-16)

The subject of police brutality and oppression of those leading a different lifestyle is a common feature of this sort of music.[17] Yet "The Battle Of The Beanfield" uses images strongly reminiscent of scenes of war and allows comparison with the well-known suppression of the community at St. George's Hill in 1650:

> As the sun rose on the beanfield
> They came like wolf on the fold
> And they didn't give a warning
> They took their bloody toll
> [...]
> And no they didn't need a reason
> It's what your votes condone
> It seems they were committing treason
> By trying to live on the road (ll. 17-20, 25-28)

8. Teaching an Alternative History

Since the spectacular events of 1989/90 when the Tories tried to reintroduce the Poll Tax which led to the eventual fall of Margaret Thatcher, things had been relatively quiet. Punk rock poet Attila The Stockbroker had linked the campaign with another significant date in the English Marxists' tradition of resistance on his *Donkey's Years* album (1991). The song "Tyler Smiles" found the obvious historical model for the massive protest against the Poll Tax in the Peasants' Revolt of 1381, sparked off by the attempt to introduce a similar tax by Richard II.

In 1994, the Criminal Justice and Public Order Bill brought mass demonstrations back to the streets of Britain. Since the new legislation was planning to virtually abolish the right to be silent, limit the right to protest and to privacy and give new powers of stop-and-search to the police, many people felt threatened and discriminated against in an unprecedented way. Once again, popular music was crucial in voicing the protest. A fine example is a compilation (a medium first used to rally support for the miners' strike in 1984) released in 1995. It was very fittingly called *The Disagreement Of The People* and contained a broad range of folk, indie rock and dance tracks (including The Pogues, Billy Bragg, New Model Army & Joolz (reciting Shelley's "Song to the Men of England"), The Poison Girls, The Oyster Band, Chumbawamba). The title plays with the Levellers' 1647 draft-constitution *An Agreement of the People* and the booklet employs a language strongly reminiscent of seventeenth-century debates:

> This government has forgotten that it holds power on trust – it doesn't rule as of right. It rules because we consent to that rule, and our consent can be withheld as well as granted. [...] Now our liberties and freedoms are under threat. No one – however high and mighty – can tell us how to live.[18]

The fullest account of England's long tradition of protest and resistance to tyranny and capitalism ever recorded was released in 1994 by Leeds indie band Chumbawamba. Their album *English Rebel Songs 1381-1914* takes a very educational approach. Its declared aim is to teach an alternative history of England which cannot be found in school books but in the orally transmitted (and therefore considered authentic) political folksongs. Youths should be made aware of their part in this great tradition. The booklet gives a preferred Marxist reading for each song and points out similarities with present causes. The result is:

> The real history of England is full of riots, revolutions, rebellions and insurrections. It's a history of perpetual class war, waged by the poor, against the state, the clergy and landlords. And unlike the history we learn in school, the history of rebellion is something we can learn from.[19]

The second track is Winstanley's "Diggers' Song" and the commentary highlights their poverty, rejection of property and eventual defeat. The moral it draws is that pacifism is not enough to shake off oppression and active resistance to state injustice is mandatory. All songs are recorded *a cappella* by seven singers which is supposed to make them sound more 'authentic', as if the oppressed of England's past were speaking directly to the listener. Chumbawamba presents a predominantly young audience with the pure socialist (SWP) interpretation of English history, untouched by revisionism or more recent trends in Marxist scholarship. Considering those far-reaching changes, it seems a brave, yet somewhat belated enterprise.

On the first album with his new band Barnstormer, *The Siege Of Shoreham* (very fittingly released with Roundhead Records in 1996), Attila The Stockbroker devoted a long track to the Diggers. "March of the Levellers / The Digger's Song / The World Turned Upside Down" combines older material into an appraisal of more than eight minutes. The first part is a 'neo-Renaissance' instrumental piece written twelve years earlier for his second album *Sawdust And Empire*. The usual rock instrumentation is expanded here to include recorders and fiddle. This opening is then followed by Winstanley's anthem sung to the same tune as the Chumbawamba version but much faster and accompanied by a single drum. Rosselson's homage to the Diggers comes last. It is delivered at breakneck speed with a full rock band. Before the closing lines of this last part, Attila includes some poetry of his own that spells out his typically strong Marxist view of history:

> At the end of the English Civil War
> When the New Model Army made the law

A host of radical movements grew
Levellers, Diggers, Ranters too
They wanted a republic and much, much more
Freedom, equality, votes for the poor
Community of land and bread for all
A new age dawning at Charles' fall
But Cromwell and his propertied friends
Had taken power for their own ends[20]

These lines show once more how valid the nineteen-seventies left-wing interpretation of the period remained among British artists even after the heated academic debates triggered by revisionism. Attila The Stockbroker has been among those who affirm this sense of history and its topicality for current political struggle at the annual Levellers Day in Burford, Oxfordshire. Since 1975, leading Socialist intellectuals and politicians (Tony Benn, Ken Livingstone) as well as artists (Billy Bragg, Leon Rosselson, Peggy Seeger) have gathered at the site of the Levellers-inspired mutiny against Cromwell. Unsuccessful as it might have been, their last stand is celebrated each May as a crucial event in England's tradition of resistance to tyranny. Twentieth-century socialists can add the mutineers to their line of ancestors and thereby explain the failure of the English Revolution by highlighting the defeat of the true revolutionary forces.

9. England's New Chains

By far the most ambitious piece of work considered in this article is the concept album *Freeborn John*, by folksinger Rev Hammer, on the life and times of charismatic Leveller leader John Lilburne. This epic and sometimes deliberately kitschy revolutionary musical was released in 1997. With its luxurious box and thick booklet, it looks rather like a classical music CD which is certainly intended. The fact that it came out in another crucial moment of recent British history, shortly before the Labour landslide victory, is no coincidence either.

It features an impressive cast of indie celebrities, including The Levellers as the Levellers, Maddy Prior as Elizabeth Lilburne and Justin Sullivan as New Model Army trooper Nehemiah Wharton. In sixteen tracks (songs and passages from contemporary documents), it tells the story of Lilburne's political life since his first conviction for 'seditious libel' in 1637. His army career during the civil war is only treated briefly (highlighting his wife's courage in "Elizabeth's Great Gallop") while the struggle against the Cromwellian settlement takes centre stage. The last five tracks deal extensively with Lilburne's defeat, exile, return and death. So the album is not so much an elevated hero worship, as an account of an individual's fight for change who is then purged by a new order, quite different from the one he had dreamt to build. This doubtlessly expressed the feelings of many left-wing activists in the wake of New Labour's victory, and its topicality has earned the musical a cult status. Rev Hammer performed parts of it at the Levellers Day in 1999, and it was put on stage for the first time on three consecutive nights at the 2005 Beautiful Days Festival.[21]

The booklet places Lilburne within a tradition that is relevant in the recent turmoil over the Criminal Justice Act when telling of his first trial for high treason: "This was perhaps the earliest recorded example of defence by the Right of Silence. He stood his ground as a freeborn Englishman and questioned the very authority of the court."[22] The Levellers are presented in a post-revisionist light by the booklet, as a progressive pressure group, yet without the socialist pathos of earlier accounts:[23]

> The Levellers were fierce individualists, their 'rights' as Freeborn Englishmen were paramount. [...] Freedom meant powers and rights as well as absence of coercion. They constantly expressed the need to check the strong and protect the weak.[24]

Throughout the album, its main character is portrayed as a bold and upright defender of the people's cause, yet also suffering doubt and eventual defeat. In a way, it sums up all the experiences of politically active men and women in the Thatcher era on the eve of the Labour victory. Its centre piece "England's New Chains" asks quite openly if it was worth all the fighting:

> Maybe time will tell
> Who survives the fire
> And maybe time will tell
> Why we've been fighting all this while (ll. 17-20)[25]

The title and chorus of this bitter ballad go back to Lilburne's pamphlet *England's New Chains Discovered* (1649) in which he had attacked the new settlement after the end of the Civil War. It is a simply structured folksong with an exorbitant instrumentation conveying a sense of disillusionment and defeat. The speaker of this soliloquy is the historic character Lilburne, who faces the debris of the recent war and the prospect of a new tyranny:

> I am a Free-born Englishman
> I am any mother's son
> I can pretend it was worth the war
> If I cut out my tongue
> And I walk in silence, 'cross the stones
> And down to Traitors Gate.
> Here we go again, it's still the same
> England's new chains.
> ... and we are held faster than before! (ll. 21-29)

But it is of course also the sad voice of the politically active contemporary of ours, looking back on years of struggle and ahead into the not very promising brave new world of New Labour.

However, Lilburne works as an historical exemplum here, too. His story is told to teach the audience about the origins of England's rebellious tradition as well as to warn them against the dangers of the eventual suppression of progressive movements by the same powers they had set their hopes on. This bitterness is at the heart of "Lilburne's Death Song":

> And as time and success have changed
> The honest shape of many men
> My time has come for Liberty
> From the last of my jails. (ll. 17-20)[26]

Thus, even this rather drippy song (culminating in a congregation singing "Now Thank We All Our God") can be read as a clarion call to beware of new leaders who might turn out to be even greater tyrants than the old ones.

10. Conclusion

It might be surprising that these songs do not personalise the enemy as, for example, Morrissey's "Margaret On The Guillotine" does. Images of class struggle abound, matching the Marxist interpretation of the Civil War as the rise of the mercantile classes which then brutally silenced dissenting voices which called for a more far-reaching transformation of society. The artists considered here fashioned themselves as part of a specifically English tradition of resistance going back to these radicals. The shining example of seventeenth-century revolutionaries informed the sense of history they were eager to communicate to their audiences. Thus, an alternative canon of English history (with heroes, villains and even texts of astonishing topicality) could be constructed. And with it a set of ideals and values quite different from those dominating Thatcher's Britain. In order to convey their vision of history to the listeners and thereby to make them feel part of a community and install them as heirs to this great tradition, the speakers took on a variety of roles: we have heard the peer, the storyteller, preacher, teacher, eye-witness and historical character. All of these aim at creating a sense of authenticity. The message they have in common is that Britain is still at war with itself and that political action is needed. They teach the lessons to be learnt from English history: not to stand idle in the face of tyranny but take political action, to know one's enemy, to beware of new leaders, and eventually to make sense of failure. Even more importantly, they provide the imagined community they address with a shared political language to articulate dissent, resistance, visions of a better future, but also doubt and defeat.

Notes

1 Blair Worden: *Roundhead Reputations. The English Civil Wars and the Passions of Posterity*, London, 2001, p. 1f.
2 See for example Henry Holorenshaw: *The Levellers and the English Revolution*, London, 1939 or David W. Petegorsky: *Left-Wing Democracy*

in the English Civil War. A Study of the Social Philosophy of Gerrard Winstanley, London, 1940; cf. Wordon: Roundhead Reputations, p. 332.

3 Christopher Hill: The World Turned Upside Down. Radical Ideas during the English Revolution, London, 1972.

4 Cf. Alastair MacLachlan: The Rise and Fall of Revolutionary England. An Essay on the Fabrication of Seventeenth-Century History, Basingstoke, 1996, p. 300.

5 Roy Shuker: Understanding Popular Music, London & New York, 1994, p. 135.

6 Dave Laing: "The Grain of Punk: An Analysis of the Lyrics". — In Angela McRobbie (Ed.): Zoot Suits and Second-Hand Dresses. An Anthology of Fashion and Music, London, 1989, pp. 74-101.

7 Quoted in David Rowe: Popular Cultures. Rock Music, Sport and the Politics of Pleasure, London, 1995, p. 56.

8 Simon Frith: Music for Pleasure. Essays in the Sociology of Pop, Cambridge, 1988, p. 123.

9 Unless stated otherwise, lyrics were taken from Leo's Lyrics Database <www.leoslyrics.com>.

10 Gang of Four: Solid Gold & Another Day / Another Dollar (EMI 8 37006 2) 1996.

11 Robin Denselow: When the Music's Over. The Story of Political Pop, London, 1989, p. 210f.

12 "England's Democratic Army", The Communist Review, Ser. IV, 1947, 171.

13 For a good Marxist overview cf. Austin Woolrych: "Putney Revisited: Political Debate in the New Model Army in 1647". — In Colin Jones (Ed.): Politics and People in Revolutionary England. Essays in Honour of Ivan Roots, Oxford, 1986, pp. 95-116.

14 Amrik Rai: "Come the Revolution ...", New Musical Express, 23 March 1985.

15 New Model Army lyrics were taken from <http://www.newmodelarmy.org/fhome.htm>.

16 Christopher Hill: The Experience of Defeat. Milton and Some Contemporaries, London, 1984, cf. his A Nation of Change and Novelty. Radical Politics, Religion and Literature in Seventeenth-Century England, London, 1990, p. 244; see also MacLachlan: The Rise and Fall of Revolutionary England, pp. 200-206.

17 Cf. Stuart Borthwick and Roy Moy's excellent introduction Popular Music Genres, Edinburgh, 2004, p. 93f.

18 V.A.: The Disagreement Of The People (Cook CD 088) 1995, 5.

19 Chumbawamba: English Rebel Songs 1381-1914 (One Little Indian/Virgin 840 906 2) 1994, 1.

20 <http://www.small-axe.com/attila/shoreham/levellers.mp3>

21 Cf.   <http://www.beautifuldays.org/BEAUTIFULDAYS2005LINE-UP.htm>.

22 Rev Hammer: *Freeborn John* (Cook CD 111) 1997, 4.
23 As for example Christopher Hill: "The Levellers". — In David Rubinstein
    (Ed.): *People for the People*. *Radical Ideas and Personalities in British
    History*, London 1973, pp. 30-36.
24 *Freeborn John*, 5.
25 *Ibid.*, 16.
26 *Ibid.*, 22.

Bibliography

Borthwick, Stuart & Roy Moy: *Popular Music Genres*, Edinburgh, 2004.
Denselow, Robin: *When the Music's Over. The Story of Political Pop*, London, 1989.
Frith, Simon: *Music for Pleasure. Essays in the Sociology of Pop*, Cambridge, 1988.
Hill, Christopher: "England's Democratic Army", *Communist Review* Ser. IV, 1947, 171-178.
---: *The World Turned Upside Down. Radical Ideas during the English Revolution*, Harmondsworth, 1991 [1972].
---: "The Levellers". – In David Rubinstein (Ed.): *People for the People. Radical Ideas and Personalities in British History*, London, 1973, pp. 30-36.
---: "Forerunners of Socialism in the 17th Century English Revolution", *Marxism Today* 21, 1977, 270-276.
---: *The Experience of Defeat. Milton and Some Contemporaries*, London, 1984.
---: *A Nation of Change and Novelty. Radical Politics, Religion and Literature in Seventeenth-Century England*, London & New York, 1990.
Holorenshaw, Henry: *The Levellers and the English Revolution*, London, 1939.
Laing, Dave: "The Grain of Punk: An Analysis of the Lyrics". – In Angela McRobbie (Ed.): *Zoot Suits and Second-Hand Dresses. An Anthology of Fashion and Music*, London, 1989, pp. 74-101.
MacLachlan, Alastair: *The Rise and Fall of Revolutionary England. An Essay on the Fabrication of Seventeenth-Century History*, Basingstoke, 1996.
Petegorsky, David W.: *Left-Wing Democracy in the English Civil War. A Study of the Social Philosophy of Gerrard Winstanley*, London, 1940.
Rai, Amrik: "Come the Revolution ...", *New Musical Express*, 23 March 1985.
Richardson, Roger Charles: *The Debate on the English Revolution Revisited*, London, 1988.
Rowe, David: *Popular Cultures. Rock Music, Sport and the Politics of Pleasure*, London, 1995.

Shuker, Roy: *Understanding Popular Music*, London & New York, 1994.

Woolrych, Austin: "Putney Revisited: Political Debate in the New Model Army in 1647". – In Colin Jones (Ed.): *Politics and People in Revolutionary England. Essays in Honour of Ivan Roots*, Oxford, 1986, pp. 95-116.

Worden, Blair: *Roundhead Reputations. The English Civil Wars and the Passions of Posterity*, Harmondsworth, 2001.

Hartmut Möller (Rostock)

Rhetorical Gestures of War and Peace in the Music of Benjamin Britten. From the *Pacifist March* to the *War Requiem*

1. *The Many Brittens and the Question of Pacifism*

As with many great composers, the relationship between the life and work of Benjamin Britten is complex and full of contradictions. Mitchell, Reed and Cooke, the editors of his selected letters and diaries, even come to the conclusion that

> one needs more than one key to unlock the many doors offering access to Britten, not only the Britten who was the predetermined 'outcast' but the many Brittens who went to make up the social being and serious citizen that he was.[1]

Many of Britten's works, songs, chamber music and operas reveal an "awareness of 'violent climates' ", as Donald Mitchell described.[2] This is particularly evident in his operas *Peter Grimes* (1942-45), *The Rape of Lucretia* (1946) and *Billy Budd* (1948-51). Even so, on what levels can we understand the comment by Britten in 1940 that he planned to make a composition "as anti-war as possible"?[3]

Benjamin Britten's pacifist attitude has been well-known and accepted in the literature up to the present. For example, David G. Greene stated in 2000 that "Britten, by contrast [to Owen], was a pacifist, and conscientiously objected to service in World War II".[4] Mervyn Cooke likewise argued that

> his pacifism was a consistent lifelong commitment, and the sincerity and intensity of its expression in the *War Requiem* ('the one musical masterwork we possess with overt pacifist meanings,' as Tippett hailed it) can never be in doubt.[5]

Indeed, it can be demonstrated that there is a continuity of musical-rhetorical gestures and types of musical expression from his pacifist works of the 1930s to his *War Requiem* of 1961: *Dances of Death, Funeral March* and *Music of Peace*. On the other hand, in real life Britten's pacifism was an articulation of his gentle spirit with no reference to real action. In 1963 he recalled in discussions with his former teacher Frank Bridge that his pacifism started about 1931: " [...] and though he didn't encourage me to take a stand for the sake of a stand, he did make me argue and argue and argue. His own pacifism was not aggressive, but typically gentle."[6] In 1942, after returning from the USA, Britten objected to service in World War II:

> Since I believe that there is in every man the spirit of God, I cannot destroy [...] human life, however strongly I disapprove of the individual's actions or thoughts. The whole of my life has been devoted to acts of creation (being by profession a composer) and I cannot take part in acts of destruction. [...] I believe sincerely that I can help my fellow human beings best, by continuing [...] the creation or propagation of music. I have possibilities of writing music for Ministry of Information films, and for B.B.C. productions, and am offering my services to the Committee for the Encouragements of Music and Art.[7]

In 1942 Britten was officially asked what he would do if the Germans invaded Great Britain. He replied, "I believe in letting an invader in and then setting him a good example. Denmark has allowed the Germans in and has not yet got them out, but time is short so far."[8]

In July 1945 Britten and the violinist Yehudi Menuhin visited the concentration camps at Bergen-Belsen, Bad Oeynhausen and other places (possibly also the camp at Haren, Emsland), giving two or three short recitals a day. Shortly before his death, Britten recalled "how shocking it was, and that the experience had coloured everything he had written subsequently".[9] As Jürgen Schaarwächter found, however, Britten's works of 1946-47 showed no relation with the experience of the German concentration camps.[10] When Yehudi Menuhin was asked if he felt that Britten did this tour because he had not participated in the collective war experience, he answered:

I think he felt that he had denied himself as a British man, as one living in that era, had denied himself an essential experience which was part of his nation, was part of his people's experience, and by taking it as it were in one fell swoop, it wasn't spread over many years – it came with a terrific power. I think that must have been a part of the motive, I'm sure. [...] His compassion was tremendous, but he had to have somehow the reality, the physical evidence of it as well. I think he needed it.[11]

2. The Composition of the War Requiem

Benjamin Britten composed his famous *War Requiem* for the opening of the rebuilt and redesigned Coventry Cathedral in 1962. At the time of its composition in 1961, Britten had completed ten operas. His musical answer to the Latin words of the *Requiem* thus tends more towards the dramatic possibilities of the genre than towards liturgical observance. Britten's *War Requiem* was not intended to be used in a Mass for the Dead. The *Requiem* text is interrupted nine times by settings of poems written by Wilfred Owen in 1917/18.

Britten's interest in Owen's poetry was first revealed in a poetry selection for a BBC radio programme in 1958. For this programme, he chose two of Owen's poems. In the same year, he also set one of these poems, "The Kind Ghosts", to music as part of his orchestral song-cycle *Nocturne*.

Britten's library contained only one edition of Owen's poems, a 1955 reprint of the 1931 edition by Edmund Blunden. This edition was Britten's principal source for all the Owen texts he used in the *War Requiem*. Britten marked the selected poems with a pencil "X". He wrote out the libretto for the *War Requiem* in one of his old school exercise books, dating from 1928. This particular one had been the schoolboy's German notebook. Britten used it from the back and upside down, using double-pages with the words of the Requiem Mass on the left and the selected Owen poems on the right.

Looking at one page from Britten's notebook (below), the Latin requiem text can be seen on the left: "Sanctus" and "Agnus". The "Lux aeterna", the official communion of the Requiem mass, is re-

From Britten's notebook (Cooke 1996, pp. 34-35).

placed by the responsory "Libera me" as the last movement of the *War Requiem*. The words "? nobis pacem" on the left page are written by Peter Pears – in the final score of the *War Requiem*, the Chorus sings the "Agnus Dei" three times, and then the solo tenor adds the non-liturgical phrase "Dona nobis pacem". On the right side of the notebook excerpt, there are two of Owen's poems, yet only the second was selected while "Arms and the Boy" was rejected.

TENOR SOLO
One ever hangs where shelled roads part
…

CHORUS
Agnus Dei

Near Golgotha strolls many a priest …

Agnus Dei …

The scribes on all the people shove …

Agnus Dei …

(from: "At a Calvary near the Ancre")

TENOR SOLO
Dona nobis pacem.

(Cooke 1996, pp. 98-99)

In the libretto, Britten combines the three stanzas of the poem with the three liturgical reiterations of the "Agnus".

Owen's poem "At a Calvary near the Ancre" develops an image known to many First World War poets and painters: Jesus Christ on the modern battlefield. This is in complete accordance with the liturgical plea to the Lamb of God.

Britten selected poems that refer to the Latin liturgical text also in the other movements of the *War Requiem*. For example, the introitus is interrupted by Owen's "Anthem for Doomed Youth". The poem asks: "What passing-bells for these who die as cattle?"

The music of the *War Requiem* has an encyclopaedic quality. It refers stylistically to the traditions of West-European art music: plainchant, Renaissance, Baroque and 19th century opera music. There are a number of parallels to Verdi's *Requiem* of 1874, which the conductor Hans von Bülow described as "Verdi's latest opera, in ecclesiastical dress".[12] When asked about historical precedents during his work on the *War Requiem*, Britten replied,

> I think that I would be a fool if I didn't take notice of how Mozart, Verdi, Dvořák – whoever you like to name – had written their Masses. I mean, many people have pointed out the similarities between the Verdi Requiem and bits of my own War Requiem, and they may be there. If I have not absorbed that, that's too bad. But that's because I'm not a good enough composer, it's not because I'm wrong.[13]

Musically, the *War Requiem* represents the culmination of Britten's middle-period style. It synthesizes many aspects of his earlier music. Therefore, echoes of Britten's earlier works come as no surprise in the pages of the *War Requiem*.

As we shall see, there are special relationships to a group of works from 1935/36 to 1940.

3. Britten and Auden

In July 1935, Benjamin Britten met the poet Wystan Hugh Auden for the first time. Auden was teaching at a preparatory school at that time. Auden stimulated Britten's interest in poetry, and he drew him to a group of avant-garde writers and artists, mostly of left-wing views, some of them Communists. All of them were disillusioned by unemployment and by the British government's attitude towards the dictators in Germany, Italy and Spain.

As well as identifying with the working class and with Communism at that time, this group of artists and intellectuals also featured various homosexual relationships among its members.

Britten with
W. H. Auden at
Tanglewood, Lenox,
Mass., August 1946

(Mitchell 1979, p. 97)

Auden and his friend Christopher Isherwood were homosexual, and so was Britten. Even after homosexuality had ceased to be a criminal offence, Britten never wrote or spoke a word about his private life. Auden's influence helped to bring out the left-wing tendencies in Britten's political thinking at that time. As Britten was too involved with his music, he did not become as politically committed as some of his friends. In 1936 he read Karl Marx, but he was most strongly attracted to the idea of pacifism that was also a central topic of this group.

Britten's strong pacifist attitude became public around 1936 when he wrote the music for a three-minute film, *Peace of Britain*, directed by Paul Rotha. The film took no political line, except for the stance that it was better for nations to negotiate than to fight. But its message was so politically inopportune that the British Board of Film Censors initially refused certification. Several newspapers and the BBC reported on this restriction – and certification was granted on the following day. In 1937 Britten worked together with Ronald Duncan on a *Pacifist March* for an organization dedicated to total pacifism: the Peace Pledge Union.

4 The printed song sheet of *Pacifist March*

(Mitchell 1979, pp. 67-68)

Ronald Duncan was the poet and playwright, and he was to become the librettist of the opera *The Rape of Lucretia* in 1946. Duncan was also the author of a book entitled *The Complete Pacifist*, and he lent Britten a book by Richard Gregg on *The Power of Non-Violence* (London 1935), which, as Duncan remembered, "influenced him considerably".[14]

Pacifist tendencies are central in the texts and in Britten's musical techniques in two works for radio: *The Company of Heaven*

(1937) and *The World of Spirit* (1938). In 1939 Britten composed a cantata, *Ballad of Heroes*, for a festival entitled "Music for the People" at Queen's Hall, London. This cantata with texts by left-wing activist Randall Swingler and by Auden honours the British volunteers killed in the Spanish Civil War. Following his friends Auden and Isherwood, Britten stayed, together with Peter Pears, in the United States from May 1939 until March 1942. There he composed the *Sinfonia da Requiem*, his only orchestral symphony. It was partly an official commission, partly a work in memory of his parents and partly an anti-militaristic statement. As Britten remarked about this work to the *New York Sun* in April 1940:

> I'm making it just as anti-war as possible [...] I don't believe you can express social or political or economic theories in music. But by coupling new music with well-known musical phrases, I think it's possible to get over certain ideas [...] One's apt to get muddled discussing such things – all I'm sure of is my own anti-war conviction as I write it.[15]

There are indeed several works from 1936 until 1940 whose texts and music are a public statement of Britten's pacifism:

1936 *Russian Funeral* for brass and percussion,
1936 *Peace of Britain*, film music,
1937 *Pacifist March,* text: Robert Duncan,
1937 *The Company of Heaven*, BBC radio project,
1938 *The World of Spirit*, BBC radio project,
1939 *Ballad of Heroes*, op. 14, cantata, text: W. Auden,
     R. Swingler,
1940 *Sinfonia da Requiem*, op. 20, orchestral symphony.

What I want to demonstrate in the rest of this article is that there is a continuity of musical-rhetorical gestures and types of musical expression in these works from the thirties to the *War Requiem* of 1962.

4. Dances of Death

By the end of 1936, Auden had decided to go to Spain, as he wanted to participate actively as an ambulance driver in the Spanish Civil War. Britten wrote in his diary on 1 December 1936: "I try to dissuade him, because what the Spanish government might gain by his joining is nothing compared with the world's gain by his continuing to write."[16] But Auden was determined to go. On 8 January 1937, the day before the poet's departure, the two men met in London. In this situation, Auden wrote down his poem "It's farewell" in a copy of Britten's first published work, the *Sinfonietta* opus 1.

Two years later Britten set this poem to music in his cantata *Ballad of Heroes*. It formed the basis of the second movement, entitled "Dance of Death".

SCHERZO (DANCE OF DEATH)
It's farewell to the drawing-room's civilised [mannerly] cry,
The professor's sensible [logical] whereto and why,
The frock-coated diplomat's social aplomb,
Now matters are settled with gas and with bomb.

The works for two pianos, the brilliant stories
Of reasonable giants and remarkable fairies,
The pictures, the ointments, the frangible wares
And the branches of olive are stored upstairs.

For the Devil has broken parole and arisen,
He has dynamited his way out of prison,
Out of the well where his Papa throws
The rebel angel, the outcast rose.

[4 stanzas]

The behaving of man is a world of horror,
A sedentary Sodom and slick Gomorrah;
I must take charge of the liquid fire,
And storm the cities of human desire.

[3 stanzas]

For it's order and trumpet and anger and drum
And power and glory command you to come.
[The graves will fly open to let you all in,
And the earth be emptied of mortal sin.]

The fishes are silent deep in the sea,
The skies are lit up like a Christmas tree,
The star in the West shoots its warning cry:
'Mankind is alive, but Mankind must die'.

So good-bye to the house with its wallpaper red,
Good-bye to the sheets on the warm double bed.
Good-bye to the beautiful birds on the wall,
It's good-bye, dear heart, good-bye to you all.[17]

This type of violent dance music for Death combines timpani, fast strings and wind instruments with the choir. It had already been used in an earlier radio cantata in 1937, in which Britten set a text from the Book of Revelation describing the war in heaven between Michael and the fallen angels. The "War in Heaven" begins with powerful timpani and dissonant string chords; the male choir is accompanied by the organ.

WAR IN HEAVEN
And there was war in heaven: Michael and his
angels fought against the dragon; and the dragon
fought and his angels,
And prevailed not; nor was their place found
any more in heaven.
And the great dragon was cast out, that old
serpent, called the Devil, and Satan, which
deceiveth the whole world: he was cast out into
the earth, and his angels were cast out with him.
And after these things I saw another angel
come down from heaven, having great power; and
the earth was lightened with his glory.
And death and hell were cast into the lake of fire.
(Revelation XX 7-9, XVIII 1, XX 14)

The numerous martial and violent passages in Britten's *War Requiem* will be illustrated by two excerpts.

The first example is the "Tuba mirum" of the "Dies irae", with single note fanfares in the brass instruments, accompanying the syllabic text of the choir, in fortissimo with a crescendo in a 7/4 measure:

Tu-ba mirum   spar- gens sonum
Per se- pulchra re-   gi-   onum
Co- get om- nes an- te   thronum,
Coget omnes ante thronum.
(*War Requiem*, score pp. 30-31)

This musical atmosphere of destruction in the "Dies irae" is taken up in the last movement, where the orchestra plays the major role by illustrating the disturbing vision. Before the beginning of the last part of the "Libera me", the solo soprano sings "et timeo", while the choir intones "dum discussio venerit atque ventura ira". The orchestra accompanies the text with gradually ascending accented notes, with a crescendo from piano to fortissimo (*War Requiem*, score pp. 194-6).

5. Funeral Marches

Britten had the opportunity to listen to a concert performance of Shostakovich's *Lady Macbeth* in March 1936. In his diary, he described the work as "tremendous [...] a most moving & exciting work of a real inspired genius." In a review, he declared that there was more music in a page of *Macbeth* than in the whole of the "elegant" output of the "eminent English Renaissance" composers.[18] His *Russian Funeral* for brass and percussion demonstrates the fruitful influence of Shostakovich and Mahler on the 23-year-old Britten. The original title was *War and Death*. This deeply impressive symphonic-poem had its premiere at the Westminster Theatre in March 1936 and was not played again until 1980. The beginning is a funeral march, influenced by Gustav Mahler, on the theme of a Russian song, which was played at the funeral of the demonstrators massacred outside the Winter Palace in 1905. This song had become a famous funeral march in memoriam of the victims of the revolution in 1905. Britten uses this melody in his *Russian Funeral*, which can be seen in the lower part of the manuscript page below.

No recording is available of Britten's *Russian Funeral*. However, this is also illustrated by the "Funeral March for a Boy" from the radio cantata *Company of Heaven* (1937). The well-known rhythmic model of the funeral march is combined with reminiscences of the music of Mahler.

Score of the Funeral March (http://www.kds-imnetz.de/kanal/2003/gedicht.htm)

A version of the funeral march is used at the beginning of the last movement of the *War Requiem*. It begins with a rhythmic skeleton of drums and percussion but soon rises up through the orchestral texture. The musical model of the funeral march is combined with the words of the chorus "Libera me".

One page from Britten's manuscript full score of *Russian Funeral* (Mitchell 1979, p. 76).

6. LIBERA ME

Britten, *War Requiem,* score (excerpt from p. 178)

Libera me, Domine, de morte aeterna,
In die illa tremenda:
Quando coeli movendi sunt et terra.
(Free me, Lord from eternal death, on that dreadful day, when
the skies and grounds shall quake.)

6. Music of Peace

In 1940, when the threat of an invasion by Hitler was imminent,
Britten was asked by the British Council to write a work for a
festivity of "the reigning dynasty of a foreign power". Britten
agreed, provided that "no form of musical jingoism" was required.[19]
The foreign power was Japan, and the festivity was the anniversary
of the foundation of the Mikado dynasty 2600 years before. Other
composers, including the German Richard Strauss, had also
received commissions. Britten sketched out his work with the title
Sinfonia da Requiem, and the Japanese approved the outline. His
intention from the onset was to "combine my ideas on war and a
memorial for Mum and Pop".[20] Britten completed the orchestra
score with three movements and sent it to Japan.

The titles of the three movements were taken from the Latin
requiem mass: "Lacrymosa", "Dies irae" and "Requiem aeternam".
Six months later, however, Britten received an outraged protest
from Japan because the Christian dogma underlying the work was
an insult to the Mikado. The work was rejected by the Japanese

with the result that the first performance then took place in New York in March 1941.

The last movement "Requiem" again refers to the music of Gustav Mahler, especially in its compassionate and luminous string texture. Meanwhile, Richard Strauss' composition *Festmusik zur Feier des 2600-jährigen Bestehens des Kaiserreiches Japan* for orchestra (op. 84, 1940.) was accepted by the Japanese government.[21]

The beginning of this movement from 1940 with the prominent bass clarinet and harp doubling is taken up again in the final movement of the *War Requiem*. The two solo voices blend at "Let us sleep now", the boys' choir sings the antiphon text "In paradisum", and they are joined by the main choir and the orchestra, together with the soprano. At this point, near the end, all the performers can thus be heard together for the first time.

TENOR AND BARITONE SOLOS: [...] Let us sleep now.
BOYS CHOIR; CHORUS AND SOPRANO SOLO: In paradisum deducant te Angeli [...] Et cum Lazaro quondam paupere aeternam habeas requiem.
BOYS: Requiem aeternam dona eis, Domine, et lux perpetua luceat eis.
CHORUS: In paradisum deducant
SOPRANO: Chorus angelorum te suscipiat
TENOR AND BARITONE: Let us sleep now...
CHORUS: Requiescant in pace. Amen.[22]

The work closes with the chiming of the bells (already heard at the very beginning) and the choir's resolution of the tritone with the words of "Requiescant in pace. Amen". F sharp is resolved to pure F major in the last chord.

In his film *War Requiem*, the British film director Derek Jarman confronts the "Libera me" with documentary footage from wars that have erupted since Britten composed his music, from Africa and Cambodia, and images of the atom bomb exploding on Hiroshima. In the finale, parallel to the music's "In paradisum deducant te Angeli" and "Requiescant in pace. Amen", the figure of Wilfred Owen appears for the last time. He holds a "flickering candle, which reveals a cavern filled with sleeping figures covered with a pall of dust".[23] As Jarman explained, he wanted to stick to his first impressions of Britten's music: "The War Requiem I heard in 1963 seemed shockingly arbitrary. I hope that my film has a similar feeling of discomfort."[24] At the end of his film, however, the feeling of discomfort resolves in accord with the music. There remains no tension between the two media at the end. While F sharp is surprisingly resolved to the conventional F major in the music, one can see a flame on the altar in the film, referring back to the perpetual flame shown right at the start.

Dances of death, funeral marches and music of peace are elements of Benjamin Britten's lifelong commitment to pacifism. The sincerity and intensity of these types of musical expression and musical-rhetorical gestures cannot be doubted. But the question remains: What kind of music was and will be in the future "as anti-war as possible"? How can the "Dona nobis pacem", the inner and the outer peace, be experienced in music?[25]

Britten, *War Requiem*, score (p. 238)

Notes

1 Mitchell, Reed & Cooke (2004: 10).

2 Donald Mitchell in Cooke (1999: 188).

3 Interview in *The New York Sun*, April 27, 1940 concerning the *Sinfonia da Requiem*, quoted in Mitchell, Reed & Cooke (2004, vol. IV, 705).

4 Greene (2000: 100).

5 Cooke (1996: 19).

6 Britten in *The Sunday Telegraph*, November 1963, quoted in Carpenter (1992: 41).

7 *Ibid.*, 1046.

8 Quoted in Mitchell, Reed & Cooke (2004: 1046).

9 Interview Tony Palmer with Humphrey Carpenter, March 22, 1991, quoted in Carpenter (1992: 228).
10 Schaarwächter (2006: 156).
11 Yehudi Menuhin interviewed by Donald Mitchell 1979, quoted in Mitchell, Reed & Cooke (2004: vol. III, 51).
12 Quoted in C. Osborne: *Verdi: A Life in the Theatre*, London: 1987, p. 233.
13 Interview in February 1969 with Donald Mitchell in: Palmer (1984: 87-96).
14 Mitchell (1979: 48).
15 See note 3.
16 Quoted in Mitchell (1979: 133).
17 Sung text; additions/variants of the original poem in W. H. Auden, January 1937; "Song fort the New Year", *Listener* February 1937; edited as "Danse macabre". W. H. Auden: *Collected Shorter Poems 1937-1957*, London, 1966, pp. 105-107. – See John Fuller: *W. H. Auden. A Commentary*, London, 1998, p. 256.
18 Quoted in Mitchell (1979: 72).
19 *Ibid.*
20 Olivier (1996: 81).
21 Cf. Schaarwächter (2006: 152).
22 Quoted in Cooke (1996: 100).
23 Jarman (1989: 42).
24 Jarman (1988: 47).
25 Cf. Hartmut Möller: "Wie kann Frieden hörbar werden?" – In Dieter Senghaas (Ed.): *Der hörbare Friede*, Frankfurt a.M. 2005, pp. 51-78.

Bibliography

Britten, Benjamin: *War Requiem* op. 66 [score], London, (No year).
Carpenter, Humphrey: *Benjamin Britten, A Biography*, London, 1992.
Cooke, Mervyn: *Britten: War Requiem*, Cambridge, 1996.
---: *The Cambridge Companion to Benjamin Britten*, Cambridge, 1999.
Frantzen, Allen J.: "Tears for Abraham: The Chester Play of Abraham and Isaac and Antisacrifice in Works by Wilfred Owen, Benjamin Britten and Derek Jarman", *Journal of Medieval and Early Modern Studies 31:3*, fall 2001, 445-476.
Greene, David B.: "The End of Religious Music", *Soundings* 83:1, spring 2000, 90-100.
Jarman, Derek: *War Requiem. The Film*, London, 1989.
Kennedy, Michael: *Britten*, rev. edition, London, 1993.
Mc Phail, Helen: *Portrait of Wilfred Owen. Poet and Soldier*, 1983-1918, Petersfield, 1993.

Mitchell, Donald: *Britten and Auden in the Thirties: The Year 1936*, London & Boston, 1979.

Mitchell, Donald, Philip Reed & Mervyn Cooke (Eds.): *Letters from a Life: The Selected Letters and Diaries of Benjamin Britten 1913-1976*, London, 2004.

Olivier, Michael: *Benjamin Britten*, London 1996.

Palmer, Christopher (Ed.): *The Britten Companion*, London, 1984.

Schaarwächter, Jürgen: " 'as anti-war as possible'. Versuch einer Annäherung an Benjamin Brittens Pazifismus", *Die Musikforschung* 59, 2006, 149-160.

Welland, Denis: *Wilfred Owen. A Critical Study*, London, 1978.

CDs

Rattle Conducts Britten, Emi 754270 2, 1991.

Britten, *The World of Spirit*, Chandos, Essex 1996.

Britten, *The Company of Heaven*, Virgin classics, Emi 2435621042, 2002.

Film

Derek Jarman (director): *War Requiem*, produced by Don Boyd, 90 min., Anglo-International Films, 1988; videocassette distributed in the United States by Mystic Fire Video, VHS 76203.

Penny Summerfield (Manchester)

Gender and Issues of Integration in Britain, 1939-45

For the past fifty years, the historiography of women in twentieth-century Britain has used equality as its benchmark. The social effects of events such as the two world wars have been evaluated in terms of the extent to which they increased or reduced equality between the sexes, and hence contributed to 'progress' for women in the twentieth century.[1] As Laura Doan points out in a review of recent histories of gender and the First World War, "the preoccupation with change" and the insistence on relating it to an undifferentiated category of 'women', has had the effect of "restricting the kinds of questions we have been able to pose".[2] An alternative objective is to address war's influence on the cultural construction of gender and the formation of gendered subjectivities in the context of the shifting material realities of wartime. Such an approach facilitates the interrogation of the impact of war on the system of gender identities and relations as a whole. A focus on 'integration' rather than 'equality' may provide a framework within which to confront these issues. Social integration is about being recognised and accepted as a member of a social unit: its antonyms are exclusion, marginalisation, segregation and differentiation. Using this definition, it is possible to ask whether cultural constructions and material realities challenged or supported the gender order, and hence promoted or inhibited the integration of women into British wartime society, and how individual women – and men – responded to these processes. This paper focuses on the Second World War, which was as much a war of the home front (women's traditional location) as the battle front: it reviews political, economic, military and domestic life from the perspective of integration.

Historians have long argued that women's contribution to the First World War earned them political citizenship in the form of partial enfranchisement in 1918 (of women over thirty, with property or educational qualifications), extended in 1928 to full enfranchisement. But the formal concession of citizenship did not guarantee political integration. On the contrary, the small number of women candidates selected to stand in elections, the even smaller number of women Members of Parliament (M.P.s), and the single woman cabinet minister in the inter-war years indicate women's marginal position in the power structure.[3] During the Second World War there were only fourteen women M.P.s amongst some six hundred men, and there were no women cabinet ministers. The rise in the number of women M.P.s to twenty four at the General Election of 1945 and the appointment of one of them as a cabinet minister suggest that the Second World War encouraged the entry of women into politics.[4] But the war did not lead to steady progress towards parliamentary participation: 1945 represented a peak not to be surpassed again until 1992.

As Alison Oram has argued, the war stimulated a revival of a type of politics in which women across parties united in defence of what they saw as women's interests.[5] These included equal compensation for war injuries, equal pay for women conscripts and for teachers, and welfare measures such as family allowances. Success was achieved in the instances of compensation for war injuries and family allowances, and was linked to the dependence of the government on women's co-operation with both the war effort and post-war reconstruction. The achievement of political citizenship thus had direct consequences for women's social citizenship, as wartime citizens with equal rights and as wives and mothers with social rights. Lack of success in the area of equal pay, however, suggests that a line was drawn when outcomes too upsetting for the social order were envisaged. The widespread practice of unequal pay constructed men and women as different types of workers with different earning needs. Equal pay would enlarge salary bills and if (as proposed) it was paid to public service employees it would increase government spending: it also threatened the authority of the male breadwinner. Political representations of the struggle tended to belittle it. Thus Churchill accused Thelma Cazalet, who tried to introduce an equal pay amendment to the Education Bill in 1944, of attempting to force "an elephant into a perambulator".[6] He did, however, authorise the establishment of a Royal Commission on Equal Pay. Its recommendations, in 1946, were for the limited application of equal pay in certain classes of the Civil Service, but even such a modest reform was politically unachievable in the post-war economic conditions. A newspaper cartoon of 1947 depicted "Miss Equal Pay" as a little girl standing beside a boy and begging two indifferent ice cream vendors (Clement Attlee, Prime Minister, and Hugh Dalton, Chancellor of the Exchequer) for "a wafer as thick as his".[7] During the war relatively few women apart from civil servants and teachers (upon whom the campaign focused) appear to have been aware of the political struggle for equal pay. The achievement through political pressure of equal pay in any sector took another ten years after the end of the war, and was limited in its application until the Equal Pay Act of 1970.[8]

Women constituted thirty-four per cent of the paid workforce on the eve of the Second World War. This proportion had remained fairly constant since the nineteenth century, in spite of fluctuations in the size of the adult female population. In the first half of the twentieth century, women were seen by economists, employers and trade unionists as a residual part of the workforce that was not as important or permanent as male labour. Women worked in sex stereotyped industries and occupations, usually only when single. Male workers were of course differentiated: they were spread across a hierarchy in which the lowest strata were casual, unskilled and episodic workers, far from integrated with the higher strata. The female workforce was also structured in this way: there were some professional and business women, as well as small numbers of women workers regarded as skilled such as upholstresses and milliners. However, in the main, women were concentrated at the lower end of the hierarchy. Whatever stratum women occupied, they were seen as less serious and deserving members of the workforce than men.

Women's lack of integration to the labour market is further indicated by their workplace concentration. Before the Second World War, one third of all women workers were domestic servants. In industry, the largest numbers worked in the group of industries classified as textiles and clothing, although numbers were increasing in engineering, metals and miscellaneous manufacturing. In these latter industries, women occupied distinct occupational niches. As Miriam Glucksman has shown, they worked predominantly on assembly lines and on repetitive machining, which was not classed as skilled work nor paid at skilled rates.[9] The robustness of the economic segregation of women is illustrated by the cases of women who aspired to occupy men's jobs. Working-class women who wanted to stay in the engineering and metals industries after the First World War were, as Gail Braybon and others have shown, rebuffed by employers and unions, and excluded by the state through the operation of unemployment benefit (or dole).[10] Even relatively well-educated women who aspired to integration were disappointed. There was a rising proportion of women clerical workers, and seven per cent of all employed women worked in the professions. But their attempts to become fully integrated by obtaining the same opportunities as men were frustrated, as were attempts to use more unusual qualifications. Victoria Drummond trained as a marine engineer at the end of the First World War, having worked in wartime as a garage mechanic. As a qualified ship's engineer she sought and found work aboard ocean-going ships in the 1920s and 30s, but was constantly disadvantaged in terms of job opportunities and promotion, and could frequently find work only under a foreign flag.[11] On the eve of the Second World War the British labour market was firmly divided by gender.

During the war there were numerous changes which did not all outlast the conflict. The shortage of workers due to the call up of men aged eighteen to fifty to the armed forces in 1939 created opportunities for women: in 1940 Victoria Drummond was promoted to Second Engineer and from 1940 to 45, in the context of the huge death toll in the merchant fleet, she served on a succession of British vessels hazardously plying the Atlantic in convoys. More generally, the exigencies of war prompted a state-managed redistribution of male and female labour across industries and occupations. Clerical work for women grew with the wartime expansion of industry and government. Domestic service shrank by nearly two million women and the numbers in the so-called 'essential' industries expanded by nearly as much. These were industries which either contributed to the production of war material, such as metals and engineering, or sustained the population in wartime, such as transport, food processing and agriculture. In engineering, the proportion of women rose during the war from less than ten per cent to more than thirty per cent: it fell at the end of the war, but at twenty-one per cent in 1950 was nevertheless higher than pre-war. Integration, however, was limited:

84

women were rapidly trained to replace men on parts of production processes which had been sub-divided and increasingly mechanised and they were regarded as semi- rather than fully-skilled.[12] Trade union responses suggest different levels of acceptance of women's integration within male-dominated types of employment. Craft unions of skilled men, such as the Amalgamated Engineering Union (A.E.U.), remained aloof as long as they could. From 1943 the A.E.U. for the first time recruited women (on a temporary basis) to increase its membership, and hence its effectiveness in collective bargaining, and to protect skilled men's jobs from dilution.[13] The response of general unions, which women had been able to join before the war, was from the start more accepting. They recruited vigorously during the war and delivered benefits to women, notably increases in pay (if not equal pay), as well as welfare benefits including shopping time, ventilation, canteens and toilets. The rhetoric (and possibly the reality) was a combination of social justice to women and protection of the rate for the job (as done by men), but one of the outcomes was a degree of feminisation of the workplace that improved conditions for both sexes. Women were not passive. In October 1943, a dramatic women's strike took place at a Rolls Royce plant near Glasgow where aircraft engines were built. The strike was a protest against a glaring discrepancy between the pay of men and women equally new to engineering who were employed on the same type of work. The Ministry of Labour noted in 1943 that women were more inclined than men to take short sharp strike action in protest at pay anomalies in wartime engineering factories. Strikes were illegal and these actions were not officially supported by the unions: another reason for recruiting women was to impose union discipline upon them.[14]

One of the problems for the unions in negotiations concerning women workers was employers' conceptualisation of the labour force as a gender-divided rather than an integrated one. From the employers' perspective, the rate for 'women's work' would always be lower than that for 'men's work', and the classification of women's work was determined not by any measure of skill, but simply by what a woman could do. However, even if they did not succeed, the readiness of the general unions to take on the problem of squaring the gender-differentiated interests of men and women workers was a new, wartime phenomenon.

As far as women's subjectivities were concerned, evidence from both Mass-Observation at the time, and oral history later, suggests that those conscripted into war industry had, in the main, low expectations of integration. They shared a stoic attitude, characterised by the phrase "we just got on with it". Women war workers interviewed in the 1990s had memories of emphasising their feminine difference in the factory, in their clothes, make up, hairstyles and the ways they interacted with men, which were often flirtatious. A woman who welded in a frock explained: "some girls wore trousers [...] but I never liked them. I didn't want to lose my identity and it was the same with my [...] friend. We never lost our identity as being girls on the job or women."[15] These women remembered accepting wartime pay differentiation, whether they later felt this was right or not. Sadie Bartlett, whose war work was agricultural labour in the Women's Land Army, remembered that "men earned their money, and you were lucky if you had any". Some took the view that it was anachronistic to consider equal pay a wartime possibility: "Now it's different, women want equality [...] but fifty years ago it wasn't heard of."[16] Such women saw 'integration' as irrelevant: even if they liked their war work, it was theirs for the duration only. Others however were more affected by the opportunities offered by new types of work for women and higher pay. Among oral history interviewees those with the most enthusiastic memories of war work drew on wartime rhetoric in recalling their experiences: "we were doing our bit", "we were all in it together".[17] Their attitude was characterised by a keenness to take on 'men's work' and by a reluctance to lose it at the end of the war. With few exceptions, they were disappointed, however. Victoria Drummond found that she had to return to work for foreign shipping companies after the war: she was no longer wanted in the British Merchant Navy. Other women who did have opportunities to continue in some variant of their war work were discouraged by the thought of being in a tiny minority. Employment exchanges, careers advisers and retraining opportunities were oriented towards placing women in conventionally feminine types of employment.[18]

The difficulties of integration were underpinned by a culture which differentiated strongly by gender. There was more than one cultural identity for women in the interwar years, yet all of them marked women as different from men. As Deirdre Beddoe has argued, there were 'flappers', depicted as single middle- or upper-class women with money to spend on fashion, cigarettes and having a good time. There were also women workers, young single women who gained a degree of independence by working for a living: they were mostly working-class, although their numbers were augmented by middle-class women who worked in clerical or professional jobs. Both groups were told by the magazines they read, the popular songs they listened to and the films they watched that this independence was a brief intermission between childhood and maturity.[19] Their destiny was to marry and become that other type of woman, the dependent and dependable wife and mother, albeit, if their husbands had the means, modern ones, with labour-saving devices such as vacuum cleaners in the house and small and well-cared for families.

In wartime, the young single woman was the target of recruitment propaganda designed to engage her patriotism and harness her energies to the war effort. She was encouraged to work in, for example, agriculture, by posters offering idealised depictions of members of the Women's Land Army guiding patient horses while in amiable discourse with friendly farmers. She was urged to join the industrial workforce by agitprop-inspired posters such as "Women of Britain, Come into the Factories", in which the war factories behind the British woman's upstretched arms emit a steady stream of planes and tanks – the products of her labour. The popular film "Millions Like Us" (1943) was designed to reinforce the message of the vital place of relatively unglamorous factory work in the national effort, combining a romantic story line with a relatively realistic depiction of the factory floor, within a framework emphasising the wartime spirit of national unity.[20] To ensure adequate recruitment of women to industry, civil defence and the women's auxiliary forces the government conscripted women aged 20-30 under the National Service Number Two Act passed in December 1941. Nothing could more clearly demonstrate that the exigencies of war required the integration of women to the public sphere in the nation's fight for survival.

Women conscripts were young and single. But the married woman also entered the employment picture in the first few years of the war. From April 1941, she was required to register (alongside single women) at Employment Exchanges for possible direction into war work. There were plenty of loopholes through which married women could slip back to hearth and home. The employment exchanges sent her away if she had a child under 14, and they could be persuaded to exempt her from war work if she had men living at home or could apply middle-class influence.[21] It was not the wartime government's intention to overturn the social order, in terms of gender or class. All the same, the Ministry of Labour's efforts to get wives into war jobs, and married women's own take up of these opportunities, for reasons of financial hardship as well as patriotism, repositioned wives socially and economically. By 1943, forty-three per cent of the female workforce was married, compared with just sixteen per cent in 1931. These women were considered legitimate members of the workforce in wartime, where formerly they had been seen as interlopers deserting their first duty as wives and mothers. Arrangements, orchestrated by the government, were made to accommodate them, such as wartime nurseries, part-time hours and unpaid shopping leave. Patriotism justified their presence, which could be made to look consistent with the conventional role of a mature woman: a recruitment poster depicted a part-time woman worker smacking Hitler's face like a mother chastising a naughty child. Economics also made sense of wives' participation. By the end of the war, employers were saying that in spite of their initial doubts, part-time married women workers were worth employing: their tolerance of boredom was higher; they were more productive during their shorter hours; they could be used on processes other workers refused to work on.[22]

After the war, married women were a source of labour which was not ignored. Government campaigns of 1947 sought to redress labour shortages in industries central to the production drive, as well as to fill vacancies for schoolteachers, by encouraging the employment of married women. And wives did not turn down these opportunities. After a fall during the period of readjustment immediately following the war, the proportion of married women in the female workforce rose steadily from forty-three per cent in 1951 to fifty-two per cent in 1961 and sixty-two per cent in 1971. Simultaneously, women became an increasingly large proportion of the total workforce. The limitations of their integration, however, are eloquently expressed in the following quotation from a labour statistician: "All of the post-war increase in women's employment is accounted for by the increase in part-time jobs" which were almost by definition women's jobs.[23] The proportion of women full-timers remained approximately one-third of all workers, as it had been for decades. Full-timers in the post-war world were, as they had been pre-war, young and single, or, a new phenomenon, they were black. Women immigrants from former British colonies worked full-time in spite of having marital partners and children. In their case, full-time work was less a mark of integration in the labour force than a sign of the segregation of the social group to which they belonged by the white host society and with it the confinement of black men to the lowest paying jobs. The issue of what constitutes integration into the workforce is clearly a complex one. However, in spite of the obvious limits to integration, women workers, married and single, were, as a result of the Second World War, a public presence which was constructed in political rhetoric and popular culture as inaugurating significant changes in the relationship of women to civil society.

If wartime industrial work with its countervailing continuities with peacetime labour relations was the scene of such changes, the Armed Forces were even more so. Women's military participation as auxiliaries to the male Armed Forces had been tried in 1917-18 and was extensively developed in the period 1939-45. Women were recruited to three women's forces, the Auxiliary Territorial Service (A.T.S., the women's branch of the Army), the Women's Auxiliary Air Force (W.A.A.F.) and the Women's Royal Naval Service (W.R.N.S.). At first the military authorities relied on volunteers, but as labour requirements mounted an element of compulsion was introduced. Under the Act of December 1941 referred to above, young single women were ostensibly given a choice between industry, the services, and civil defence, although in practice they were sent to wherever the shortages were greatest when they were called up. In 1944, there were 468,800 servicewomen.

The depiction of women in military service as 'auxiliaries' indicates the limits of their integration into military life. They were there to help and support the male military rather than to engage in 'active service' themselves. At the heart of this gender differentiation was the requirement that women (but not men) must sign a letter of consent before handling lethal weapons. But this functional boundary could not be firmly drawn, for reasons of technical change as well as labour shortage. For example, A.T.S. women who worked on anti-aircraft batteries were supposed to aim but not fire the guns, but by the end of the war technical changes had made the distinction almost meaningless.[24] In short, women's auxiliary functions did not extend only to sustaining the bodies of the men who used such machinery at the battle front but were deeply implicated in military activity. Furthermore, these women possessed some of the symbols of military identity, notably uniform, badges and ranks. Official recruitment posters emphasised the parallels between men's and women's service. The film "The Gentle Sex" (1943) showed women joining the A.T.S. and playing a vital part in army manoeuvres.[25] Oral history evidence suggests that many women in the services understood and relished this relatively heroic role "as close to the front line as a woman could get", enjoyed wearing trousers and dungarees, and thought of themselves as "one of the boys".[26]

The biggest constraints on women's integration into the military were fourfold. Firstly, the notion that women could not participate in combat or active service persisted in spite of evidence to the contrary. Secondly, the women's services were throughout the war separate single-sex organisations, which worked with the male forces on gunsites or aerodromes, but which were always differentiated, in terms of rules, discipline, rewards, and lines of command. Thirdly, military femininity was institutionalised in requirements concerning uniforms and appearance: servicewomen might wear 'masculine' overalls and battle dress when working, but must put on service dress – skirt and tunic – when in public. Glamour had to be restrained: protests in Parliament against depictions of A.T.S. members as sexually alluring led to the withdrawal of a poster, "Join the ATS" by Abram Games, which portrayed a blond A.T.S. member in elegant profile. But femininity was at the same time officially and unofficially cultivated. The film referred to above, "The Gentle Sex", expressed the idea that women could fight in a war and yet remain gentle, lovable and man- and marriage-oriented. Fourthly, after 1945 the women's auxiliaries were vastly reduced in size, so for the majority of their members the experience of being a servicewoman was confined to the war, after which it lived on only in memory. Nevertheless, as Tessa Stone and Lucy Noakes have shown with reference to the W.A.A.F. and the A.T.S. respectively, the auxiliary forces were not disbanded as they had been at the end of the First World War, and their technical and combatant functions were not removed.[27] Both in practice and in terms of women's subjective understandings of the significance of their contribution, membership of the services positioned women publicly as they had never been positioned before.

There was, however, a wartime military organisation in which integration barely began. Women demanded a place in the Home Guard, the key British organisation for home defence in the event of an invasion. The Home Guard was a force of volunteers formed rapidly and enthusiastically in May 1940 when one and a half million men joined. They were part-time soldiers, required to put on and take off their military identity with their uniforms for a few hours each week, unless the advent of an invasion necessitated their full-time service. After a three-year political campaign led by the Labour M.P. Edith Summerskill, women were grudgingly permitted by the War Office to join this force. By this time, April 1943, the threat of invasion had lessened: women were admitted strictly as non-combatant auxiliaries, to do clerical work, cooking and driving. They were given as little of the symbolic status of Home Guards as possible – no financial compensation, no weapons, no uniform apart from a brooch badge.[28]

There were 32,000 Women Home Guard Auxiliaries in 1944. These women were wives, mothers, women below conscription age and women war workers – a cross-section of the women of the home front. But, in contrast to women in industry and in the auxiliary armed forces, women's role in home defence received little cultural recognition at the time and has been almost forgotten in both popular culture and historical accounts since the war. Gender integration was apparently possible (if partial) in the cases of industry and the armed services, but apparently all but impossible where home defence was concerned. Three reasons can be suggested, all of which relate to the defence of major gender divides. First, women would have had to be armed if they were to join the Home Guard in resisting an invasion. Thus their integration would have been more complete than in either of the other two cases, at the expense of the traditional differentiation of male combatants and female non-combatants. Secondly, arming women could have undermined another central gender identifier, that women gave life rather than taking it. Thirdly, integration of women with men in defence of hearth and home would have challenged the traditional gender contract: in wartime men bore arms and risked their lives to protect women and children who embodied the values for which the war was being fought. The semiotics of official photographs of Home Guards waving good-bye to wives and children at home would have been profoundly different had the wife been leaving for duty with her husband.

The extensive mobilisation for war of both single and married women was in tension with the perceived social necessity of maintaining that gender contract. Government ministries and the Church were concerned about the potentially susceptible morality of wartime women. The wife and the girlfriend were the targets of campaigns against 'careless talk', which depicted them as particularly unreliable with military or industrial secrets. As Sonya Rose has shown, there were fears that girls and young women were being corrupted by the growth of both wartime earnings and opportunities for fun. The influx of allied servicemen stationed in Britain in the run-up to D-Day, who included black Americans, was felt to be a sexual threat, and the 'good-time girls' who became too intimate with the 'G.I.s' were condemned in the press.[29] Lone wives suspected of forming extra-marital liaisons were seen not only as immoral but, more profoundly, as disloyal, since they threatened their servicemen-husbands' morale. The film "Waterloo Road" (1944) depicted an army private deserting his tank regiment in order to put an end to his wife's suspected infidelity: the narrative condoned his actions while emphasising the risk to the war effort caused by both his emotional turmoil and his temporary desertion.[30] Venereal disease, illegitimacy and divorce rates rose, apparently signifying a decline in sexual morality. But official histories adopted a congratulatory tone towards the wartime social services for containing and controlling the social disruption arising from the supposed unleashing of feminine sexuality. There was concern about men's sexuality too, but male infidelity, particularly the use of prostitutes by British servicemen throughout the world, was condoned. End of war films, notably "Brief Encounter" (1945), emphasised the need for and merit of restraint among women, and (like the New Look in fashion) presented an image of the modern woman which was deeply traditional.[31]

Expectations of the wartime housewife were not only that she would remain faithful. She was also required to contribute to the war effort by public and private efforts that were potentially contradictory. She was supposed to do full- or part-time paid war work and additionally to undertake unpaid voluntary work, for example in the Women's Voluntary Services for Air Raid

Precautions.[32] She was expected to maintain a welcoming home for husbands, sons and other menfolk, who returned unpredictably after long absences. She had to contribute to the collective survival of bombing by blacking out her house and erecting air raid shelters. Alternatively, if she lived in an area deemed not to be at risk, she was expected to take in evacuee children. She had to ensure that her (extended) family was well fed on meagre rations for which it took hours to shop, and was urged to cultivate her garden to boost supplies. She was required to 'make-do-and-mend' her own and her family's clothing, which, like food, was rationed; to contribute to National Savings; and to avoid extravagance and thus defeat the 'Squanderbug'. The wartime housewife belonged to the most silent group in terms of leaving a record of her wartime experiences. Possibly, she was too busy and fatigued to keep a diary or write a memoir, although there are some of both in the Imperial War Museum and the Mass-Observation Archive. The most celebrated representation in film of the wartime wife and mother is Jan Struther's fictitious, middle-class "Mrs Miniver" (1942).[33] Less well-known is the real working-class Barrow housewife, Nella Last, whose Mass-Observation diary was first published in 1981.[34] The war enhanced the social visibility of both women, but in neither case did integration as a wartime citizen alter these wartime housewives' traditional roles.

Women in industry and the armed services were publicly praised. Thus in 1941, Victoria Drummond was honoured with the Lloyds War Medal for Bravery at Sea and an M.B.E. for her fortitude under fire in the Atlantic (Her medals did not, however, ease her post-war job-seeking difficulties.). In contrast, congratulations for the wartime housewife were sparse. A *Daily Express* cartoon of 1945 shows the medals she might have been awarded: making an affectionate joke of her wartime trials and tribulations, it rewards her for queuing, shopping, receiving evacuees, dodging bombs, darning and maintaining throughout a 'stiff upper lip'.[35] On the other hand, politicians promised her more tangible rewards as part of the post-war welfare state: improved housing and education, family allowances paid direct to her, a national health service, and social insurance that would take account of her needs, were central to a post-war settlement that would make her life better without transforming her role.

To conclude, the extent of and resistance to the integration of women into the political, economic and military structures of wartime Britain reveal the fundamental social parameters of Britain in the Second World War. The weak points on the boundaries of the social and cultural order of the 1940s, where women could be admitted and accepted as a permanent presence, were the lower strata of the industrial, clerical and professional labour force, and the auxiliary services which supported the male military forces. Women's exclusion from the public sphere was reduced by the Second World War. But their integration was neither a process which continued smoothly thereafter, nor by any means complete. Women's admittance to politics was marked by marginalisation, and their involvement in industry and the military was characterised by segregation. Domesticity continued to be considered a woman's central and gender-delimited concern; government agencies endeavoured to control women's sexuality; and popular culture worked overtime to maintain the differentiation of the sexes.

Notes

1 See for example Gail Braybon: *Women Workers in the First World War*, London, 1989; Gail Braybon & Penny Summerfield: *Out of the Cage: Women's Experiences in Two World Wars*, London, 1987; Arthur Marwick: *Britain in the Century of Total War: War, Peace and Social Change 1900-1967*, London, 1968; Arthur Marwick: *War and Social Change in the Twentieth Century: A Comparative Study of Britain, France, Germany, Russia and the United States*, London 1974; Alva Myrdal & Viola Klein: *Women's Two Roles: Home and Work*, London, 1956; Harold L. Smith: "The Effect of the War on the Status of Women". – In H. L. S. (Ed.): *War and Social Change: British Society in the Second World War*, Manchester, 1986; Penny Summerfield: "Approaches to Women and Social Change in the Second World War". – In Brian Brivati & Harriet Jones (Eds.): *What Difference Did the War Make?* Leicester, 1993; Richard M. Titmuss: *Essays on 'The Welfare State'*, London, 1958; Deborah Thom: *Nice Girls and Rude Girls: Women Workers in World War I*, London, 2000.
2 Laura Doan: "A Challenge to 'Change'? New Perspectives on Women and the Great War", *Women's History Review* 15:2, 2006, 338.
3 Margaret Bondfield was Minister of Labour, with a Cabinet seat, 1929-31.

4 Ellen Wilkinson was Minister of Education, with a Cabinet seat, 1945-47.
5 Alison Oram: "'Bombs Don't Discriminate!' Women's Political Activism in the Second World War". – In Christine Gledhill & Gillian Swanson (Eds.): *Nationalising Femininity: Culture, Sexuality and British Cinema in the Second World War*, Manchester, 1996.
6 Pamela Brookes: *Women at Westminster: an Account of Women in the British Parliament 1918-1966*, London, 1967, p. 140.
7 *Daily Express*, 2 June 1947, "I Want a Wafer as Thick as His" by Strube.
8 Harold L. Smith: "The Problem of 'Equal Pay for Equal Work' in Great Britain", *Journal of Modern History* 53, 1984.
9 Miriam Glucksman: *Women Assemble: Women Workers and the New Industries in Inter-war Britain*, London, 1990.
10 Gail Braybon: *Women Workers in the First World War*, London, 1989.
11 Cherry Drummond: *The Remarkable Life of Victoria Drummond, Marine Engineer*, London, 1994.
12 Penny Summerfield: *Women Workers in the Second World War: Production and Patriarchy in Conflict*, London, 1989.
13 Clare Wightman: *More than Munitions: Women, Work and the Engineering Industries 1900-1950*, Harlow, 1999.
14 The National Archives, PRO Lab 10/281, 'Causes of Industrial Unrest', 3 November 1943.
15 Penny Summerfield: *Reconstructing Women's Wartime Lives: Discourse and Subjectivity in Oral Histories of the Second World War*, Manchester, 1998, p. 142.
16 *Ibid.*, 128 and 131.
17 *Ibid.*, 82-92.
18 *Ibid.*, Chapter Six.
19 Deidre Beddoe: *Back to Home and Duty: Women Between the Wars 1918-1939*, London, 1989.
20 "Millions Like Us", Gainsborough Pictures, September 1943. Producer, Edward Black; Directors, Frank Launder and Sidney Gilliat.
21 Margaret Allen: "The Domestic Ideal and the Mobilisation of Woman Power in World War II", *Women's Studies International Forum* 6, 1983.
22 Penny Summerfield: *Women Workers in the Second World War*, London, 1989, pp. 141-146.
23 Jane Elliott: "Demographic Trends in Domestic Life, 1945-87". – In David Clark (Ed.): *Marriage, Domestic Life and Social Change*, London, 1991, p. 102.
24 Gerard DeGroot: "Whose Finger on the Trigger? Mixed Anti-aircraft Batteries and the Female Combat Taboo", *War in History* 4, 1997; Lucy Noakes: *Women in the British Army: War and the Gentle Sex 1907-1948*, London, 2006, pp. 19-21.
25 "The Gentle Sex", Two Cities-Concanen, April 1943. Producers, Derek de Marney and Leslie Howard; Director, Leslie Howard.

26 Penny Summerfield: *Reconstructing Women's Wartime Lives*, Manchester, 1998, pp. 136-138.

27 Tessa Stone: "Creating a (Gendered?) Military Identity in the Women's Auxiliary Air Force in Great Britain in the Second World War", *Women's History Review* 8, 1999; Lucy Noakes: *Women in the British Army*, London, 2006, Chapter 7.

28 Penny Summerfield: "'She Wants a Gun Not a Dishcloth!': Gender, Service and Citizenship in Britain in the Second World War". – In Gerard DeGroot & Corinna Peniston-Bird: *A Soldier and a Woman: Sexual Integration in the Military*, Harlow, 2000; Penny Summerfield & Corinna Peniston-Bird: *Contesting Home Defence: Men, Women and the Home Guard in the Second World War*, Manchester, 2007 (press).

29 Sonya Rose: *Which People's War? National Identity and Citizenship in Wartime Britain 1939-1945*, Oxford, 2003, pp. 75-78.

30 "Waterloo Road", Gainsborough Pictures, 1944. Producer, Edward Black; Director, Sidney Gilliat.

31 "Brief Encounter", Pinewood Films, 1945. Producer, Noel Coward; Director, David Lean.

32 James Hinton: *Women, Social Leadership and the Second World War: Continuities of Class*, Oxford, 2002.

33 "Mrs Miniver", Metro-Goldwyn-Mayer, 1942. Producer, Sydney Franklin; Director, William Wyler.

34 Richard Broad & Susie Fleming (Eds.): *Nella Last's War: A Mother's Diary 1939-45*, Bristol, 1981.

35 *Daily Express*, 21 May 1945, "Entitled to All Six" by Strube.

Bibliography

Allen, Margaret: "The Domestic Ideal and the Mobilisation of Woman Power in World War II", *Women's Studies International Forum* 6, 1983, 401-412.

Beddoe, Deidre: *Back to Home and Duty: Women Between the Wars 1918-1939*, London, 1989.

Braybon, Gail: *Women Workers in the First World War*, London, 1989.

Broad, Richard & Susie Fleming (Eds.): *Nella Last's War: A Mother's Diary 1939-45*, Bristol, 1981.

Brookes, Pamela: *Women at Westminster: an Account of Women in the British Parliament 1918-1966*, London, 1967.

Daily Express, 2 June 1947, "I Want a Wafer as Thick as His" by Strube.

Daily Express, 21 May 1945, "Entitled to All Six" by Strube.

DeGroot, Gerard: "Whose Finger on the Trigger? Mixed Anti-aircraft Batteries and the Female Combat Taboo", *War in History* 4, 1997, 434-453.

Doan, Laura: "A Challenge to 'Change'? New Perspectives on Women and the Great War", *Women's History Review* 15:2, 2006, 337-343.

Drummond, Cherry: *The Remarkable Life of Victoria Drummond, Marine Engineer*, London, 1994.

Elliott, Jane: "Demographic Trends in Domestic Life, 1945-87". – In David Clark (Ed.): *Marriage, Domestic Life and Social Change*, London, 1991, pp. 85-108.

Glucksman, Miriam: *Women Assemble: Women Workers and the New Industries in Inter-war Britain*, London, 1990.

Hinton, James: *Women, Social Leadership and the Second World War: Continuities of Class*, Oxford, 2002.

Noakes, Lucy: *Women in the British Army: War and the Gentle Sex 1907-1948*, London, 2006.

Oram, Alison: "'Bombs Don't Discriminate!' Women's Political Activism in the Second World War". – In Christine Gledhill & Gillian Swanson (Eds.): *Nationalising Femininity: Culture, Sexuality and British Cinema in the Second World War*, Manchester, 1996, pp. 53-69.

Rose, Sonya: *Which People's War? National Identity and Citizenship in Wartime Britain 1939-1945*, Oxford, 2003.

Smith, Harold L.: "The Problem of 'Equal Pay for Equal Work' in Great Britain", *Journal of Modern History* 53, 1984, 652-672.

Stone, Tessa: "Creating a (Gendered?) Military Identity in the Women's Auxiliary Air Force in Great Britain in the Second World War", *Women's History Review* 8, 1999, 605-624.

Summerfield, Penny & Corinna Peniston-Bird: *Contesting Home Defence: Men, Women and the Home Guard in the Second World War*, Manchester, 2007 (press).

Summerfield, Penny: "'She Wants a Gun Not a Dishcloth!': Gender, Service and Citizenship in Britain in the Second World War". – In Gerard DeGroot & Corinna Peniston-Bird: *A Soldier and a Woman: Sexual Integration in the Military*, Harlow, 2000, pp. 119-134.

Summerfield, Penny: *Reconstructing Women's Wartime Lives: Discourse and Subjectivity in Oral Histories of the Second World War*, Manchester, 1998.

Summerfield, Penny: *Women Workers in the Second World War: Production and Patriarchy in Conflict*, London, 1989.

The National Archives, PRO Lab 10/281, 'Causes of Industrial Unrest', 3 November 1943.

Wightman, Clare: *More than Munitions: Women, Work and the Engineering Industries 1900-1950*, Harlow, 1999.

Films

"Brief Encounter", Pinewood Films, 1945. Producer, Noel Coward; Director, David Lean.

"Millions Like Us", Gainsborough Pictures, September 1943. Producer, Edward Black; Directors, Frank Launder and Sidney Gilliat.

"Mrs Miniver", Metro-Goldwyn-Mayer, 1942. Producer, Sydney Franklin; Director, William Wyler.

"The Gentle Sex", Two Cities-Concanen, April 1943. Producers, Derek de Marney and Leslie Howard; Director, Leslie Howard.

"Waterloo Road", Gainsborough Pictures, 1944. Producer, Edward Black; Director, Sidney Gilliat.

Doris Teske (Weingarten/Leipzig)

Working With Experience.
The Presentation of the Two World Wars and Teaching Matter

1. Introduction

When in the popular 1970s comedy series *Fawlty Towers*, Basil Fawlty coined the phrase 'Don't mention the War' while just doing that in the most inappropriate situations, British and non-British viewers saw the Second World War (not to mention the First World War or 'Great War') as a thing of the past. These two wars which had re-defined the outlook of the world and produced a watershed in art, thought, and the life of the individual, were by then neglected by a majority of people as of no immediate influence on the present. Today, however, this view has changed, as many conflicts are brought home to us by television and the refugees from wars and civil wars all over the world, as armed forces are deployed to various trouble spots, and as our countries are threatened by terrorists who justify their actions with the wars raging in their countries and our involvement in them. War is again perceived as a contemporary phenomenon, and the two World Wars once more are seen as moments in recent history from which lessons can be drawn for the future. As a topic they have recently been taken up by contemporary fiction and history writing, in films and in paintings. In reaction to this new interest, but also under the impression that the last eye-witnesses of the two World Wars will soon be dead, new museums such as the *Historial de la Grande Guerre* at Péronne (1992), the *In Flanders Fields Museum* at Ypres (1993) and the *Imperial War Museum North* (2002) have been established. Temporary exhibitions on the two World Wars have focused on the memory of the survivors and on the current influence of developments initiated in the war years (see the 2004 exhibition of

Deutsches Historisches Museum at Berlin, which sees the First World War in close connection with the year 1989). One of the most important considerations in connection with this revival of interest is the question how the important and harrowing experience of war can be rendered and mediated, so that wars are seen and experienced as bitter reality, not as incidents in history.

The (European)[1] concern with the two World Wars is defined by two basic views, namely the question of matter and narration. The First World War devastated whole regions and destroyed the life in them, maimed and killed an unimaginably large number of soldiers, and left the surviving average soldier traumatised by the experience. It re-defined material and thought at home and at the front according to the needs of a total war. The Second World War gave these developments an even more terrible form, resulting in the destruction of many cities and civilian lives and virtually redrawing the map of Europe. Thus, to cope with the shocking experiences of modern warfare war, victims would focus on objects, using them as fix points, and attaching to them a symbolic meaning even as they became fractured, distorted or perverted. Others would deal with the traumatic experience by creating narratives, presenting the unimaginable in a shape in which it could be endured.

The two ways of coping with war experiences developed into various traditions. The material aspect of war defined new formats of visual presentation, rituals of memory, and the reduction of experience into emblematic objects.[2] On the other hand, narrative patterns of endurance, comradeship and heroism were shaped, which again were subsumed under narratives of national identity. Physical objects which carried with them the aura of war were collected, and museum and private exhibitions developed around them the idea of the sacral. Memorial spaces for the two World Wars united both the material and the narrative position, as the various forms of grieving centred in the physical object around which rituals developed, and which was included in narrative traditions of remembrance. Finally, the written sources of the world wars (official pieces of information and propaganda as well as personal memoirs) became themselves objects of rituals of remembrance, while the narrative patterns were dissociated from their original sources and would be found in a wealth of material such as children's stories, war novels and films, or even commercials.[3]

Monuments, museums, pieces of art and everyday objects have become central for a culture rediscovering the importance of material reality. Objects, which initially had been collected as trophies and lucky charms, as souvenirs or as emblems of certain aspects of war, had found their way into public collections even before the end of the First World War. Today, their immediate function needs to be recovered, while additional meanings are attributed to them, not only connecting through them with the experience of an earlier generation,[4] but developing new perceptions of the past.

The narrative and the material aspect of the World Wars are increasingly brought together in order to mediate the war experience. This is done prominently in history museums and in history teaching. Both museum and classroom focus on the idea of experience, not only by narrating the experience of war participants in order to create empathy with the individual, but by bringing the idea of war close to the visitors and pupils by initiating an immediate, though virtual experience of the past.

2. Experience, Object and Narration

Experience is a complex notion influenced by diverse traditions in philosophy and psychology. The term is used in Aristotelian philosophy and in empiricist thinking, in modern science and in hermeneutics and phenomenology. In its many shades of meaning, experience results from what is perceived by the senses, what is learned in the interplay of action and knowledge, what is defined by emotions, cognitive reasoning and religious or moral consideration, and what is created by the aesthetics, the aura of and the – presumed – knowledge about a piece of art. For this paper, experience will be defined as the encounter with the other, in which a situation, a person or an object presents itself to the subject, followed by the process of ordering and explaining, in which the sensory and other input is ordered, integrated in previous knowledge, or structured along patterns already known. Experience starts at a fixed moment, whereas the process of evaluation and re-evaluation has no definite ending as it can cover decades of learning and change.

Experience has often been divided into an original, immediate or primary experience, and a secondary (formalised or mediated) experience. In the context of World War 1 and World War 2, primary experience would be confined to soldiers in action, close-by observers, and civilians who became immediate victims of war actions. They all would have physical experiences of the war actions, immediately reacting to the physical materiality of trench and other war sites, focusing on objects which became central factors of their experiences, and becoming war "matériel" themselves.[5] Civilians at the home front are often added to this list, as they would have been affected by food and fuel shortages, the loss of family members, and changes in their own life style (most obvious, the war employment of women, blackouts, gas and bomb attack precautions and panics, and the evacuation of children during war time). Again, they would have an immediate relation to objects of everyday life gaining a new meaning in the changed circumstances and to new objects connected to the new situation.

The authentic primary experience, however, is seldom pure or original. It can be argued that former experiences and formulas for narrating experience influence the perception of reality, functioning as a filter which defines what can be perceived at all. Likewise, the traumatic sense impressions need to be filtered, categorized and connected before the various bits of information form a pattern which can be understood. In the therapeutic retelling of the war experience certain aspects are exaggerated while others are left out. When these impressions are communicated, they are once more filtered and re-defined, sometimes even submerged: They are shaped by conventions of language, narrative formulas and shared meaning, but they are also defined by the narrative situation, such as ideas about what is expected by the listeners and what is beyond their understanding.[6]

The retelling of experience could be called a secondary, mediated experience, involving processes of depersonalisation and abstraction, or a contrary focus on the detail, the concrete and anecdotal. This retelling can become so convincing that the original experience is substituted by it, and that others accept it as their own experience without having been in the situation. Most of the later telling of war experiences thus was not a direct reframing of authentic experience, but a substitution of it, as the original experience of the War had been silenced, ignored or ritualised.

Many veterans were not able to express their traumas, just as the unspeakable war horrors made it almost impossible to retell their trench experience in the context of the family or of a community scarred by the loss of many young men.[7] Their return home often resulted in a complete break between their personal war experience and the ordinary life resumed afterwards – for many perhaps their only way to regain their sanity after horrid impressions. The general view of war, in contrast, became sanitised, formalised and ritualised, resulting in individual or family myths[8] or in the adoption of dominant narratives, mainly the headquarter interpretations of war as duty, adventure and strategy, which came to define an ubiquitous memory culture. Dominant national patriotic narratives continued the propaganda of the war years which had been defined by headquarters and staff as well as by the recruiting machinery.[9]

The use of ritualised narratives is part of a memory culture which soon came to define all memory of the First World War.[10] This memory culture originally answered the need for remembrance by the bereaved and found its expression in commemorative services, plaques, and in the trench tourism of the 1920s. The ritual of mourning, however, became increasingly prone to ideological use. Both the idea that the cause of war actually was worth dying for and the belief that these deaths would ensure that such carnage would never happen again held high potential for patriotic redefinitions. "Taking up the torch" after the war dead (quoting John McRae's "In Flanders Fields") could be done in various ways and for various purposes.[11] It was made use of by national institutions, shaping a narrative of national identity and togetherness. In the Armistice commemorations shown by BBC television on every 11th of November, this idea of the nation worth fighting for has survived until today: As the two minutes of silence are observed, pictures of Big Ben, the London Cenotaph, local memorial monuments, a view of London, close-ups on veterans and servicemen, families of war dead, the Royal family, political leaders, Parliament, shots of the stock exchange, city streets, and a church service shape a visual union of all Britons.[12]

The Second World War created a different idea of experience and participation as the civilian society was involved in the war to a higher degree, many larger British cities becoming military targets of the Blitz and the V1 and V2-raids. The resulting large-scale destructions, the evacuations and the long-term effects of civilian war efforts such as food rationing and female work defined it as a 'Civilians' War'. In the retelling of the individual experiences as secondary experience, however, an overpowering state propaganda effectively suppressed divergent narratives in order to maintain national unity around the war effort or 'The People's War'.[13]

Parallel to the changes of the narration of the war experience, the perception of war objects changed. After functioning as fix points, as therapeutic objects, and as souvenirs for the soldiers, the objects changed their meaning and function when they became symbols of remembrance for war widows and grieving communities.[14] Saunders describes the new role of such objects in the ritual of private memory, when physical objects replaced memory and functioned as (at the same time tangible and sacral) links to the dead.[15]

With the eventual passing away of the generations of war participants and with the rejection of most of the dominant narratives in the postmodern condition, it could be argued that the contemporary view of the World Wars is defined by a third kind of experience, which could be called tertiary, creative or virtual. The existing objects and narratives of war are disconnected from their old context, as there is little shared knowledge between current viewers and the people originally experiencing the two World Wars. However, the wish to make sense of objects and to attach meaning to events and things of the past, as well as the wish to use existing narratives for one's own end is very much present. With the postmodern tenet that there is no marked difference between fantasy and the perception of reality, or between real life and virtual reality, the new encounter with the historical objects and the recreation of the past are rated as not categorically less authentic or valuable than the original (filtered and mediated) experience. With this change in attitude, the presentation of objects in exhibitions and the presentation of narratives in various text forms are given a new meaning.

3. The Teaching of History and of World War History

The causes and development of the two World Wars and the long-term changes effected by them form an integral part of History teaching in both German and British schools. They feature in the

History and Politics curricula of most German *Bundesländer* at a rather late stage,[16] as minor features embedded in the context of nationalism, militarism and the Nazi system. The British school curriculum, as described on the national standards website,[17] tends to put more emphasis on the war experience at an earlier stage. In key stages 1 and 2 in History, in which the pupils shall connect to events in the past and become aware of their position in time and space, the Second World War is listed as one period of encounter.[18] When answering the basic question, 'What was it like for children in World War 2', subtopics such as the Evacuation, food shortages and the Blitz are mentioned as features in which British children were affected. Another topic for the History teaching at key stages 1 and 2 is 'What are we remembering on Remembrance Day', which focuses on the relevance of the two World Wars for today. In the advanced History classes at key stage 3 and key stage 4/GCSE level, several objectives are to be met beyond the encounter with the historical other, the empathy with people in other situations and the awareness of difference through time. Here, the structural approach shows aspects of the First World War as part of a longer development and as defining historical change, in which various groups of 'players' can be identified. In addition, different sources are presented for assessment by the pupils, illustrating the bias and incompleteness of certain information. Finally, ideas of memory and remembrance are used for individual work at key stage 4.

The teaching of history has changed parallel to the paradigm shift in the academic discipline of History: The school subject has increasingly focused on everyday culture and the mentality of common people. Less importance is attached to historical facts and eminent persons, or to abstract approaches explaining chronological or cause-effect relations, continuities or structural change. Instead, new emphasis has been given to the understanding of the past through personal experience, by following an ordinary person's point of view and knowledge and by involving the pupils' senses and emotions.[19] Through identification with one person and the discussion of exemplary cases (furthered in specific work tasks involving dilemma situations and role plays), the learning process is facilitated. As the past is recovered with authentic material (or material perceived as authentic), a virtual experience is shaped: the past is re-enacted and experienced as if original, as the individual re-lives the experience of another historical person.[20]

4. The Mediation of War Experience – Some Examples

In the following, various materials will be considered which while mediating the war experience shape a form of tertiary or virtual experience. School text books and additional reading for the school context take up the idea of a virtual, mediated experience with their focus on empathy. Additional material supporting school education can be found on the Internet, notably on the educational pages published by the BBC, where questions of authenticity and of virtual experience as immediate experience are central. Finally, the permanent exhibitions at the Imperial War Museum (IWM) and IWM North take school children as their major clientele who define the exhibitions as well as some of the additional information material (see, for example, the temporary exhibition 'The Children's War' which focuses on British children's experiences of the Second World War). With the exposition of the real objects of war, a reconstruction of war sites and eye-witness accounts by various participants, mediated and virtual experience is at the centre of the exhibitions. In all the mediations of war experience mentioned, forms of tertiary experience are created, as the children's interest, imagination and creativity is involved and ways are shown to relate to experience in an individual and authentic way.

❖ Roderick Hunt & Alex Brychta: *What Was It Like*? Oxford, 2001.

The Oxford Reading Tree programme offers teachers as well as parents additional material for slow and developing readers for unguided reading at key stages 1 and 2. *What Was It Like?* gives children an impression of the bombing of cities and the evacuation of children during World War 2. The booklet follows a format established in earlier books of the same series about the Romans, the Egyptians, or Robin Hood: After some introduction of a link between the present and the past, a magic key moves the children protagonists into the past, which they experience first hand, participating and intervening in a short moment in history. The stories always end with the return to the present time and a rounding off by the children.

The text on the Second World War, however, introduces important changes: After their first contact with the topic (preparing a play, wearing the clothes of that era, and talking to their grandmother, who experienced the Second World War as a child), the four children note that although they have become aware of the hardships of the time, they have difficulties in connecting to the past. In the ensuing time travel, they do not experience a well-defined story, but incidents defining the life of children at the time of World War 2: the children stay in an underground shelter, they see the results of an air raid with fires in the street, are forced to wear gas masks and are almost split up under evacuation. In contrast to the playfulness of other texts in the series in which the children remain in control of the action around them, this story shows the children in a situation where they feel afraid, and where they can only react. They are put in a hierarchy, and they are moved around obeying adult commands and not knowing about their future. However, safety is reintroduced when the children move back into their own time. The two pictures framing this return are similar: the guardian overseeing their evacuation is substituted by their grandmother in the present, who stands in the same position with the same pose – thus the time travel is explained as a shared fantasy about the past.

❖ Richard Radway: *Britain 1906-1918*, London, 2002.

At key stage 3, material on World War 1 is usually included in textbooks narrating the main events of a longer period. Although this is also the case with *Britain 1906-1918* by Richard Radway, most of the textbook revolves around the First World War and its impact on the nation. The War chapters are divided into a part covering the redefinition of civilian life during the War: shortages and their impact on everyday life, the British government's intervention in production and commerce and shaping of a wartime economy, the mobilisation of the civilians as to the war effort, the threat of war on British soil (presenting the Zeppelin attacks in a format comparable to the World War 2 bombings), and the women's role in World War 1. Another group of topics is concerned with the government's propaganda and the initial reactions of volunteers, but also with the re-writing of the realities of trench warfare for the public. Finally, the results of the World War 1 are discussed.

The text focuses on the main events in the period. While the central text renders some basic data, assesses certain details and presents a general storyline, the marginal text is concerned with various sources such as propaganda posters, photographs and diary entries, interviews, or letters. The central text of the chapter: "The Impact of War on Civilians" connects and contrasts the warfare and personal experience of World War 1 with earlier wars. It relates the wartime economy (the destruction of merchant shipping) to general trends in food production (the dependence on food imports), and it describes how the government increasingly intervened in the market and how the popular reaction thwarted these measures. The marginal text illustrates and supports the main narrative, but also functions as an emotional counterpoint by putting individual experience in contrast to the official, nationwide view.

In the pages on food shortages, three text sources stand against two government posters and a photograph of unclear origin. The short memory snippets are by common people, not eminent persons. They present a narrow, personal experience or repeat local or family myths. With the various sources in the marginal text, critical source analysis is introduced, as the text sources differ in their validity and objectivity. Although the topic introduced and the biographical format give the pupils the opportunity to connect, this is not the focus of the text. The emotional aspect of the sources is not made explicit, just as the individual experience of certain aspects of war experience is only mentioned in passing. The tasks given at the end of the main text are focusing on these extra sources, but only to connect and compare them with the main text. The emotional aspect of these sources is rather made a negative point in their evaluation.

❖ Dale Banham & Christopher Culpin: *The Trenches*, London, 2002.

In this in-depth textbook on the First World War, Dale Banham and Christopher Culpin present a first introduction to source analysis. The starting point is the propaganda film *The Battle of the Somme*, which was released in August 1916, celebrating a British victory long before the attack had to be halted because of the little gains made in spite of high casualties. In a fictitious situation, the pupils become part of a TV team which has to prepare a new film on World War 1. In single steps, in which they have to find reliable sources for their project, the difference between propaganda and fact, between idealised presentation and complex reality is shown. Special emphasis is put on how the viewer is influenced by the use of suggestive and loaded language, by the order of presentation and the inclusion/exclusion and framing of material. This critical view of contemporary sources is continued for other material as well, such as photographs, interviews, letters and memories, paintings, cartoons, and fictional literature. Tasks such as finding and evaluating the information given, assessing the validity and objectivity of source material, or choosing and adapting material to create an emotional response in the viewer/reader lead the pupils to a better understanding of historical research. Again, personal reminiscences, letters or diary entries are seen as not providing a complete and objective view of the events of the First World War. However, this textbook rates them as important for a complete understanding of the time, and it shows the complexity and bias of all kinds of sources, including the sources presenting themselves as objective.

❖ The BBC Internet Pages Concerning the Two World Wars

The BBC as a quasi-governmental institution offers a wealth of websites for public information and education seeing its function as a national memory container in which the last of the war generation can store their knowledge for the use of younger generations.[21] Some of the BBC educational pages are specifically intended to be used along with other school material, following the needs created by the school curriculum. These materials are devised as support for history teachers and as self-access learning material. Both the pages on the First World War (BBC Schools Online 2005) and the pages on the children's experience of the Second World War (BBC Primary History 2005) present varied sources such as photographs, official and private letters, posters and diary entries while the narratives and the tasks help structure the experience.

The main point of view of the World War One pages is that of the ordinary person involved, as dramatised diaries are presented and the belongings of individuals are shown. Virtual tours give an idea of how it felt to be a soldier in the trenches and in the war at sea. In the further pages, as well as in the evaluation of events, however, the official perspective of the headquarters is presented as the central one, its focus on tactics ignoring the plight of the common soldier. The views of contemporary historians are presented as inherently more important than the individual perceptions by the participants, even though they include the experience of the individuals as central. A specific group of pages intended for key stage 3 pupils focuses on the experiences of the soldier, the sister at home, the survivor/prisoner of war and the observer, inviting empathy while these views are compared and evaluated. Finally, some interactive programmes are included, such as a computer game on strategy – choosing the right weapons for a special task, a prepared programme of shooting – a cognitive revision, as to what was achieved and how little this actually meant in the bigger picture.

The "Children in the Second World War" website was created by the BBC as an addition to its School TV programme on the children's experience of the Second World War. As a source container and a learning platform for key stage 2 pupils, it shows a similar diversity of material, although this time the BBC is more concerned with using material aspects of the war for school activities, less on the use and evaluation of statements of the war participants. Based on copies of authentic materials, such as photographs of a (reconstructed) wartime home, ration coupons or shop catalogues of the time, the children have to solve problems of everyday households: to plan which clothes to buy or to mend on the few coupons available, or to decide which objects to pack in case of an evacuation. Here, the action of the pupils is meant to translate into an understanding what life was like during those years. This would result in an empathy with wartime families trying to get by.

❖ The Imperial War Museum and Imperial War Museum North

In the mediation of the two World Wars, museums and temporary exhibitions have played a major role, starting as early as 1914 with the exhibition of war material and battle trophies at the Berlin Zeughaus. Collections of war memorabilia were started in many countries, the British War Museum resulting from the most comprehensive initiative (initiated in 1917, opened at its first site at Crystal Palace in 1920).[22] Recently, museums presenting the two World Wars have had a new upsurge, the most prominent example in Britain being the famous Daniel Libeskind building housing the Imperial War Museum North at Manchester (2002). The challenge for the contemporary museums is to initiate an intergenerational exchange, not only to accommodate the last survivors of the war years but to appeal to young people, interesting and informing them. At the same time, teaching material and examples from the collections have been made accessible via Internet, giving the opportunity for an increased amount of self-access learning and personal encounter with the historical objects.

The major concern of museums is not to render information but to facilitate the visitor's access to the past, creating a specific experience of a virtual past.[23] Thus, information, entertainment and emotional presentation have to be arranged in a spatial structure around the material objects, and need to address different visitors. As the exhibitions focus on the material objects, decisions have to be made how things will be presented in which format: an arrangement of similar objects in classes or categories can give a sense of the completeness and value of the collection, the exhibition of a single, cleaned object can evoke the aura of the original and its beauty or appropriateness of design, an arrangement of things found together or connected to the same situation might stress the function of the object or tell a story concerning its onetime user. Together with the general structure of the exhibition, the lighting arrangements and the textual commentaries, these decisions influence the reactions of the visitors.

The Imperial War Museum at London unites several galleries which allow for different approaches to the topic. The focal space, however, which also gives meaning to the rest of the collection, is the central inner court in which large objects are exhibited – various vehicles and weapons, many of them exhibited because of the

111

importance of this specific type of weapon, but some also exhibited because of their symbolic meaning (such as the gun from which the first British shot was fired in World War 1, or the boat *Tamzine* which stands for the evacuation of troops from Dunkirk). This collection suggests a celebratory view of the war effort and the technical innovations accompanying it. Several of the other galleries are more critical but they can only partly dispel the uncritical main impression.

Both the First and the Second World War are presented in the format of showcases in chronologically arranged themed display areas with short descriptions of the exhibits, accompanied by large-scale illustrations of the timeline and commentaries telling the main narrative of events. In addition, both a trench typical for the 1916 Western front and a London scenario of 1940 (an air-raid shelter and a destroyed street) have been re-created in order to give the visitor a first-hand impression of the sites of war. Sound, light, and smell effects are included in these presentations, and some replicas of showcase exhibits are positioned at central points of the galleries. Both the First World War and Second World War expositions, however, create very different emotions in the viewer: the trench experience can be walked through individually – even though on fixed lines – at one's own pace, without any reference to the pressures the soldiers were under when carrying out orders during an enemy attack. The air-raid shelter and the London street after an air-raid, in contrast, can only be visited in a group, which in itself creates some idea of the feelings experienced at that time – being thrown together with strangers and depending on them in a moment of stress, feeling the tension and confinement in the shelter, and experiencing the disorientation in a street where things are turned upside down.

Several of the features of the Imperial War Museum are repeated in the new Imperial War Museum North at Manchester. Mainly geared for school visitors, it shows a similar interest in the large weapons hall. This time, the experience of dislocation and danger is shaped as part of the presentation itself in audiovisual presentations (so-called 'Big Pictures' on war weapons, on reasons and justifications of wars, and on children in the war) which are shown at regular intervals. As images of war are projected unto the walls and objects of the darkened exhibition, the rapid changes of lighting and the surround sounds of war recreate the auditory and visual experiences of war participants. In the permanent exhibition, sensory experience plays a major role in the introductory part, where the smells and tactile experiences of the trenches are brought close to the pupils in an 'action station': The children have to identify objects in black boxes and to make guesses as to trench life.

Authentic objects connected to the World Wars are made accessible to the senses and to immediate experience of the visitors in various ways: In the themed silos, they are displayed in rather traditional ways, for example, by showing them in showcases and presenting them as objects of art or as examples for a class of objects. The time stacks offer the opportunity to personally handle the original objects such as letters, keep-sakes, military equipment, or garments and explore their history. In other areas such as the 'Experience of War' area, authentic material of individual war participants can be called up in order to understand the individual's experience of World War 2. Finally, radio and film coverage as well as contemporary print material can be accessed in a gigantic living-room structure. All these formats give the individual visitor the opportunity to experience authentic material at their own pace and in their own way. The experience created in this room thus becomes authentic, as it cannot be defined or planned in advance, neither by the museum nor by the visitor. The visitor undergoes an active learning process, in which he or she will develop his or her own answers to the objects, finding individual points of contact by choosing which person's history to look at, or by selecting a certain theme or object.

The focus on individual research, which in IWM North is included in the exhibition space, has its origin in the history of the IWM, which from the beginning was to function as a container of memories and objects concerning the First World War. This is continued with the virtual extension of the IWM (IWM collections archive, 2005). Here, part of the central collections can be accessed from without with the help of Internet search tools, including the photograph archive, the collection of interview recordings, the manuscripts and transcripts of personal letters and diaries donated to the Museum, the official material deposited and the collection of sketches and poems. The research in this virtual museum and in virtual objects exhibited, to which pupils are invited when visiting

113

the IWM web pages, becomes a way towards an original, individual experience of war actions and war as a national past.

5. Conclusion

At a moment in time when the original experience of the two World Wars cannot be recovered in interpersonal exchange, the question of learning from past experience has become all the more pressing, as new military conflicts and crises of terrorism have shattered our beliefs in a non-violent future. A tertiary or virtual experience of past events, is seen as the way to have children of today connect to the lessons of the past. The materials presented in this paper accordingly show different positions as to how this tertiary experience can be created and to what effect it can be used.

What Was It Like uses the idea of the fantasy trip as a way of covering the distance between present and past. With fantasy, the difference in experience can be reduced, and children can empathise with the historical other. By imagining themselves in the position of the other and acting out certain situations, the experience becomes real for the younger children.

In the school texts for key stages 3 and 4, this movement from fantasy to reality is not supported, so that learning has to be facilitated by other experiential strategies. One of them is to present the experience of the other in a personalised form (in diaries, letters, interviews, narratives directed to the listener/reader), so that the children can relive certain decisive moments in the lives of individuals or come close to the dilemmas and the everyday decisions of ordinary people in the past. Traditional conceptions of the historical discipline, however, which grade sources and historical narrations on the grounds of their objectivity, validity and completeness of presentation of facts, jar with these experiential forms of teaching. *The Trenches* shows a solution to this problem, combining both the personal and the critical approach: By putting the reader in an active role in present time, i.e. well outside the war action, it keeps up a critical distance to the material presented, while facilitating the learning through direct involvement and experience. The pupils find their own personal position with regard to the material as they are put in the position of reporters/researchers, and they learn to regard the interpretation of past events as an ongoing process. Discussing their own formats of presentation, they can develop a deeper understanding of the existing material and the role that the format of presentation plays.

The immediate experience of research and of presentation, including the development of own formats of presentation, is of central importance for the mediation of war experience by Internet. This is obvious in the web pages created by the BBC and the Imperial War Museum. While exercises involving the action of choosing and combining are seen as valid for the key stage 2 pupils, the tasks for key stage 3 and GCSE students focus on individual research, on finding objects and materials, evaluating them, using them to present aspects of war or to tell specific stories. The representation of physical objects in the virtual classroom of the Internet becomes a moment of authentic learning.

The new relationship between the virtual and the authentic as well as between experience and learning that shows in Internet-supported learning situations, is also an important feature of current museums and exhibition formats. Here, the object can be made the anchor of a personal experience, which is immediate and authentic in itself, even though the object can be a simulacrum, a simplified version of the complex object or sometimes even a (virtual) reconstruction. Reconstructions of the past become acceptable in the mediation of the past, being all the more effective if the new and authentic experience created by them echoes the original experience without trying to substitute it as the same. The role of the fabricated/simplified and the virtual as capable of creating authentic experience shows in the Trench and Blitz Experience galleries at the London Imperial War Museum and the IWM North lightshows: Both the recreations and the sound-and-lightshow give visitors the opportunity to experience an idea of war, although in very different formats. While the walk-through recreations of the London museum fabricate experience, the sensations given in the Big Picture lightshows, though highly abstract, are just as immediate. Finally, the experience of searching to understand the past and to shape an individual view out of the wealth of contradictory narratives become most authentic as they are acted out in a museum which symbolically as well as literally functions as a container of material objects and memories, with various narratives and interpretations defining its structure and its format of presentation.

Notes

1 For its purpose, this paper focuses on the Western and Central European, mainly the British perception of the two World Wars. Features ranging centrally are the trench war on the Western Front, the Dunkirk and Battle of Britain experience, and the bombings of British and German cities.

2 Nicholas Saunders: "Material Culture and Conflict. The Great War, 1914-2003". – In N. S. (Ed.): *Matters of Conflict*, London & N.Y., 2004, pp. 5-25.

3 Michael Paris: *Warrior Nation. Images of War in British Popular Culture, 1850-2000*, London, 2000.

4 Saunders (2004: 5)

5 *Ibid.*, 9.

6 Gerd-Walter Fritsche convincingly analyses the diversity of war experience by looking at the war letters of two writers from widely different backgrounds (G.-W. Fritsche: "Bedingungen des individuellen Kriegserlebnisses". – In Peter Knoch (Ed.): *Kriegsalltag*, Stuttgart, 1989, pp. 114-152.).

7 Especially affected were the communities from which the so-called 'Pals' Battalions' were drawn, when the youths of one area who had no specific family attachment to one regiment had signed up together and died together in the same action.

8 These individual and family stories and myths are the central concern of Oral History – a rich historical source, but a problematic one as well. How strong family myths and how close and uncritical (popular) oral history can be is shown in recent popular TV series on both world wars, where the children of war participants are interviewed as 'witnesses', even though they were babies around the time of the events. Biographical material on individual experiences (sometimes recorded many years after the event, with all the problems this brings) shows how many diverse emotional states the soldiers were going through: of physical and mental (spiritual) exhaustion, danger and fear, personal and trained violence. Other feelings listed by Max Arthur (Max Arthur (Ed.): *Forgotten Voices of the Great War*, London, 2002.) and Richard Holmes (*Tommy. The British Soldier on the Western Front 1914-1918*, London, 2004.), were comradeship, patriotism, pride in achievement or specialisation, hate, running berserk, or the conviction of doing the necessary.

9 Michael Paris, for example, shows how values such as personal leadership, heroism, comradeship and self-sacrifice, endurance and good humour, or fairness and good judgement, which had been defined long before 1914, were used to re-tell the World War throughout the interwar years, although they actually had been rejected or found missing by many common soldiers in the trenches, see Paris (2000: *passim*).

10 For a close observation of the material aspects of this memory culture, see Saunders (2004).

11 See Jay Winter: *Sites of Memory, Sites of Mourning. The Great War in European Cultural History*, Cambridge, 1995, pp. 78-116.

12 For a view of the Remembrance Day rituals, see the BBC website on the topic: (BBC Remembrance, 2005). Adrian Gregory (*The Silence of Memory. Armistice Day 1919-1946*, Oxford & Providence, 1994, p. 9.) shows how the first ideas of an Armistice commemoration ritual already stressed "the greater things we hold in common" (Fitzpatrick's memorandum on a two minute's silence, 1919).

13 Angus Calder's *Myth of the Blitz* still remains the most influential criticism of this myth, which even has been called "hegemonic cultural formation" (Sonya Rose: *Which People's War? National Identity and Citizenship in Britain 1939-1945*, New York, 2003, p. 21.).

14 Nicholas Saunders has coined the term 'memory bridge' for this development, see Nicholas Saunders: "Apprehending Memory: Material Culture and War, 1919-1939". – In John Bourne, Peter Liddle & Ian Whitehead (Eds.): *The Great World War, 1914-1945*, vol. 2, London, 2001, pp. 477-483.

15 Saunders (2004: 13-15).

16 See, for example, the curriculum of Hessia with its detailed description of the topic for year 9 pupils (Lehrplan Online Hessen 2006).

17 See the DES Standards Website (Department for Education and Skills 2005)

18 Other periods featuring in the Curriculum are the Roman Age, the Viking Age, and The Victorian Age.

19 Especially the development of oral history workshops has made a difference in the schoolrooms, as the personal narrative has become very important for the connection of present and past. Recent introductions to World War 1 also include the sensory approach. See Peter Schulz-Hageleit: *Geschichtsbewusstsein und Zukunftssorge. Unbewusstheiten im geschichts- wissenschaftlichen und geschichtsdidaktischen Diskurs*, Herbolzheim, 2004 and Bernd Mütter & Uwe Uffelmann (Eds.): *Emotionen und historisches Lernen. Forschung – Vermittlung – Rezeption*, Frankfurt/M., 1992, passim.

20 Although this movement can be found in both British and German discussions on the teaching of History, there are clear differences as to the extent to which the experiential and experimental approach has been realised in the schoolroom. In British schools, the empirical tradition has long favoured the use of sensory perceptions, learner agency, the setting of research tasks, and the importance of empathy created by the use of case stories, and the pedagogical use of adapted original sources. In Germany, the totalitarian abuse of History as '*Gesinnungsfach*', a subject used to indoctrinate the pupils, has made teachers and educationalists more wary of the emotional factor.

21 On the web pages of the BBC, for example, some extracts from e-mails are published which were sent in from various war participants answering an invitation by the World War 2 People's War project of the BBC and Open University (2005).

22 For the history of the Imperial War Museum and the considerations leading to its establishment, as well as the influence of the buildings in which the collection was located (Crystal Palace, Imperial Institute and Bethlem Royal Hospital), see Paul Cornish: "'Sacred Relics': Objects in the Imperial War Museum 1917-1993". – In: Nicholas Saunders (Ed.): *Matters of Conflict*, London & N.Y., 2004, pp. 35-50. Other war museums were less celebratory of the war effort of a single nation, most notably the private *Anti-Kriegsmuseum* established by Ernst Friedrich at Berlin in 1925.

23 Cornish (2004) adds further objectives for the early war museums, such as being a memorial for the war victims, celebrating national identity and making statements on the war causes and guilt.

Bibliography

Agena, Meint: "'Habe unter Tausend kaum einen Helden entdecken können'. Dominik Richerts Erlebnisbericht über den Ersten Weltkrieg", *Geschichte Lernen* 110, 2005, 26-31.

Arand, Tobias: "Die 'Urkatastrophe des 20. Jahrhunderts' fällt aus. Der Erste Weltkrieg und seine Behandlung im Geschichtsunterricht", *Geschichte, Politik und ihre Didaktik* 31, 2003, 210-216.

Arand, Tobias: "Ausgewählte Museen zum Ersten Weltkrieg", *Geschichte Lernen* 110, 2005, 58-61.

Arthur, Max (Ed.): *Forgotten Voices of the Great War*, London, 2002.

Banham, Dale & Christopher Culpin: *This is History! The Trenches. A First World War Depth Study for Key Stage 3*, London, 2002.

BBC, Remembrance <http://www.bbc.co.uk/religion/remembrance/ – 20.07.2006>.

BBC Schools Online, World War One <http://www.bbc.co.uk/schools/ worldwarone/ – 07.11.2005>.

BBC Primary History – Children in the Second World War <http://www.bbc.co.uk/history/ww2children/home.shtml – 23.10.2005>.

BBC Scotland, Around Scotland, Scotland During the Second World War <http://www.bbc.co.uk/scotland/education/as/ww2/ – 17.11.2005>.

BBC & Open University, WW II The People's War <http://www.open2.net/ peopleswar/peopleswar.html – 20.11.2005>.

BBC History Homepage, Wars and Conflict <http://www.bbc.co.uk/history/war/ – 07.11.2005>.

Beier, Rosmarie (Ed.): *Geschichtskultur in der Zweiten Moderne*, Frankfurt/M., 2000.

Borries, Bodo von: "Von gesinnungsbildenden Erlebnissen zur Kultivierung der Affekte? Über Ziele und Wirkungen von Geschichtslernen in Deutschland". – In Bernd Mütter & Uwe Uffelmann (Eds.): *Emotionen und historisches Lernen*, Frankfurt/M., 1992, pp. 67-92.

Brötel, Dieter & Hans Pöschko (Eds.): *Krisen und Geschichtsbewusstsein. Mentalitätsgeschichtliche und didaktische Beiträge*, Weinheim, 1996.

Calder, Angus: *The People's War. Britain 1939-1945*, London, 1996 [1969].

Calder, Angus: *The Myth of the Blitz*, London, 1995 [1991].

Clio Online <http://www.erster-weltkrieg.clio-online.de/site/lang__de-DE/1/ – 20.07.2006>.

Corneließen, Christoph: "Was heißt Erinnerungskultur? Begriff-Methoden-Perspektiven", *Geschichte in Wissenschaft und Unterricht* 54, 2003, 548-563.

Cornish, Paul "'Sacred Relics': Objects in the Imperial War Museum 1917-1993". – In Nicholas Saunders (Ed.): *Matters of Conflict*, London & N.Y., 2004, pp. 35-50.

Deary, Terry: *Horrible Histories: The Frightful First World War*, London, 1998.

Deary, Terry: *Horrible Histories: The Blitzed Brits*, London, 1994.

Demantowsky, Marko: "Geschichtskultur und Erinnerungskultur – zwei Konzeptionen des einen Gegenstandes. Historischer Hintergrund und exemplarischer Vergleich", *Geschichte in Wissenschaft und Unterricht* 55, 2004, 11-20.

Department for Education and Skills, The Standards Site, History at Key Stage 3 <http://www.standards.dfes.gov.uk/schemes2/secondary_history/ – 23.10.2005>.

Deutsches Historisches Museum & Rother, Rainer (Eds.): *Der Weltkrieg 1914-1918. Ereignis und Erinnerung. Begleitmaterial zur Ausstellung*, Berlin, 2004.

Dines, Peter & Peter Knoch: "Deutsche und Britische Erfahrungen im Bombenkrieg 1940-1945". – In Dieter Brötel & Hans Pöschko (Eds.): *Krisen und Geschichtsbewusstsein*, Weinheim, 1996, pp. 53-75.

Erdmann, Elisabeth: "Treppensteigen in der Toga. Sinnlich-emotionale Erfahrungen im Museum". – In Bernd Mütter & Uwe Uffelmann (Eds.): *Emotionen und historisches Lernen*, Frankfurt/M., 1992, pp. 153-163.

Fast, Kirstin (Ed.): *Handbuch museumspädagogischer Ansätze*, Opladen, 1995.

Fritsche, Gerd-Walter: "Bedingungen des individuellen Kriegserlebnisses". – In Peter Knoch (Ed.): *Kriegsalltag*, Stuttgart, 1989, pp. 114-152.

Gardiner, Juliet: *The Children's War. The Second World War Through the Eyes of the Children of Britain*, London: Imperial War Museum, 2005.

Gregory, Adrian: *The Silence of Memory. Armistice Day 1919-1946*, Oxford & Providence, 1994.

Gygi, Fabio "Shattered Experiences – Recycled Relics: Strategies of Representation and the Legacy of the Great War". – In Nicholas Saunders (Ed.): *Matters of Conflict*, London & N.Y., 2004, pp. 72-89.

Hinz, Hans-Martin (Ed.): *Der Krieg und seine Museen*, Berlin, 1997.

Holmes, Richard: *Tommy. The British Soldier on the Western Front 1914-1918*, London, 2004.

Hunt, Roderick & Alex Brychta: *What Was It Like?*, Oxford, no date [Stage 8, KS 1].

Imperial War Museum London: *The Imperial War Museum London*, London, 2004.

Imperial War Museum, Collections and Archive <http://collections.iwm. org.uk/ – 11.11.2005>.

Imperial War Museum London, The Children's War exhibition <http://london.iwm.org.uk/childrenswar/ – 20.08.2005>.

Imperial War Museum North <http://north.iwm.org.uk/ – 20.11.2005>.

Kavanagh, Gaynor: *Dream Spaces. Memory and Museum*, London etc., 2000.

Knoch, Peter (Ed.): *Kriegsalltag. Die Rekonstruktion des Kriegsalltags als Aufgabe der historischen Forschung und der Friedenserziehung*, Stuttgart, 1989.

Knoch, Peter: "Luftkrieg 1940-1945. Massenvernichtung im Erlebnis von Zeitzeugen und im Nacherleben von Jugendlichen heute". – In Bernd Mütter & Uwe Uffelmann (Eds.): *Emotionen und historisches Lernen*, Frankfurt/M., 1992, pp. 255-280.

Korff, Gottfried *et al.* (Eds.): *Museumsdinge. Deponieren – Exponieren*, Köln, Weimar & Wien, 2002.

Korff, Gottfried: "Die Eigenart der Museums-Dinge: Zur Materialität und Medialiät des Museums". – In G.K. (Ed.): *Museumsdinge,* Köln, Weimar & Wien, 2002, pp. 17-28.

Krumeich, Gerd: "Konjunkturen der Weltkriegserinnerung". – In Rainer Rother (Ed.): *Der Weltkrieg 1914-1918*, Berlin & Wolfratshausen, pp. 68-73.

Lehrplan Online Hessen, Geschichte <http://www.lpo-hessen.de/go/ ausgabe.asp?q=603&modus=22&nav=9 – 20.07.2006>.

Loewy, Hanno & Berhard Moltmann (Eds.): *Erlebnis – Gedächtnis – Sinn. Authentische und Konstruierte Erinnerung*, Frankfurt/M., 1996.

Münch, Matti: "Leben in den Schützengräben. Eine Annäherung über die Sinne", *Geschichte Lernen* 110, 2005, 10-16.

Mütter, Bernd & Uwe Uffelmann (Eds.): *Emotionen und historisches Lernen. Forschung – Vermittlung – Rezeption*, Frankfurt/M., 1992.

Nevermann, Knut: "Zur Zukunft historischer Museen", *Standbein, Spielbein. Museumspädagogik aktuell* 67, 2003, 14-15.

Paris, Michael: *Warrior Nation. Images of War in British Popular Culture, 1850-2000*, London, 2000.

QCA National Curriculum Online, History <http://www.standards.dfes.gov.uk/ schemes2/history/his9/501983?view=get – 23.10.2005>.

Radway, Richard: *Britain 1906-1918*, London, 2002.

Reese, Armin: "Unkontrolliert –aber beeinflussbar? Das historische Kinder- und Jugendbuch als Vermittlungsinstanz für Emotionen". – In Bernd Mütter & Uwe Uffelmann (Eds.): *Emotionen und historisches Lernen*, Frankfurt/M., 1992, pp. 181-190.

Rose, Sonya: *Which People's War? National Identity and Citizenship in Britain 1939–1945*, New York, 2003.

Rother, Rainer & Deutsches Historisches Museum: *Der Weltkrieg 1914-1918. Ereignis und Erinnerung*, Berlin & Wolfratshausen, 2004.

Rüsen, Jörn: "Historisch trauern – Idee einer Zumutung". – In J.R. (Ed.): *Zerbrechende Zeit. Über den Sinn der Geschichte*, Köln, Weimar & Wien, 2001, pp. 301-324.

Saunders, Nicholas: "Apprehending Memory: Material Culture and War, 1919-1939". – In John Bourne, Peter Liddle & Ian Whitehead (Eds.): *The Great World War, 1914-1945*, vol. 2, London, 2001, pp. 476-488.

Saunders, Nicholas (Ed.): *Matters of Conflict. Material Culture, Memory and the First World War*, London & N.Y., 2004.

Saunders, Nicholas: "Material Culture and Conflict. The Great War, 1914-2003". – In N. S. (Ed.): *Matters of Conflict*, London & N.Y., 2004, pp. 5-25.

Schulz-Hageleit, Peter: *Grundzüge geschichtlichen und geschichtsdidaktischen Denkens*, Frankfurt/M., 2002.

Schulz-Hageleit, Peter: *Geschichtsbewusstsein und Zukunftssorge. Unbewusstheiten im geschichtswissenschaftlichen und geschichtsdidaktischen Diskurs*, Herbolzheim, 2004.

Schwan, Torsten: "Denk mal. Funktionen emotionalen Lernen für den Geschichtsunterricht am Beispiel einer Stunde zum Napoleon-Bild", *Geschichte in Wissenschaft und Unterricht* 55, 2005, 19-31.

Simon, Werner: *Fachdidaktik kompakt: Geschichte und Sozialkunde für die Sekundarstufe I*, Hamburg, 2002.

Winter, Jay: *Sites of Memory, Sites of Mourning. The Great War in European Cultural History*, Cambridge, 1995.

Zacharias, Wolfgang: "Orte, Ereignisse, Effekte der Museumspädagogik. Horizonte des musealen Bildungsauftrages und Spekulationen zur Topographie kultureller Erfahrung". – In Kirstin Fast (Ed.): *Handbuch museumspädagogischer Ansätze*, Opladen, 1995, pp. 71-97.

Christian Schmitt-Kilb (Rostock)

The Suez War and the Shaping of a Postimperial English Identity (with a Comment on Kazuo Ishiguro's *The Remains of the Day*)

1. Introduction

According to the 1989 *Encyclopaedia Britannica*, the "Suez Crisis" (a Suez War is no entry) marks a "crucial juncture in the history of the Middle East". After a short and, from a non Anglo-French perspective, patriotically whitewashed description of events in October and November 1956 – whitewashed in such a way that the collusion between Israel, France and Britain remains more than necessary in the dark – the article ends on a rather melancholic note with the remark that: "England and France, less fortunate [than Egypt and Israel], lost most of their influence in the Middle East as a result of the episode."[1] This is undoubtedly true, albeit understated, because the long term results for both England and France amounted to much more than their loss of influence in this part of the world: namely their significant loss of influence on the world stage and their degradation to, as one might call it, second division players in world politics.

To qualify this statement, it has to be granted that the Suez Crisis was neither the only nor the major cause for this gradual development. What it was, though, is the single most important event which induced both the political caste and the majority of the population to *realise* that Britain's status as a world power was of the past and that from now on major decisions were taken elsewhere. The fact of the reluctant acknowledgement is important here: After Suez Britain was forced "to come to terms with her second-class status in the world".[2] Thus the event's importance lies, at least for Great Britain, on the level of signification rather than that of the actual historical referent: For the national psyche[3], the collective imagination, the symbolic content of Suez as signifier or symbol for this degradation is arguably more central than the event itself.

Approaching the war and its consequences with semiotic terminology does not, however, mean to ignore the more than 1000 Egyptians, many of them civilians, who were killed in only a couple of days nor the sufferings of the many injured, who are hardly ever mentioned in the history books. The importance for Britain and Britain's self-image, nevertheless, lies elsewhere. Although it was probably the shortest military conflict ever fought which received its own proper name, the country which decided to initiate the Suez War differed in important respects from the country that came out of it. Never before did an overwhelming military success, which it undoubtedly was, have such devastating consequences for the victorious side. Coming back to the above quoted entry in the *Encyclopaedia Britannica*, a crucial juncture it was not only in the history of the Middle East, but at least as much in the history, especially in the history of mentalities, of Great Britain.

Before considering the long-term repercussions of the event, which are ingeniously captured in Kazuo Ishiguro's 1989 novel *The Remains of the Day*, I want to focus on the Suez Crisis as such. After a short outline of the major events, I shall concentrate on the way in which the conservative Eden government attempted to sell its politics both to the British public and to the President of the United States, Dwight D. Eisenhower – in the first case via the press and in the second via private correspondence between Prime Minister and President. Both discourses reveal the extent to which parts of the British public and Britain's leading politicians based their assumptions and decisions on ideas about Britain which were no longer supported by the realities of the time.

2. Historical Preliminaries

The Suez Canal, originally financed by France and Egypt, opened to traffic on 17 November 1869. It provides the shortest maritime route between Europe and the Indian and western Pacific oceans. Only six years after its completion, in 1875, internal debts forced the Egyptian government to sell its share to the British. In 1882, British troops protected the canal during a civil war in Egypt, and in

1888, the Convention of Constantinople, signed by all major European powers, declared the canal a neutral zone under the protection of the British. Free passage was guaranteed to all in time of peace and war. The canal's management was placed in the hands of the Suez Canal Company.

The Anglo-Egyptian treaty of 1936 made Egypt virtually independent, but Britain reserved rights for the protection of the canal. Only after World War II did Egypt begin to press for evacuation of foreign troops. As a consequence of Egypt's repudiation of the 1936 treaty in 1951, Britain agreed to withdraw. In June 1956, the British completed their evacuation of armed forces from Egypt and the canal zone.

Since its opening, the canal had been of major strategic and economic importance, as, on the one hand, the link between Britain and India and as a major trading route and one of the most important providing lines for European oil on the other. Even after India had gained independence in 1947, it remained received wisdom that Britain's position in the Near and Middle East was dependent on the control of the Suez Canal, which the *Observer* considered "the main artery of the Commonwealth".[4] In 1952, officers in the Egyptian army overthrew the monarchy under King Farouk, who had previously employed a British puppet government. Abandoning policies which were co-operative with European powers, the new government desired to take up a more nationalistic and assertive stance. This led to conflict with Israel and the European powers over the Suez Canal at the end of which stood the nationalization of the canal by Egyptian President Minister Gamal Abdel Nasser on 26 July 1956. Foreign canal shareholders were compensated at current market prices when the privately owned Suez Canal Company was replaced by the Egyptian Canal Authority. In August, British oil and embassy officials were expelled from the country.

Nasser's move was partly inspired by Arab nationalism, partly by larger political issues. It has to be judged in the light of the cold war which gained momentum in these years. Both Israel and Egypt had been seeking to secure arms in the preceding months and years to prepare for a military showdown. When Egypt turned down an American offer and announced that Czechoslovakia would supply weapons, America and Britain withdrew money to finance the prestigious Aswan Dam. Egypt's dismissal of the British forces from the Suez region was a consequence of this withdrawal. In the eyes of the huge majority of the Egyptian population, Nasser turned into an Arab hero.

The British Prime Minister Anthony Eden regarded the nationalisation of the canal as unacceptable and was determined to reverse it, while US President Eisenhower was strictly opposed to the use of force. In the months that followed, a secret meeting between Israel, France and Britain took place. Details only emerged years later as records of the meeting were suppressed and destroyed. All parties agreed that Israel should invade and that Britain and France would subsequently intervene, instruct the Israeli and Egyptian armies to withdraw their forces from either side of the canal, and then place an Anglo-French intervention force in the canal zone.

The invasion began on 29 October 1956 when Israeli forces acted according to the plan and invaded the Gaza Strip and the Sinai Peninsula. Again in accordance with the plan, Britain and France issued a twelve-hour ultimatum to Israel and Egypt to withdraw to a line ten miles away from either side of the canal. As expected, Egypt rejected the ultimatum which demanded a withdrawal within their own sovereign territory. Nasser's refusal was in the following used as a pretext for a joint invasion to regain control of the canal and topple the hated Egyptian President. On 30 October, the United States introduced a resolution in the UN Security Council calling for a ceasefire and a withdrawal of Israeli forces from Egypt which was vetoed by Britain and France. In the world's first helicopter-borne assault, the United Kingdom and France began to bomb Egypt on 31 October to force the reopening of the canal. Nasser responded by sinking a number of ships then present in the canal to block the passage, while at the same time the oil pipeline from Iraq to Lebanon was blown up by Syrian engineers. Moreover, Saudi Arabia broke off diplomatic relations with Britain and imposed an oil boycott.

On 5 November, British and French troops landed in Port Said and Port Faud. The operation to take the canal was highly successful from a military point of view, but a political disaster. The Soviet Union warned Britain that the Suez crisis might lead to a world war and made reference to Soviet rockets aimed at Paris and London. America, on the other hand, put severe economic pressure on Britain and France. With the loss of Middle Eastern oil, Britain was dependent on New World supplies. At the same time, massive withdrawals of sterling made Britain dependent on an International Monetary Fund loan. The US government refused an increase in oil supplies and withheld support for an IMF loan unless there was an immediate ceasefire. On 6 November, Britain and France agreed to a humiliating ceasefire.

In the following months, UN forces (from which Britain and France were excluded) arrived in Egypt and before the end of the year, the last remaining British troops left Egypt. While this happened, Eden went on a holiday to Jamaica to recover from health problems he had suffered under the strain of the crisis. Continuing illness combined with his seriously weakened political position resulted in his resignation on 9 January 1957. Eden's resignation marked, at least until the Falklands War, the end of the last attempt Britain would ever make to establish, as Scott Lucas writes, "that Britain did not require Washington's endorsement to defend her interests".[5]

3. Confronting Parliament, Public, Press and President: Eden Overstrained

The wars fought in recent decades, particularly Vietnam and the Gulf Wars, have been increasingly debated in the light of crisis media management. The role of mass media, public opinion and their mutual influence on each other and on the actual military and political decision makers has moved to the centre of interest not only in academic discourse but also in the circles directly involved in the conduct of wars: politicians and the military. British Prime Minister Anthony Eden's attempts to control and manipulate the mass media during the Suez crisis have often been judged a complete disaster, an example for future leaders how not to do it. Resulting from ignorance of the power and importance of public relations, so the story goes, Eden and Britain had lost the Suez war not on the battlefield (which is of course true) but on the information front. While Nasser's was a totalitarian regime dependent for its survival upon propaganda, that is, on its ability to tell lies, democratic governments like the British were, even at times of crisis, beholden to their people and therefore forced to stick to the facts. Until today, the myth that the British printing press as the flagship of the open society was the real victor of the conflict survives. That this is far from being the truth has been revealed in a recent study by Tony Shaw who closely analyses what happened between Downing Street and Fleet Street between July and November 1956.

Right from the beginning, Suez was staged as a public event. This was taken care of, on the Arabic side, by Nasser whose live speech on the radio in which he announced the nationalization of the Suez Canal Company on 26 July 1956 was a calculated media act. Nasser unusually spoke in the Arabic of the streets, thus making clear whose cause he was about to defend, and he made use of a powerful rhetoric with the message that those listening ought to "defend our nationalism and our Arabism".[6]

Eden saw the affront as a chance for himself. He was under pressure in his own country, even in his own party because large parts of the population were not convinced at all that the diplomatic course he had been steering in the recent past in Middle East matters had been to Britain's advantage. Now he could prove himself as a man of action. On the other hand, he knew that Nasser had not even technically broken the law. The Egyptian leader's announcement to compensate the foreign shareholders at a fair rate was a clever move. How could Eden then brand Nasser as an international criminal and even threaten him with armed force outside the UN?

It has to be explained at this stage that it was not formally illegal for Nasser to nationalize the canal as long as he stuck to the treatise of 1888 to keep the canal open for all ships. Eden had to marginalize the legality issue and, at the same time, convince the nation and the world that even the use of armed force outside the UN, were appropriate. What this meant in practice was according to Shaw "a twin-track policy of rapid military preparations supported by a propaganda campaign vilifying Nasser and whipping up public opinion in favour of the use of force". And Shaw continues:

> The key to this policy was for the government to dissemble. Were the public to discover Eden's real purpose, whole sections of opinion that trusted him as a 'man of peace' would be alienated. The trick, therefore, was to have the public opinion-formers do the government's bidding whilst the latter stuck to the line that its only objective was to 'restore' international control of the Suez Canal. This called for media

manipulation of the highest calibre, not to mention Machiavellian nature.[7]

The result was an intensive propaganda campaign launched by the British government with the help of the media with the aim to whip up public opinion in favour of the use of force. At the same time, the government itself had to appear as merely interested in the restoration of international control of the Suez Canal. The result of this difficult strategy, and the miscalculations involved, can be evaluated if one confronts the government's media campaign with Eden's personal correspondence with Eisenhower at the same time.

The British press reacted immediately and with unbridled aggression in the early days after Nasser's declaration. The front-page leader of the *Daily Mail* on 27 July was entitled "Hitler of the Nile", the *Daily Express* on the same day saw "A Time To Resist", "No more Adolf Hitlers" shouted the *Daily Herald* one day later on the front page and declared there was "no room for appeasement" while the liberal *News Chronicle* conceded that "the British government will be fully justified in taking retaliatory action".[8]

It should not be overlooked, though, that the call for action was accompanied by criticism launched at Eden's policy in several conservative papers. The argument was that Nasser's policy was to be expected as the British policy of the recent past had contributed to Nasser's power. A more uncompromising course would have prevented Nasser from nationalising the canal in the first place. The *Daily Express* sums it up in its first leader on 27 July: "Is Britain going to tolerate this new arrogance? With each act of surrender to Nasser the task of resistance has become harder."[9]

Eden's actions on 27 July, the day after Nasser's declaration, shall be looked at in some detail in order to shed light on the double strategy which the Prime Minister was to follow in the weeks to come. In the morning, he made a statement in parliament giving away nothing of his deep anger with Nasser. There he said:

> The unilateral decision of the Egyptian Government to expropriate the Suez Canal Company, without notice and in breach of the Concession Agreements, affects the rights and interests in many nations. Her Majesty's Government are consulting other Governments immediately concerned, with regard to the serious situation thus created. The consultations will cover both the effect of this arbitrary action upon the operation of the Suez Canal and also wider questions which it raises.[10]

In the afternoon of the same day, he met for the first time with Iverach McDonald, foreign and deputy editor of *The Times*. Quite bluntly, he wanted the paper to help in the creation of a war mentality in the wider public, and thus his tone was much harsher here. He told McDonald that the government was willing to act alone and to use force without the UN or other nations, if necessary. After McDonald had been briefed, the paper adopted an extremely hardline pro-force stance. A whole series of editorials resembled, sometimes down to the very words used, what Eden had told McDonald in their first meeting. For example, the editorial of 1 August entitled "A Hinge of History" warned of the threat to the West's interests throughout the Middle East should Nasser be allowed to get away with it and the danger of getting involved in "legal quibbles" concerning Egypt's right to nationalize the Suez Canal Company, a phrase which Eden also used in his first and supposedly confidential cable to Eisenhower later the same day (see below).

Thus Eden's initial meeting with McDonald was very successful and his strategy clear. Both had got what they wanted: the journalist his inside information and Eden the support of the print media without public knowledge of his involvement. This set the pattern for the next weeks, in which Eden used selected press members as instruments for publicizing policies on which the cabinet were agreed but to which it had not publicly committed itself.

Later the same day, Eden wrote the already mentioned letter via cable to Eisenhower in which he explained his point of view thus:

> Apart from the Egyptians' complete lack of technical qualifications, their past behaviour gives no confidence that they can be trusted to manage it with any sense of international obligation. [...] We should not allow ourselves to become involved in legal quibbles about the rights of the Egyptian Government to nationalise what is technically an Egyptian company, or in financial arguments about their capacity to pay the compensation which they have offered. [...] As we see it, we are unlikely to attain our objective by economic pressures alone. My colleagues and I are convinced that we must be ready, in the last resort, to use force to bring Nasser to his senses. For our part, we are prepared to do so. I have this morning instructed our Chiefs of Staff to prepare a military plan accordingly.[11]

Ironically, in his own memoirs, Eden later quoted extensively from the aforementioned editorial in the *Times* as evidence of "a general conviction throughout the country that Nasser must not be allowed to get away with his theft and that we should be fully justified in taking forcible steps to prevent him".[12] He remained quiet, however, about the fact that he was quoting his own words and his own convictions delivered via McDonald.[13]

Eisenhower's response on the same day was an attempt at moderation. "While we agree with much that you have to say", he writes, "we rather think there are one or two additional thoughts that you and we might profitably consider." (155) And a few days later, he specified these thoughts, highlighting public opinion as one major parameter which needs to be taken into account. On 31 July 1956, he cautions that

> [i]f unfortunately the situation can only be resolved by drastic means, there should be no grounds for belief anywhere that [...] legal rights of a sovereign nation were ruthlessly flouted. [...] Public opinion [...] would be outraged should there be a failure to make such efforts. Moreover, initial military successes might be easy, but the eventual price might become far too heavy. (156)

Eden, on the other hand, kept on reminding the President of the parallels between the disastrous appeasement policy of the thirties and what may happen in the Middle East. On 5 August he writes: "I have never thought Nasser a Hitler: he has no warlike people behind him. But the parallel with Mussolini is close. Neither of us can forget the lives and treasure he cost us before he was finally dealt with." (158)

Parallel to the almost daily correspondence with Eisenhower (Eisenhower ironically and condescendingly referred to it as "a transatlantic essay contest".[14]), in which he tried to impose on Eisenhower his view that ultimately the use of force will be necessary, Eden continued his attempts to influence public opinion via the press. Although he was looking for Eisenhower's consent, he acted as if Britain was – in terms of world political importance – still on a par with its transatlantic ally. What is of importance to my argument here is that the October collusion between Israel, France and England which finally triggered the Suez war, was acted out in the imperial spirit of the nineteenth century, even though a careful reading of Eisenhower's letters in the months leading up to the war might have led Eden to the conclusion that the President no longer considered the Prime Minister an equal partner. Eden rejected the charge of implicit imperialism in another letter to Eisenhower on 30 October 1956: "I can assure you that any action which we may have to take [...] is not part of a harking back to the old Colonial and occupational concepts. We are most anxious to avoid this impression." (181)

Several British historians later blamed Eisenhower for keeping England in the dark about his attitude prior to the outbreak of the war. On the evidence of the letters, nevertheless, this is hardly sustainable. Eisenhower was most clear about his own position. He was convinced that the use of force would be the worst possible option, and his letter dating from 2 September already underlines this:

> I am afraid, Anthony, that from this point onward our views on this situation diverge. As to the use of force or the threat of force at this juncture [...] I regard it as indispensable that if we are to proceed solidly together to the solution of this problem, public opinion in our several countries must be overwhelming in its support. [...] American public opinion flatly rejects the thought of using force. [...] The use of force would, it seems to me, vastly increase the area of jeopardy. (162-163)

But Eden had by then manoeuvred himself into a position in which his remaining options were those of a shameful retreat (which would have cost him his job) and the use of force (which cost him his job nevertheless), between the acknowledgement of the fact that Britain's status in the world was no longer that of an imperial power and the denial of this fact. Eden chose the second option with the results that have been outlined above.

While a huge split went through the British public as to the right reaction towards Nasser's act, large parts of the press continued to uphold the impression, briefed by Eden, that a huge majority of the population asked for military action. On 27 August, *The Times* entitled its editorial "Escapers' Club" and wrote:

> Nations live by the vigorous defence of their interest. [...] Doubtless it is good to have a flourishing tourist trade, to win test matches, and to be regaled by photos of Miss Diana Dors [TV and radio celebrity of the fifties] being pushed into a swimming pool. But nations do not live by

circuses alone. The people, in their silent way, know this better than the critics. They still want Britain great.[15]

That this was a gross misrepresentation of the actual state of affairs became obvious right after the beginning of the invasion. On 4 November 1956, the British capital saw one of the hitherto largest political protest meetings. People from different social classes and political convictions protested against the use of force showing that support for Eden's war was far from being as widespread as *The Times* had claimed over and over again.

Without displaying too much backbone, the paper fundamentally changed its tone immediately after the outbreak of hostilities. William Haley, one of the editors and the author of the "Escapers Club"-article only a month ago, now claimed that the paper had favoured a peaceful solution right from the start. And the conservative *Daily Mail*, which had called for a crusade against the "Hitler of the Nile", now asserted that they had always supported the view that the "rule of the white topee" was definitely over and had been so even before the crisis. In the light of this development, it can at best be called self-irony, at worst cynicism when *The Times* made what they considered as the best of the crisis, namely that John Stuart Mill as an observer of the Suez crisis and the Suez war would have been proud of the British democracy, especially regarding the freedom and independence of the press.

The example of Eden's attempt at double or even triple dealing (if one considers his personal performance on 27 July *vis-à-vis* the public, the press and the President of the United States) shows how thinking along imperial lines was still vital and revivable in times of crisis and that both the press and the government were prone to tie into that discourse. Kunz observes that "[i]t was intolerable to a man like Eden, born in the last century and come to maturity at the apogee of empire, that an upstart like Nasser could strip Britain of one of its most glorious imperial possessions".[16] In the end and with the help of a changing climate in world politics, this is exactly what Nasser achieved – with consequences for England (and *Great Britain*) and its sense of identity which can be described in sociological, historical or even psychological terminology but which might be grasped more directly and more emphatically in Kazuo Ishiguro's 1989 novel *The Remains of the Day*.[17] As a coda to the previous pages concerning Suez, I want to turn to that novel in order to highlight on the one hand how new layers of meaning come to the fore when the text is read against the backdrop of the Suez crisis and on the other how the long-lasting repercussions of the crisis might be understood better if confronted in the context of the history of an (albeit fictional) individual.

4. The Aftermath of Suez: The Remains of the Day

The Remains of the Day is narrated in the first-person by an English butler named Stevens. The time of the narration is July 1956, the days around the beginning of the Suez crisis. Stevens gets the permission by his employer to take a six-day road trip to the West Country of England – a region to the west of Darlington Hall, the house in which Stevens resides and has worked for thirty-four years. Until recently the house was owned by the now-deceased Lord Darlington. The present owner, a rich American gentleman called John Farraday, is proud to own a house with "features going back centuries" and "a real old English butler" who has served "a real English lord". (124)

Much of the narrative is comprised of Stevens's memories of his work as a butler before, during and just after World War II. It is gradually revealed that Lord Darlington sympathized with the Nazis, even arranged and hosted dinner parties between the German and British heads of state to help both sides come to a peaceful understanding. Stevens always maintains that Lord Darlington was a perfect gentleman and that it is a shame his reputation has been stained simply because he misunderstood the Nazis' true aims: "Lord Darlington was a gentleman of great moral stature. [...] I gave thirty-five years' service to Lord Darlington [...] and I am today nothing but proud and grateful to have been given such a privilege." (126)

The Remains of the Day is a story primarily about personal regret: throughout his life, Stevens puts his absolute trust and devotion in a man who makes drastic political and personal mistakes. In the totality of his professional commitment, Stevens moreover fails to pursue the one woman with whom he could have had a fulfilling and loving relationship. His formality cuts him off from intimacy, companionship, and understanding. The novel also voices regret concerning the supposedly good old days when

English Lords owned English Halls – even though Stevens in the end realizes that the good old days were not without blemish after all. For himself, this means the reinterpretation and ultimately utter devaluation of the life he has lived: "I trusted in his lordship's wisdom. All those years I served him, I trusted I was doing something worthwhile. I can't even say I made my own mistakes. Really – one has to ask oneself – what dignity is there in that?" (243) Knowing the significance which dignity holds in Stevens' mental universe, the measure of his self-depreciation can hardly be overestimated.

Even though Stevens' personal issues are in the foreground, the private emotions of the narrator/main character are in the novel short-circuited with larger historical issues. Ishiguro himself denies his interest "in history per se"[18] and the critic James Lang underlines that as a political event, Suez "remains entirely obscured in Ishiguro's novel".[19] Nevertheless, there are many obvious and important links to England in the thirties and the mid-fifties which ground the text firmly in the historical context of its time. First there is the time – Mr Farraday has bought the house at the time when Eden came to power, and the six days in July 1956, when he undertakes the trip, coincide with the outbreak of the crisis. Moreover, Eden is named several times as one of the persons who visited Darlington Hall prior to the war, a reference which highlights the potentially dangerous parallels between the appeasement politics of the thirties and Eden's choices as Prime Minister in the present. Eden's pro-war propaganda in the months leading up to Suez relied heavily, as has been shown, on this comparison.

In one central episode of the novel, Ishiguro subtly hints at the political muddle the oppositional Labour Party found itself in during the crisis because they did not have a clear stand on decolonisation and thus on the imminent Suez crisis. On the third day of his journey, Stevens runs out of fuel[20] and ends up in the village of Tavistock where he is engaged by the talkative Labour-bent Harry Smith in a debate about politics and the dignity of man. Smith on the one hand supports the idea of democracy. He points to World War II in which, he claims, "we won the right to be free citizens. And it is one of the privileges of being born English that no matter who you are, no matter if you're rich or poor, you're born free. [...] You can't have dignity if you're a slave." (186) Never mind his plea for democracy, he asks Stevens (whom he takes to be an influential gentleman) to put fellow villager Dr. Carlisle in the right about the latter's misguided ideas concerning "all kinds of little countries going independent". (192) Democracy for Britain and the clinging to imperial ideas were not mutually exclusive even for the left.

Most importantly, however, and less obvious is the novelistic take on the changed relationship between England and the United States, which also implies a changed attitude of Englishmen to their own history. The transfer of Darlington Hall, which here serves as a metonymy for the British aristocratic heritage, to an American, the source of whose power, importantly, is not gentility but money is of symbolic importance. Farraday in this respect represents not only America, but more specifically the new world power of capitalism, and Stevens, once a representative in his own marginal way of the British colonisers, has become colonised himself by the power of capital: a fact that Farraday demonstrates to him after Stevens has mistakenly led a visitor to believe that he is only a "mock" butler:

> Indeed Stevens, I told [Mrs Wakefield] you were the real thing. A real old English butler. That you'd been in this house over thirty years serving a real English lord [...] I mean to say, this *is* a genuine grand old English house isn't it? That's what I paid for. And you're a genuine old fashioned English butler, not just some waiter pretending to be one. You're the real thing aren't you? That's what I wanted, isn't that what I have? (124)

Stevens, as Farraday's outburst makes clear, has been bought and sold as a "real" English commodity. The value of his Englishness no longer lies in his agency as a dignified servant of great powers, but in his capacity to look genuine and to be desirable as a product. The fact that Stevens presents himself, in only a short period of time, as "the real thing" which he really is and was, namely the butler of Darlington Hall, as a "mock butler" who is currently employed by Mr Farraday but has not served Lord Darlington, and as the Lord himself (in conversation with the villagers) emphasises the identity crisis in which he finds himself trapped. In this sense, the condition of Stevens resembles that of Britain which also has troubles to adapt to the changed political realities, has to give up old patterns of thought and acknowledge the fact that the power and influence of (transatlantic) money has superseded the power of (English/British/Old Europe's) tradition.

Already in the 1930s, Senator Lewis who is the only American guest at one of Lord Darlington's political meetings, is furious and disillusioned about the degree of naiveté involved in the European's old-fashioned approach to solve problems of world importance. He bursts out:

> You gentlemen here, forgive me, but you are just a bunch of naïve dreamers. And if you didn't insist on meddling in large affairs that affect the globe, you would actually be charming. Let's take our good host here. [...] His lordship here is an amateur. [...] He is an amateur and international affairs today are no longer for gentlemen amateurs. The sooner you here in Europe realize that the better. All you decent, well-meaning gentlemen, let me ask you, have you any idea what sort of place the world is becoming all around you? The days when you could act out your noble instincts are over. Except of course, you here in Europe don't seem to know it. [...] You here in Europe need professionals to run your affaires. If you don't realize that soon you're headed for disaster. A toast, gentlemen. Let me make a toast. To professionalism. (102)

The degree of professionalism which Lewis toasts to and pleas for in the pre-war years is not sufficiently established even in the mid-fifties with the result that an English Prime Minister continues to act as if the rules of the empire were still internationally accepted and respected. "By 1956", as one critic points out, "the 'American century' is under way, and Stevens has travelled the open road of his own country as the means by which he can finally confront the changes that lie ahead for Britain in the post-Eden, post-imperial era."[21] *The Remains of the Day* ingeniously highlights the mixture of melancholy and regret which has accompanied the process of decolonisation, the end of the notion of empire and the necessity to develop a new sense of self. It shows how these categories are tangible on a personal and a public level. The Suez war as a symbolic and a real watershed in English self-conception has paved Stevens' and Eden's followers' ways.

Notes

1 *Encyclopeadia Britannica*, 15th edition, vol. 11, Chicago *et al.* 1989, p. 353.

2 Robert Hewison: *In Anger: British Culture in the Cold War, 1945-1960*, New York, 1981, p. 127.

3 It is the national psyche of the English rather than that of the British which I am speaking of, if there is such a thing at all. Krishan Kumar's *The Making of English National Identity* (Cambridge 2003) is only the most recent of a number of publications which reject the very notion of a fully-fledged English national identity, let alone a British one. On the other hand, the involvement of the whole of the United Kingdom, that is, of Scotland, Ireland and Wales in the history of colonialism (of which Suez of course is a part) has to be taken into account. This would speak for a usage of Britain/British rather then England/English when talking about 'national' consciousness. I have, nevertheless, decided at times to stick to England/English, prominently so in the title, even though I am aware of the implicit problems. The fact that my reading of Kazuo Ishiguro's novel below provides a genuinely English example of post-imperial identity crisis supports this decision.

4 *Observer*, October 21, 1951, p. 4, Quoted in Gerhard Altmann: *Abschied vom Empire. Die innere Dekolonisation Großbritanniens 1945-1985*, Göttingen, 2005, p. 129.

5 W. Scott Lucas: *Divided We Stand: Britain, the US and the Suez Crisis*, London, Sydney, Auckland, Toronto, 1991, p. 324. – A propos the Falklands: During the 1982 Falklands crisis British ministers, civil servants and the military were haunted by memories of Suez. Admiral Sir Terence Lewin, chief of the Defence Staff, remembers as "his worst moment of the crisis" his report to Prime Minister Thatcher about the loss of two helicopters at the start of the operation. "It did not take too much imagination", he writes, "to see the thought going through her [Thatcher's] mind: 'Is this going to be another Suez?'" As opposed to Suez, though, the major world powers did not get involved due to the absence of either economic or military interests. Lewin's quote in Tony Shaw: *Eden, Suez and the Mass Media: Propaganda and Persuasion During the Suez Crisis*, London, New York, 1996, p. 1.

6 Quoted in Shaw, p. 5.

7 *Ibid.*, 10.

8 All quotes in Shaw, pp. 23-24.

9 *Ibid.*, 24.

10 *Ibid.*, 26.

11 Peter G. Boyle: *The Eden-Eisenhower Correspondence, 1955-1957*, Chapel Hill & London 2005, p. 154. Further references to this edition will be included in the text.

12 Quoted in Shaw, p. 27.

13 Or maybe he even did not remember correctly – negotiating on the same day with the press, parliament and Eisenhower about the same issue but with different intent may have overstrained his memory.

14 Dwight D. Eisenhower: *Waging Peace*, New York, 1965, p. 77.

15 Quoted in Shaw, p. 57.

16 Diane Kunz: *The Economic Diplomacy of the Suez Crisis*, Chapel Hill, 1991, p. 79.

17 Kazuo Ishiguro: *The Remains of the Day*, London, 1989. Further References to this edition will be included in the text.

18 "I would search through history books in the way that a film director might search for locations for a script he has already written. I would look for moments in history that would best serve my purposes, or what I wanted to write about. [...] I didn't have a strong emotional tie with [...] British history, so I could just use it to serve my own purposes." Kazuo Ishiguro: "The Novelist in Today's World: A Conversation" (Interview with Kenzaburo Oe) *Boundary* 2:18.3, 1991, 109-122, 115.

19 James M. Lang: "Public Memory, Private History. Kazuo Ishiguro's *The Remains of the Day*", *Clio* 29, 2000, 143-165, 152.

20 If I am right that the ageing Stevens with his pre-war *Weltanschauung* may be read as a metonomy for a feeling of Englishness shared by large parts of the population, the passage may be interpreted as symbolic for the actual situation England found itself in – fuel, that is oil, was what the Suez conflict was really about, and the British government finally had to give in because the United States made it clear that England would also literally run out of fuel soon if it continued its military engagement in Egypt.

21 John P. McCombe: "The End of Anthony Eden: Ishiguro's Remains of the Day and Midcentury Anglo-American Tensions", *Twentieth Century Literature: A Scholarly and Critical Journal*, 48:1, 2002, 77-99, 97.

Thomas F. Schneider (Osnabrück)

'Lost Generation' of the 1990s.
Confrontations with the 'Other' in Bosnia and at Home in Peter Kosminsky's Television Mini Series *Warriors* (1999)

Peter Kosminsky's 1999 two part three hours television mini series *Warriors*,[1] produced for the BBC, was a highly awarded[2] fictional representation of the participation of British soldiers in UNPROFOR peace units in Bosnia in the early nineties. Although heavily pointing also at the 'before' and 'after' of the soldiers' actions in that war, the film's reviews focused on the question whether the representation of military actions including 'ethnic cleansing' were realistic or not – especially as the marketing of the movie heavily focused on 'based on the testimony of soldiers who served in Bosnia'.

This paper will discuss the use of stereotypes of war representation in *Warriors* in relation to the tradition of the 'Lost Generation' theme, and in relation to the tradition of other 'homecoming' feature films like *Coming Home* (Hal Ashby, USA 1978), or *The Deer Hunter* (Michael Cimino, USA 1978) and others. The criteria effective in the discussion on this outstandingly successful television series on the British military engagement in the Yugoslavian Civil War(s) will be subject for investigation with a special focus on the relation between reality and representation.

Warriors tells the story of a tank crew as part of a 'peacekeeping' UNPROFOR unit in Bosnia in winter 1992/93 during 'Operation Grapple One'. The main characters are shaped on the basis of their military ranks: two Lieutenants (Lt. John Feeley/Ioan Gruffudd, and Lt. Neil Loughrey/Damian Lewis), one Sergeant (Sgt. Andre Sochanik/Cal Macaninch), and two Privates (Pvt. Alan James/Matthew MacFadyen, and Pvt. Peter Skeet/Darren Morfitt).

Warriors is heavily structured by a before-and-after frame (see the structure survey at the end of this paper) with the process of experiencing the Bosnian war in-between. The 'before' section of 20 minutes shows the protagonists within their social contexts, that is a middle-class background for the lieutenants (while one of them is living in the barracks), a farming background for the sergeant, and a working-class context at Liverpool for the privates which is characterized by football and disco amusements. The backgrounds are representatively located in Liverpool, London, Scotland and Wales.

The 25 minutes 'after' section shows the protagonists after their Bosnia experience (with the exception of Pvt. Skeet) in their former social environment (family, barracks, farm, football stadium, etc.) not coming to terms with the impressions of the Bosnian war. Finally, Lt. Feeley (on his way to a new mission in Northern Ireland) tries to commit suicide, but is eventually saved by his comrades.

The Bosnia section of approximately two hours is structured in nine episodes of military missions and eight in-between sequences of rest, reflection and retardation of suspense.

Especially in the second half of the movie (and second part of the series), the sequences of rest more and more intermingle with the mission sequences, while at the beginning a clear distinction is made between inside (the camp, and barracks respectively) and outside (the war), especially because one of the plot lines focuses on the unfulfilled 'love' story of Lt. Feeley and the wife of his Bosnian Muslim landlord, Almira (Branka Katic), which is contrasted by the love affair of Lt. Loughrey and the interpreter Minka (Sheyla Shehovich).

The mission sequences deserve most interest because here the movie's image of the Bosnian war is shaped, which is the basis for disillusionment and despair of the protagonists after their return to Britain. It should be highlighted that throughout the movie no information is given neither on the reasons for the outbreak of the Yugoslavian Civil War in Bosnia nor on the objectives of the fighting parties. In other words: the movie refers to a preformed image of the Bosnian war and to the audience's pre-knowledge about that war. It should also be kept in mind that the movie was produced four years after the end of that war and about seven years after the events referred to in the movie. Thus the movie does not present a new image of that war, but its primary objective seems to be a representation of the all-day experience of British

142

UNPROFOR soldiers in Bosnia. The movie does not explain anything but rather gives the impression that it only wants to (re-) present a 'reality' outside the media coverage of the Bosnian war, which at the time of the movie's release was common knowledge as a stereotype.

Therefore, the movie's objective was not to comment on the Bosnian war or its commemoration, but – taking into account the actual political situation – to interfere in the NATO (and British) engagement and operations in the Kosovo crisis in 1999.[3]

The nine mission sequences function as a guide to the Bosnian war for the protagonists as well as for the audience. The movie is nearly never leaving the perspective of the British soldiers (or the Bosnian persons closely related to them).

Mission 1 (28:00, 10 min.): November 1992, Croatian checkpoint, first destroyed buildings and lootings, expulsion of civilians. A British soldier saves a child by taking her into the tank.[4]

Mission 2 (40:00, 8 min.): Serbian checkpoint with expulsed Muslim civilians; women are checked (which is a clear hint to raping and 'rape camps'). British soldiers save a woman and escort the Muslim civilians.

Mission 3 (50:00, 8 Min.): Patrol in a village where fighting takes place. A bullet of unknown origin kills Pvt. Skeet.

These first three missions focus on the movie's distinction between perpetrators (Croatian and Serbian militia and military) and victims (Muslim civilians and militia). It is also made clear that the British troops (No troops of other nationalities as part of UNPROFOR are shown throughout the movie!) are not allowed to interfere in any situation because, as an UN official (Rik Langrubber/Carsten Voigt, either German or Dutch) points out, they then would support 'ethnic cleansing' and become a party to the war. The movie indicates that the 'ethnic cleansing' is already taking place and – with the killing of Pvt. Skeet – that the British troops are already unwillingly a party to the war.

The movie clearly focuses on the moral aspect prior to the political aspect of the UNPROFOR mission. It suggests that the British troops are capable, willing and able to help and save (Muslim) civilians, but are not allowed to interfere because of the military structure of the UN high command and within the British troops. This leads to a moral dilemma for the protagonists: to be condemned to act as 'observers' instead of 'warriors' – which is what they had been trained to do. Within this framework, the movie operates and shows its protagonists' action and struggle against these limitations.

Mission 4 (60:00, 25 min.): Serbian checkpoint, the mission is to patrol a Muslim village (Sase) and to evacuate wounded civilians. After a night of waiting, the troops are allowed to enter the village, which is shortly afterwards attacked by shrapnel fire. The Serbian commander (who is portrayed as a completely unreliable and dangerous, that is 'uncivilized' person) explains to the UN official that Muslim troops would attack their own people in order to secure the stay of the UN troops. The Sase village civilians are guarded by one Muslim militiawoman, who – after the retreat of the UN troops is commanded – leads the civilians into the woods to an insecure fate.

A young man slightly wounded and wearing a 'Manchester United' t-shirt is taken into the tank. As the tank reaches the Serbian checkpoint again, the UN official gives order to let the Serbian commander check the tank. Pvt. James (reference to his social football background) and Sgt. Suchanik (reference to an ID-check and questionnaire of his family origin the night before by the Serbian militia – he is the son of a Polish father and a Serbian mother) are responsible for hiding the young man, and they first refuse to hand him over, but they have to obey (UN) orders. The young man is led by the Serbian militia into the woods as a 'POW' (presumably to be executed). Pvt. James is starting to cry.

At the end of part one of the movie, a first failed attempt to break out of the suggested framework is extensively presented, repeating and manifesting the perpetrator/victim structure again. Presenting a single Muslim militiawoman in the Sase village to protect the civilians is heavily underlining this structure: this weak (Bosnian) party of the conflict should be supported by the British troops, instead of arguing with the UN officials and 'uncivilized' Serbian militia.

The second part (*Mission 5*, 86:00, 8 min.) starts in April 1993 with a visit of Lt. Feeley and Almira to a place, where during World War II Croatian Ustaša imprisoned and killed Serbian and Jewish civilians in a concentration camp. This indicates the movie's only attempt to approach the historical origins of the conflict – but in this case just the conflict between Serbs and Croatians, and not between these two ethnic groups on one side and the Muslims on the other

(Almira is Muslim). An actual conflict between Croatians and Serbians is not indicated throughout the movie.

Returning to the camp, Lt. Feeley observes Croatian militia looting the house of an elderly Muslim family at the outskirts of the village of Ahmici. Referring to his UN status, he interferes. Meanwhile in a parallel sequence, Lt. Loughrey with other British soldiers is visiting a Muslim family in the centre of Ahmici.

Thus the movie now opens up a new part of the limiting framework. The British troops fraternize with Bosnian civilians outside the camp and outside the military structure (Loughrey already has established his love affair with the interpreter Minka.). Because of the good-bad scheme manifested in part one, these people consequently can only be Muslim civilians. Moreover, the movie suggests that a distinction can be made between military and civilian structures and in this case refers to a pre-modern image of warfare, although the Croatian militia appears in three civilian Mercedes Benz's.

Mission 6 (96:00, 11 min.): On the next day (21 April 1993), the British troops return to Ahmici and find the elderly Muslim family killed respectively crucified, and the other visited Muslim family burned alive to death in the basement of their house. Buildings of other ethnic inhabitants (Croatians in this case) are not affected by the massacre. This sequence is extensive in presenting mutilated, tortured, raped, etc. civilians, which had almost been omitted in the preceding part of the movie.

These two mission sequences are remarkable in at least two points: Firstly, the movie here clearly and explicitly refers to one of the key events in the history of British military intervention in the Bosnian war: the Ahmici massacre of 21 April 1993. According to British and UN sources, British troops 'discovered' the massacre committed by Croatian militia, which was then widely covered by British media.[5] Thus the movie let its protagonists become participants of one of the best-known events of the Bosnian war, presumably on the same level of public knowledge and mythification as the 1993 Srebrenica massacre.[6]

Here, on the other hand, the movie contradicts its own and its protagonists' perspectives up to this point: now it is not the 'ordinary' Bosnia experience represented by the movie, but the experience of an event which became part of the media world and media history. Moreover, by representing such a widely known event, the movie supports its legitimisation and claim to authenticity. Cynically spoken, it is not any massacre but *the* massacre relevant for the British public (as it is 'Srebrenica' for the Dutch public etc.).

Secondly, within its own discourse framework the movie offers a completely new 'reason' for the massacre: The movie suggests that the elderly Muslim family undoubtedly was killed because of the interference of Lt. Feeley. It is just a short step to transfer this causality to the killing of the visited Muslim family and furthermore to the commitment of the complete massacre (which is an event in world media history). Although the movie is clearly indicating that the massacre was planned and prepared at least before the night of the visit of the British troops, the sequences support the discourse of dangerous and forbidden interference in this conflict. More and more the audience is asked what for the troops were sent to Bosnia and if their mere presence is an interference, not to speak of personal relations and fraternization.

Consequently, the next two missions focus on these points: *Mission 7* (115:00, 6 min.) repeats the 'ethnic cleansing' assistance argument by showing Muslim civilians in the town of Travnik hiding in basements. In a parallel sequence, Almira and her daughter are brought to the camp (and thus 'saved') by Lt. Feeley (while her husband takes part in the war as a Muslim militiaman).

Mission 8 (123:00, 8 min.) shows the British troops at night evacuating, against their orders, the Travnik Muslim civilians. Returning to the camp, they learn that Almira and her daughter were killed, who had returned to their house to pick up some family souvenirs.

Again, within the movie's discourse, interference produces death, but this time the movie switches from an anonymous level to a personal level because Feeley was hoping to take Almira with him to Britain and was in love with her. At this stage of the movie, the nameless and countless victims have not only got a face (as the young man with the 'ManU' t-shirt at the end of part one), but are individualized by a name and by a direct relation to one of the protagonists. The audience's identification is now completely and emotionally directed to the victim part of the framework: at this point, Lt. Feeley finds a Muslim priest to celebrate the funeral of the two women, which is the first time that cultural differences between the British and the Bosnians are shown and are not

146

obscured by the attempt of the Bosnians to appear as Western culture influenced as possible (by drinking alcohol, playing Play Station etc.). The movie indicates that the 'victims' now have become part of the British part in the conflict (and vice versa) and thus suggests that the distinction between 'peacekeeping' forces and civilians according to the UN regulations of the mission is absurd more than ever.

Mission 9 (133:00, 10 min.) consequently leads to the culmination of this development of the discourse: The British troops show up at a site of an exchange of Muslim militia and/or male civilian execution victims who were killed by Croatian militia, who are still present. The militia want to abduct Muslim women, and Pvt. James is forced by the Croatian militia commander to investigate a truck full of corpses to find the only man who is still alive. Not surprisingly, he finds Almira's heavily wounded husband there, and he ends up in a macho monologue (similar to macho Serbo-Croatian language shown before in the movie) with the militia commander with the objective to provoke the commander to use violence against him, which would allow Pvt. James to kill him according to the UN regulations.

Again in a parallel and for the first time flashback montage, the movie presents an investigation commission on this event in Great Britain after the war (in preparation of court proceedings at the International Criminal Tribunal for the former Yugoslavia (ICTY) at The Hague). One question is whether Pvt. James interfered in the overall war (according to the UN regulations) with his action or not (and of course he did). But at least Almira's husband (who lost a leg) could be saved, and the corpses were exchanged and could be buried – and Pvt. James is said to be a 'hero' by his officer Engel.

The mission sequences of the movie end with a solution to the limitation established in the first three missions: by ignoring the UN restrictions and by assimilation to the warfare structure (indicated by language), it is possible for the British soldiers to conduct the humanitarian mission. Clinging to the UN regulations means to interfere willingly or unwillingly in the conflict by presumably producing additional casualties. In these sequences, the movie takes a clear standpoint pro military intervention and contra UN 'peacekeeping' missions.

The overall 'before' and 'after' structure contradicts this interpretation only at first sight. The disillusion and despair of the

147

protagonists after returning home refer to the experienced events and not to the overall situation in Bosnia; they are the consequences of the limitations and unwillingly produced casualties (indicated by short flashbacks of Feeley and James). Thus it only makes sense that Lt. Feeley, willing to commit suicide in the barracks in Britain, is saved by other soldiers and that the movie can end with a picture of warmness and shelter when Lt. Feeley is in the arms of a 'comrade'.

That James is hysterically condemned by a woman in a supermarket – "one should keep him locked away" – or that Lt. Loughrey beats his pregnant fiancé because he confuses the noise of his lawn-mower with the noise of a tank can be neglected because these sequences refer to a level of the movie directed to the audience's pre-understanding of 'misunderstanding' the British soldiers who participated in the Bosnian war. This 'misunderstanding' operates within the discourse of the 'lost generation' tradition. This 'lost generation' tradition is helping the audience to locate the Bosnian war within a preformed story (or stereotype) of representing war experience since the First World War.[7] But in Peter Kosminsky's movie *Warriors* the question is explicitly posed why these British soldiers are nearly unable to return to their semi-civil life after the operation. In this movie, it is not the experience of war in general (as it would be in the 'lost generation' tradition), but the experience of helplessness, powerlessness and the confrontation with a type of warfare they were not trained to conduct or to come to terms with. Kosminsky neither questions the institution of the military nor the legitimacy of war in general. He questions the way of preparing soldiers for such a conflict and thus – and because of his explicit good/bad scheme – takes a clear standpoint pro military intervention.

Warriors in some parts takes up the representation of 'homecoming' in former feature films like Hal Ashby's *Coming Home* (USA 1978).[8] The opening 'before' sequence resembles the one hour opening Polish wedding sequence in Michael Cimino's *The Deer Hunter* (USA 1978),[9] both sequences are an attempt to draw a sketch of the 'before' social structure which is destroyed by the war experience. While in *The Deer Hunter* this destruction is shown in the social group of Polish immigrants in a working-class setting in Pennsylvania, in *Warriors*, it is the lower-class football background of Pvt. James and Skeet (which is a strong cliché) or the wedding problems of Lt. Loughrey and his fiancé or the farm problems of Sgt. Suchanik after the accidental death of his brother. Both movies point at the contrast of civilian violence (hunting, disco brawl) and war violence shortly afterwards, but they also point at social bindings and social shelter, which at the end of the movie *Warriors* are substituted by social shelter in the military.

But more than referring to stereotypes of 'homecoming' sujets of the 'lost generation' tradition (as mentioned above), Kosminsky's movie perfectly fits into the movie representation of UN missions since the late 1990s.[10] In feature films like *Underground* (Emir Kosturica, Yugoslavia/France/Germany/Hungary 1995), *Welcome to Sarajevo* (Michael Winterbottom, GB/USA 1997), *Black Hawk Down* (Ridley Scott, USA 2001), *Behind Enemy Lines* (John Moore, USA 2001), *Nikogarsnja zemlja/No man's Land* (Danis Tanovic, Slovenia 2001), and presumably many others, the UN 'peacekeeping' forces are portrayed as helpless and insufficiently prepared for the warfare they are confronted with. Moreover, the UN restrictions are preventing a solution of the conflict or are structurally responsible for the 'humanitarian catastrophe'.

Especially *Behind Enemy Lines* and *Black Hawk Down* operate with this stereotype to present a 'solution' for the overall 'helplessness' problem of the UN forces – which is the ordinary and 'effective' military action (in these two cases of the US army). Both movies, which were sponsored by the US military, promote military comradeship ('no one's left behind'), and also deconstruct UN reputation. In *Behind Enemy Lines*, Gene Hackman (as an US general) simply ignores the UN rules of the mission and gets rewarded by discovering and proving a war crime committed by Serbian militia. In *Black Hawk Down*, the UN mission (in Somalia) simply functions as a background for the attempt to replace the pictures of burned GI corpses in the streets of Mogadishu in 1993 by a story of heroism and comradeship; and in the end the military action is welcomed by the Somali civilians.

It seems as if Peter Kosminsky's movie is targeting at such a 'solution' by pointing at the consequences of helplessness and at the possibility of diverse, non UN-restriction ruled action – in the context of the 1999 Kosovo War and the NATO (including British) engagement in favour of the then Albanian 'victims'. It's clearly cynical that the credits of *Warriors* end with an insert pointing out: "UN did not endorse or sponsor this programme in any way".

It should be clear that such a good/bad or perpetrator/victim scheme presented in *Warriors* or other movies mentioned above has nothing to do with the reality of the Bosnian or any other war. The good/bad scheme in media representations of war (in movies as well as in literature or other print or audio-visual media) is a stereotyped vehicle to promote military engagement and to justify and to legitimise the interference of the 'good' party (being in every case the soldiers from the country of those who produce the representations). It is a well-known mode of propaganda to first distinguish the parties in a war in a good/bad scheme, which is accompanied by a hierarchy of cultural difference. To deny the enemy's competence in terms of civilization then enables your own troops as well as your own public to support warfare and at least to accept casualties (physically as well as humanitarian values). The content and structure of *Warriors* is a striking example of this propaganda mode and method.

Kosminsky himself admitted in an interview that the objective of the movie was to change the character of 'peacekeeping' UN operations:

Thema dieses ehrgeizigen und spannenden Fernsehfilms ist unser zwiespältiges Verhältnis zum Krieg. Wir wollten eine Debatte über die Berechtigung von Militäroperationen zur Friedenserhaltung in Gang bringen. Denn hierin wird die vorrangige Aufgabe der Soldaten des 21. Jahrhunderts bestehen. Als wir *WARRIORS – EINSATZ IN BOSNIEN* drehten, wurden britische Truppen ins Kosovo geschickt. Bei Ende der Dreharbeiten waren andere Kontingente in Timor im Einsatz. Wenn wir weiterhin unsere Soldaten als Friedenspolizei in die ganze Welt entsenden, müssen wir uns langsam überlegen, welchen Auftrag wir diesen jungen Männern mit auf den Weg geben. [...] Ich wollte keinen Film über den Bosnienkrieg machen, ich fühle mich dafür nicht qualifiziert. Mich interessierten die Blauhelme. Ich fragte mich, was es für diese jungen Frauen und Männer bedeutete, sich plötzlich inmitten eines Krieges zu befinden, der nicht der ihre war. Ich wollte wissen, was es heißt, eine Kampfausbildung hinter sich zu haben und dann ohnmächtig zuschauen zu müssen, wie Menschen ihre Nachbarn ermorden. Die Soldaten der ersten Blauhelm-Missionen mussten tatenlos zusehen, wie die unmenschlichsten Grausamkeiten begangen wurden. Als die NATO das Kommando übernahm, änderte sich die Situation: Es wurde möglich, auch mit Waffengewalt Frieden zu stiften.[11]

This means in the end, that *Warriors* is not a movie about the Bosnian war or British troops in the UNPROFOR mission, but the attempt to change British and/or international policy in the context of UN missions. Although Kosminsky claimed that he had interviewed 80 (respectively 90) veterans of the UNPROFOR mission, and despite the marketing of the movie that emphasized that it is "based on the testimony of soldiers who served in Bosnia",[12] many reviews emphasize, that Kosminsky fictionalised the subject: "Needless to say, the fictionalized docudrama format raises more issues of creative license than Kosminsky's former talking-head approach, but the dramatic manipulations are an important part of the achievement."[13] That means: "The facts of ethnic cleansing are well known, but Kosminsky's triumph is to make a jaded audience feel their impact."[14] The focus is not on 'authenticity' in respect of the 'facts' of events and military action but on 'authenticity' of impact and emotion. This indeed is an innovation and a change in the genre of modern war film, which distinguishes *Warriors* from most its antecedents.

The pre-dominant claim for 'authenticity' in the war movie genre is fulfilled in this production by referring to testimonies of veterans ('based on') and historical events like the Ahmici massacre, and by the use of 'authentic' tanks, and actors and actresses from former Yugoslavia (with an appropriate accent). The 'authenticity' effective in the reception is that of emotion, regardless of historical 'truth'.[15] The reliability of the veterans and Yugoslavian actors and actresses is given by their own experiences, which ensure the 'authenticity' of emotions, which is superior to the old claim for 'authenticity'.

And perhaps this is the reason why Kosminsky at last succeeded in having the Ministry of Defense cooperate in the production of the movie – as Kosminsky put it:

> The main reason for their [the MoD] defensiveness was that it was very difficult to see the film I was proposing as anything other than a criticism. But I was completely open about my intentions, that I wanted to look at it from the human angle, to get a debate going about the nature of peacekeeping and its effect on individuals, as we enter a new century when there is going to be a lot more of it going on. I also made it clear that I was going to focus entirely at platoon commander level and below. In general I think they just didn't feel threatened by it.[16]

Suddenly, the former critic of British military engagement,[17] Kosminsky, in 1999 turned into an agent of a new British military intervention policy, because – and this is finally the crude argumentation – this new policy (which is in fact the old policy) would not produce such men in despair as in the old 'peacekeeping' units. The idea (and stereotype) of the 'lost generation' which for centuries has been identical with the idea of pacifism, peace keeping, and the prevention of war, is turned into its opposite: only military action and killing would avoid traumatic experiences.[18] Or as Kosminsky put it right before the premiere in 1999: "I think the progressive forces in the Army will like this film because it is forcing the serious consideration of the issues."[19]

And Kosminsky was soon correctly understood and supported by political commentators like Neal Ascherson in *The Observer*:

> What about dying? Public voices used to bray on about heroism and sacrifice. But the private British view is that death is a family matter. That's why young soldiers – more responsible than they have ever been – are less willing to risk it. But Britain is not yet a 'body-bag' culture in which every war-widow feels entitled to sue the colonel for criminal negligence. That was the Tory government's misreading of the public mood at the time of Bosnia. The British are more grown-up than that – and so are their soldiers.[20]

The British military engagement in the 1999 Kosovo crisis and in the 2003 Iraq War proved and proves that Kosminsky's intention to change British public's opinion and Ascherson's interpretation have become a guideline for British military intervention policy. But a story of the 'lost generation' of the first decade of the 21st century still has to be written.

Notes

1 All information on the content refers to the 1999 BBC video edition of *Warriors*, in which the two-part series structure is eliminated. For the TV presentation of 20 and 21 November 1999, both parts had approximately 85 minutes. All information on cast and crew refer to the International Movie Database: <http://www.imdb.com/title/tt0119873/ – 18 October 2005>.

2 The movie received the following awards: "Best Drama Serial" and "Best Sound", BAFTA TV Award (2000); Golden FIPA in category "Fiction" (2000); "Best Single Drama", Broadcasting Press Guild Award (2000); "Best Mini-Series", Golden Nymph, Monte Carlo TV Festival (2000); Prix Italia in category "Fiction – Serial" (2000); "Best Sound", "Best Music", and "Best Costume Design", RTS Television Award (2000); WGC Award for Pete White (1998). "Best Single Film", UK Broadcast Press Guild (2000); "Best Television Drama", South Bank Show Awards (2000). See <http://www.imdb.com/title/tt0119873/awards – 18 October 2005>.

3 See here and in general on New Labour's change in war politics Holger Rossow's article in this volume.

4 'Warrior' is the correct name of the tank shown, but of course the title operates with the audience's expectation of soldiers as warriors.

5 See <http://news.bbc.co.uk/2/hi/europe/603420.stm, 14 February 2000 – 18 October 2005>; <http://www.ohr.int/ohr-dept/presso/bh-media-rep/summaries-tv/bhtv/default.asp?content_id=634, 16 April 2000 – 18 October 2005>; <http://www.cnn.com/WORLD/Bosnia/updates/9604/17/massacre/, 17 April 1996 – 18 October 2005>; report of the 1998 UN trial at <http://www.un.org/icty/indictment/english/kup-1ai980209e.htm>; about the media coverage, see <http://www.balkan-archive.org.yu/kosta/mediji/mediji-MWF-11.html (1994) – 18 October 2005>.

6 Srebrenica is mentioned in part one as the place where the Sase village civilians are trying to escape to. Of course, the audience knows about the Srebrenica massacre and thus can be sure that the Sase village inhabitants had been killed.

7 See for stereotyped story telling in war movies, Rainer Leschke: "Von den Schwierigkeiten vom Krieg zu erzählen – Zur medialen Choreographie eines gesellschaftlichen Ereignisses". – In Waltraud 'Wara' Wende (Ed.): *Krieg und Gedächtnis. Ein Ausnahmezustand im Spannungsfeld kultureller Sinnkonstruktionen*, Würzburg, 2005, pp. 306-327.

8 See James Campbell: "Coming Home: Difference and Reconciliation in Narratives of the Return to 'the World'". – In Richard M. Slabey (Ed.): *The United States and Viet Nam from War to Peace*. Jefferson, NC, 1996, pp. 198-207.

9 Of the extensive literature on this movie see, Frank Burke: "Reading Michael Cimino's *The Deer Hunter*. Interpretation as Melting Pot", *Literature/Film Quarterly* 20:3, 1992, 249-259; Robert E. Bourdette Jr.: "Rereading 'The Deer Hunter'". – In Owen W. Gilman Jr. & Lorrie Smith (Eds.): *Critical Essays on Literature and Film of the Vietnam War*, New York, London, 1990, pp. 165-188; John Hellman: "Vietnam and the Hollywood Genre Film. Inversions of American Mythology in 'The Deer Hunter' and 'Apocalypse Now'". – In Michael A. Anderegg (Ed.): *Inventing Vietnam. The War in Film and Television*, Philadelphia, 1991, pp. 56-80; Eben J. Muse: "Romance, Power, and the Vietnam War: Romantic

Triangles in Three Vietnam War Films", *Durham University Journal* 86:2, 1994, 307-313; Leonard Quart: "'The Deer Hunter'. The Superman in Vietnam". – In Linda Dittmar & Gene Michaud (Eds.): *From Hanoi to Hollywood. The Vietnam War in American Film*, New Brunswick & London, 1990, pp. 159-168.

10 It would be too far reaching, however, to assume that *Warriors* functioned as a blueprint for this representation.

11 Original source not identified, quoted at <http://archives.arte-tv.com/fiction/ warriors/dtext/apropos.htm – 19 October 2005>.

12 See Video jacket of the 1999 edition.

13 Nicholas J. Cull: "Warriors", *The American Historical Review* 106:1, 2001, quoted at <http://www.historycooperative.org/journals/ahr/106.1/mr_3.html – 19 October 2005>.

14 *Ibid.*

15 See for example Paul Hoggart in the *Times Newspapers Limited*, 22 November 1999: "Having identified this terrible subject, Kominsky chose fiction rather than documentary because of its greater human force. In dramatic terms, he has followed the same pattern as the Holby City team-writer dramatising the effect on the nurse of being stabbed by a teenage drug-thief. But if this technique is a craft, Warriors forged it into compelling art, through its sheer depth and intensity"; and Tony Purnell in *The Mirror*, 22 November 1999: "He [Ioan Gruffudd] captured the feeling of helplessness and guilt shared by all the men who were under strict orders and unable to intervene. Tempers flared. Tears flowed. Upper lips trembled. This was Army life for real for a change."

16 Jasper Rees: "When Men of War Keep Peace", origin unknown, 13 November 1999, quoted at <http://www.matthew-macfadyen.co.uk/ press2.html – 19 October 2005>.

17 As in *The Falklands War – The Untold Story* (1987), *Afghantsi* (1988), *Shoot to Kill* (1991/92), *No Child of Mine* (1997), and recently in *The Government Inspector* (2005).

18 For a slightly critical response to the movie see, Hannah Mcgill in *The Scotsman*, 20 November 1999: "The argument behind dramas like *Warriors* is that fictionalising the horrors of war brings them home to an audience in a more immediate way than news reports can. It's ironic – we're so accustomed to responding emotionally to the travails of fictional characters in fictional situations, and so desensitised to the messier narratives shown on the news, that the recent past of our nation means more to us when it's transposed into drama. In the case of *Warriors*, the civil war in Bosnia even provides the frame for a classic love-among-the-landmines storyline. It's a hard-hitting film, and sensitively performed; but bowing to the public appetite for a photogenic romance [...] seems a cop-out. The ultimate difficulty with this kind of drama is that war doesn't operate on the level of individuals; it requires that nations be regarded as homogenous masses. If

you admit that every individual has a history, a home life, love affairs and long-cherished loyalties, it gets kind of difficult to drop bombs on them. *Warriors* only makes sense if you admit that soldiers from every side in every war are young, confused, brutalised and homesick."

19 *Press Association News*, 3 November 1999.
20 Neal Ascherson: "People Still Bleed in 'Virtual' War", *The Observer*, 21 November 1999.

Peter Kosminsky: *Warriors* (1999) – Structure

Sequence	Min.	Content
Part One		
Before	19:00	Protagonists in their social environments
Vitez barracks	8:00	Instructions and regulations
Mission 1	10:00	Croatian check-point
Mission 2	8:00	Serbian check-point, expulsed Muslim civilians
Mission 3	8:00	Fighting in village, death of Pt. Skeet
Mission 4	25:00	Serbian check-point at bridge, Sase village, shrapnel fire, boy with 'ManU' t-shirt, check-point, delivering of boy as POW
Part Two		
Mission 5	8:00	Visit to Ahmici family, Croatian militia and old civilians
Mission 6	10:00	Ahmici massacre discovery
	8:00	Tensions between soldiers, love affairs
Mission 7	8:00	Travnik: civilians in basements, 'saving' of Almira and her daughter
Mission 8	8:00	Travnik: evacuation of civilians at night, discovery of murder of Almira and daughter, funeral

Mission 9	8:00	Croatian militia: exchange of corpses, Pvt. James discovers and saves Almira's husband
	3:00	Travnik: Feeley's visit to Almira's husband
After	22:00	Protagonists in their social environment – 'lost generation' motifs, Feeley's suicide attempt

Holger Rossow (Rostock)

New Labour at War: the Rhetoric of Community, Responsibility, Values, Ethics and Morality – Kosovo Revisited

1. Introduction

> How had it all gone so wrong? The missionary Blair, the man who had travelled light in opposition, who had known little of the world, had convinced himself that he, the Prime Minister, could change that world. Blair had acquired a passion for military intervention without precedent in modern British political history and without parallel internationally. Five wars in six years was a remarkable record.[1]

In a speech at the Lord Mayor's Banquet in November 1999, Blair referred to Dean Acheson's remark that Britain had lost an Empire but not yet found a role and proclaimed that the search can now end:

> We have got over our Imperial past – and the withdrawal symptoms. No longer do we want to be taken seriously just for our history, but for what we are and what we will become. We have a new role. [...] It is to use the strengths of our history to build our future not as a super power but as a pivotal power, as a power that is at the crux of the alliances and international politics which shape the world and its future. Engaged, open, dynamic, a partner and, where possible, a leader in ideas and in influence, that is where (*sic*) Britain must be.[2]

When New Labour came to power in 1997, it seemed to be clear that they were determined to develop a different course for UK foreign policy. This determination had become obvious already in the presentation of their foreign policy priorities in the election manifesto. The centrepieces of the manifesto "Britain will be better with new Labour", however, were education and the economy, clearly not foreign policy. What was standing out was the ambitiousness of the envisaged foreign policy – even for an election manifesto:

> Britain, though an island nation with limited natural resources, has for centuries been a leader of nations. But under the Conservatives Britain's influence has waned. With a new Labour government, Britain will be strong in defence; resolute in standing up for its own interests; an advocate of human rights and democracy the world over; a reliable and powerful ally in the international institutions of which we are a member; and will be a leader in Europe. [...] A new Labour government will [...] restore Britain's pride and influence as a leading force for good in the world. With effective leadership and clear vision, Britain could once again be at the centre of international decision-making instead of at its margins.[3]

The most problematic aspect of the new orientation was the approach towards human rights issues: "We will make the protection and promotion of human rights a central part of our foreign policy."[4] The determination of New Labour to follow a different trajectory in foreign affairs was also evident in ministerial speeches in the first months following the election victory. Arguably, the most notable – but definitely the most controversial – was delivered by Robin Cook, the Foreign Secretary, on 12 May 1997. In his Mission Statement, he announced that: "Our foreign policy must have an ethical dimension and must support the demands of other peoples for the democratic rights on which we insist for ourselves."[5] Robin Cook insisted that a new direction had been adopted in foreign affairs, one which broke with the policy of the outgoing Conservative administration:

> Today's Mission Statement sets out new directions in foreign policy. It makes the business of the Foreign and Commonwealth Office delivery of a long-term strategy, not just managing crisis intervention. It supplies an ethical content to foreign policy and recognises that the national interest cannot be defined only by narrow realpolitik. It aims to make Britain a leading partner in a world community of nations, and reverses the Tory trend towards not so splendid isolation.[6]

The New Labour government had a fairly good idea what the principles and priorities of its foreign policy were to be in an *ideal context* but it was rather unprepared for the challenges thrown up by the *real world* in general, the Kosovo crisis in particular and the perceived need to intervene militarily in the affairs of a *sovereign* state *without* the express authorisation of the Security Council of the United Nations.[7] Dunne and Wheeler point out that it was

> NATO's intervention to protect Kosovar Albanians in March 1999 [which] brought the use of force to the top of the government's foreign policy agenda as ministers grappled with the complex moral, legal and strategic dilemmas.[8]

What was missing from New Labour's early policy documents was the question whether and in which circumstances it would be justifiable to use force in defence of human rights.[9] The answer to this question could not be postponed for long and finally had to be given as a result of the crisis in Kosovo. Blair's various speeches, interviews and public statements in the context of the crisis showed that he was very much aware of the problem. In his "Doctrine of the International Community" speech delivered in Chicago on 23 April 1999, he stated that "[t]he most pressing foreign policy problem we face is to identify the circumstances in which we should get actively involved in other people's conflicts".[10]

The following analysis is based on the – admittedly contested – assumptions that conditions in Kosovo at the time of the intervention were not only unacceptable but that Europe in view of its own history could not – and should not on principle – tolerate genocide, mass expulsion or ethnic cleansing, and that NATO was therefore justified to ignore the sovereignty of the Federal Republic of Yugoslavia. It is not the purpose of this paper to discuss the (also hotly debated) question whether the military option should or could have been avoided but rather to look more closely at the development of the Kosovo discourse against the backdrop of Cook's announcement that Britain's foreign policy "must have an ethical dimension".[11]

Although the analysis focuses strongly on Blair, who played a front role in the Kosovo crisis, it needs to be emphasized that he did not act independently or in circumvention of the relevant government institutions – as he did in other policy areas. Riddell, for example, stresses that Blair, during the Iraq war in 1998 and in the Kosovo conflict, "was scrupulous in working through the Defence and Overseas Policy Committee of the Cabinet [...]. The full Cabinet was also kept informed in both these cases."[12]

The paper discusses New Labour's rhetoric of ethics, values, community and responsibility in the context of the Kosovo War and argues that the Kosovo discourse can only be analysed and comprehended if it is embedded in a more general discursive structure which developed around the idea of an 'international community' based on ethics, common values and shared responsibilities in a global environment.

The analysis opens with a brief outline of the unfolding of events in Kosovo, of the *objectives* of the Kosovo intervention and the *criteria* for interventions in sovereign states as proposed by Tony Blair. This is followed by the main part of the paper which is devoted to a close analysis of selected aspects of the Kosovo discourse itself.

2. Character of the Kosovo War

The war in Kosovo, for Europeans and to a lesser degree also Americans, differed from other locations of ethnic strife and mass killings because it echoed Europe in the period preceding the Second World War and the war itself: "forced migration, the separation of families and the slaughter of men, the way nationalism can trump all other arguments and emotions, and the horror of the large-scale bombing of towns and villages".[13] Pond wrote in 1999 that

> [f]or Europeans, the war in Kosovo was existential. It put to the test all the continent's gains of the previous fifty years, and especially of the post-Cold War 1990s. It challenged the assumption that at last, at the end of a terrible century, voluntary cooperation had triumphed over Nazi and Communist coercion. It exhumed the savage ethnic Balkan wars of bygone eras, even those before the forgotten Great War.[14]

According to estimates of the United Nations about 200,000 Kosovo Albanians had been displaced and were living in the open by early August 1998.[15] The pathetic pictures of their plight were broadcast to the homes of people across Europe and around the world. The pictures and the historical parallels – real or assumed – produced an increasing pressure to intervene on behalf of the Kosovar Albanians. Allusions to the similarities between the Second World War and Hitler, on the one hand, and the situation in

Kosovo and Milošević, on the other, were frequently employed by those who defended military actions against Serbia – that the comparison was out of all proportion did not really matter. Blair, for example, argued that

> [t]his is a just war, based not on any territorial ambitions but on values. We cannot let the evil of ethnic cleansing stand. We must not rest until it is reversed. We have learned twice before in this century that appeasement does not work. If we let an evil dictator range unchallenged, we will have to spill infinitely more blood and treasure to stop him later.[16]

The comparison of World War II and Hitler with Milošević and Kosovo, which is explicit here, could also be observed in many other speeches and political commentary.

The actual bombing attacks against Serbia started on 24 March 1999, and it became quickly obvious that the Serb forces used the NATO intervention as an excuse to intensify their programme of ethnic cleansing. This in turn lead to a dramatic increase in the number of refugees trying to escape to Albania and Macedonia. Kampfner argues that: "[t]hese apocalyptic scenes changed the whole context of the intervention".[17]

The war against Serbia was fought as much militarily as it was fought through the media. The crucial role of the media, of course, was far from new in conducting a war but Vickers argues that

> [w]hat was new about Kosovo was the degree to which member states and NATO attempted to use political communications techniques usually reserved for domestic politics and election campaigning to bolster public support for their actions. This happened both in the US and in Britain.[18]

Vickers believes that "Blair had only one overall aim – having started military action, to see it through and finish it, while not damaging the government's ability to govern and see its domestic programme through".[19] Blair himself was fully aware of the significance of the media: "When you fight an action like this in modern politics, in our modern media world, you're fighting it on television."[20]

3. Objectives of the Kosovo War

The Kosovo discourse, as far as New Labour was concerned, was part of an intricate web of various objectives and motivations. Here one needs to distinguish between the more limited ones, which directly related to the fate of the Kosovar Albanians, the Serbs and Milošević, and the wider concerns, which cannot be discussed in detail here but were clearly also affecting the British government. The latter included the wish to strengthen the position of Britain in the European Union and to support the idea of a common foreign and security policy of the European Union including a common defence policy. Further aspects were the relationship with the USA and the ambition to play a more prominent and active role in world affairs again. The decision to intervene in Kosovo was clearly also influenced by the envisaged new role of NATO in the 21st century. In the words of Javier Solana, "[i]naction in the face of the Kosovar plight would have undermined our policies, the credibility of Western institutions, and the transatlantic relationship".[21]

The limited objectives were formulated by NATO and repeated again and again by Blair:

> We have five objectives: a verifiable cessation of all combat activities and killings; the withdrawal of Serb military, police and paramilitary forces from Kosovo; the deployment of an international military force, the return of all refugees and unimpeded access for humanitarian aid; and a political framework for Kosovo building on the Rambouillet accords. We will not negotiate on these aims. Milošević must accept them.[22]

The conditions for Milošević were characterised by Blair as "the minimum conditions consistent with upholding the values of civilisation against the barbarity that has happened in Kosovo".[23]

4. Blair's Criteria for Foreign Interventions

Blair was fully aware of the foreign policy problems raised by the decision to intervene in the affairs of sovereign states:

> The most pressing foreign policy problem we face is to identify the circumstances in which we should get actively involved in other

people's conflicts. Non-interference has long been considered an important principle of international order. And it is not one we would want to jettison too readily. One state should not feel it has the right to change the political system of another or foment subversion or seize pieces of territory to which it feels it should have some claim. But the principle of non-interference must be qualified in important respects.[24]

Although the principle of non-interference is re-affirmed as being central to international affairs, it is argued that it can or, indeed, *must* be qualified in important respects. According to Blair, whose views on this particular problem were shared by other European leaders, intervention would be justified under the following circumstances:

> Acts of genocide can never be a purely internal matter. When oppression produces massive flows of refugees which unsettle neighbouring countries then they can properly be described as 'threats to international peace and security'.[25]

The Prime Minister seemed to have no doubts that the situation in Kosovo not only justified but necessitated the projection of force and the violation of Serbia's sovereignty: "No one in the West who has seen what is happening in Kosovo can doubt that NATO's military action is justified."[26] Although this statement did not really describe the situation correctly, the publicly expressed lack of doubt clearly helped to galvanise support for the intervention at home *and* abroad. Blair, however, also acknowledged that

> [l]ooking around the world there are many regimes that are undemocratic and engaged in barbarous acts. If we wanted to right every wrong that we see in the modern world then we would do little else than intervene in the affairs of other countries. We would not be able to cope.[27]

The fact that there are plenty of undemocratic regimes engaged in acts of violence against their own populations at any given moment raises the morally difficult question when and whether NATO or perhaps in the future the European Union should intervene. The decisive question following logically and inevitably from Blair's position is on which criteria the decision to intervene in sovereign states should be based. He proposed five major criteria that need to be applied before the decision can be taken. Although they were formulated in the context of the Kosovo crisis, they were presented as generally applicable:

1. Are we sure of our case?
2. Have we exhausted all diplomatic options?
3. Are there military operations which we can sensibly and prudently undertake?
4. Are we prepared for the long term in order not to have to return for a repeat performance?
5. Do we have national interests involved?[28]

Blair admitted that these were not "absolute tests" but insisted that "they are the kind of issues we need to think about in deciding in the future when and whether we will intervene".[29] Dunne and Wheeler draw attention to the omission of the question of authorisation by Blair:

> For intervention to have the force of law and legitimacy it should be authorised by the UN Security Council, since this is the only body that is empowered to mandate force for purposes other than self-defence. The Blair government has argued that its use of force has a secure basis in international law. It accepted that military intervention lacked the express Security Council authorisation but claimed to be enforcing existing Security Council resolutions.[30]

The Blair government admitted the lack of an *express* authorisation of the Security Council but argued that the intervention was backed by international law and existing Security Resolutions:

> We would have welcomed the express authorisation of the UN Security Council through a resolution before the NATO air campaign. This would have represented the strongest possible expression of international support. But discussions at the United Nations in New York had shown that such a resolution could not be achieved. Nevertheless, the UK and our NATO Allies, and many others in the international community, were clear that as a last resort, all other means of resolving the crisis having failed, armed intervention was justifiable in international law as an exceptional measure to prevent an overwhelming humanitarian catastrophe in Kosovo.[31]

Among those who did not follow this line of argument were the permanent members of the Security Council Russia and China who argued that the intervention of NATO was not covered by the UN charter and setting a dangerous precedent to be emulated by others – a view shared by many other non-western countries. "By analogy," write Dunne and Wheeler, "one could ask how NATO states would respond if a coalition of willing Arab countries were to use force against Israel without the consent of the Security Council but with a host of condemnatory resolutions as their cover?"[32] But – in reference to reservations Kofi Annan had about the lack of a Security Council mandate for the intervention – they also point out that

> [w]here Annan and Blair are in definite agreement is that there is a 'developing international norm' of humanitarian intervention and that identifying the circumstances under which an armed response is justified poses a fundamental challenge to the international community.[33]

The sovereignty of states had been, at least in theory, guaranteed by international law since the League of Nations. Though it could be argued that the United States, the Soviet Union and many other countries had militarily and in various other ways intervened in sovereign states before, the war in Kosovo was different from all those precedents because it has given, writes Beedham, the world a new rule: "Here was an alliance of the democracies defying the 20th century's sacred principle of sovereignty in order to insist that a dictator should not brutalise one part of his sovereign country."[34]

5. Assessment of Blair's Criteria

It would perhaps not be unfair to argue that, for example, the humanitarian crisis and the mass killings in Rwanda and Sudan at the time did obviously not affect the national interests of the UK, NATO members or the USA in the same way as Kosovo because they refrained from actively interfering in any effective way. Blair acknowledged that the situation in Kosovo did differ from other locations because national interests were affected when he stated that it made "a difference that this is taking place in such a combustible part of Europe".[35] Not surprisingly, the reconstruction of the Balkans was also considered to be in the interest of Britain and "not an act of simple generosity. It is also in our own self-interest. Unless we remove the causes of conflict we will keep having to return to the region, and put the lives of our servicemen and -women at risk again and again."[36]

In a joint interview with Javier Solana, NATO Secretary General at that time, Blair also gave strategic reasons for the NATO intervention in the Kosovo crisis – coupled with a feeling of moral outrage:

> We know the history of the Balkans, we know that instability and civil war in one part of the Balkans very often spills over into other parts, it can destabilise the entire region. So there are all those strategic reasons and they are important and I don't wish to diminish them in any way at all. But I think there is a proper sense of moral outrage at what Milošević has done that we should not shy away from but should be proud of feeling.[37]

Elsewhere, Blair emphasised that the intervention was "military action for a moral purpose as much as a strategic interest".[38]

Blair insisted with regard to events in Kosovo that "[w]e cannot allow that to happen, not on Europe's doorstep without acting".[39] An important aspect of such a stance is whether this might mean in the future that arguably much more barbarous acts in, for example, Africa will be allowed to happen simply because neither NATO nor European Union members feel that their national interests are endangered.

6. The Core Elements of the Kosovo Discourse: Community, Responsibility, Values, Ethics and Morality

6.1 Introduction

The following analysis of the core elements of the Kosovo discourse precedes from the assumption that New Labour's rhetoric of responsibility, values, ethics and morality in the context of the crisis was developed as part of a more general discursive structure the foundations of which were provided by the idea of an 'international community'.

6.2 Community

The emphasis on the idea of 'communities' both on the national and the international level had been central to the carefully managed public image of New Labour already before the Kosovo crisis. The *Strategic Defence Review* of 1998, for example, states with regard to the envisaged role of Britain in international affairs that

> [w]e do not aspire to be a world policeman; many of our important national interests and responsibilities are shared with others, particularly our Partners and Allies in the European Union and NATO. We also attach immense importance to the international community as a whole working together through the many multinational organisations, above all the United Nations.[40]

The idea of an 'international community' was proclaimed in its most comprehensive and systematic form by Blair in his "Doctrine of the International Community" speech in 1999 mentioned above in which he claimed that

> [w]e are witnessing the beginnings of a new doctrine of international community. [...] Just as within domestic politics, the notion of community – the belief that partnership and co-operation are essential to advance self-interest – is coming into its own; so it needs to find its own international echo.[41]

Membership in this 'international community' for new 'applicants' would be based on a subscription to what was defined as its core values: liberty, the rule of law, human rights and an open democratic society. Blair left no doubt in 1999 that Serbia clearly did not fall into the latter category when he stated that

> until Serbia embraces democracy, until Serbia has a Government, which wants to live with its neighbours in peace, Serbia will not be part of that modern Europe. [...] We want a modern democratic Serbia to be part of a modern democratic Europe. But the choice rests with Serbia.[42]

6.3 Responsibility

The concept of 'communities' was closely connected with the notion of 'responsibilities' underlying not only the policies of the Labour

Party but also general trends on the global level. In a speech at the World Economic Forum in 2000, Blair claimed that

> [a]longside the advance of global markets and technologies we are seeing a new search for community, locally, nationally and globally that is a response to change and insecurity, but also reflects the best of our nature and our enduring values. With it is coming a new political agenda – one that is founded on mutual responsibility – both within nations and across the world.[43]

The Secretary of State for Defence, George Robertson, wrote in the introduction to the *Strategic Defence Review 1998*:

> The British are, by instinct, an internationalist people. We believe that as well as defending our rights, we should discharge our responsibilities in the world. We do not want to stand idly by and watch humanitarian disasters or the aggression of dictators go unchecked. We want to give a lead, we want to be a force for good.[44]

Blair extended this notion of 'responsibility' also to other 'Europeans' when he warned in a speech at the Royal United Services Institute that "[w]e Europeans should not expect the United States to play a role in every disorder in our back yard".[45]

6.4 Values

According to Chandler, the Labour government's *Strategic Defence Review* in 1998 made it clear that the absence of strategic cold war threats faced by the UK "has allowed foreign policy to be driven more directly by a search for policy initiatives seen to symbolise a clear projection of values".[46] This was also expressed by Blair in Chicago in 1999:

> No longer is our existence as states under threat. Now our actions are guided by a more subtle blend of mutual self interest and moral purpose in defending the values we cherish. In the end values and interests merge. If we can establish and spread the values of liberty, the rule of law, human rights and an open society then that is in our national interests too. The spread of our values makes us safer.[47]

The re-defined concept of sovereignty, mentioned above, was also reflected in the new NATO concept that differed radically from that of the Cold-War NATO. Blair told the House of Commons on 26 April 1999 at the height of the Kosovo conflict that

> [w]hile NATO's fundamental role will remain the defence and security of the allies, there was an equally strong consensus on the need for a more capable and flexible Alliance, able to contribute to security throughout the Euro-Atlantic area and to promote the values of democracy, human rights and the rule of law for which it has stood since its foundation.[48]

Whether 'democracy', 'human rights' and 'the rule of law' had really been central to the self-image and the objectives of NATO is a completely different matter, which cannot be addressed here, but the purpose of the organization really had been changed:

> The purpose is no longer for America to help the European democracies defend their borders against Russia. It is for Europe and America to march side by side to the wars they will very likely have to fight outside their borders in the century ahead. NATO, formerly an American arm round Europe's shoulder, is becoming an organisation capable of projecting global force.[49]

6.5 Ethics and Morality

Blair and other members of his administration frequently claimed that New Labour had a new foreign policy that was distinct from that of both Conservative and Labour governments in the past. Wickham-Jones argues that one of the distinctive features of that policy "would be an emphasis placed by the new government on the moral stance of its policy".[50] The German magazine *Die Zeit* wrote in 2003 that Blair, like no other Western head of government, embodies the new type of an 'ethical interventionist' who proceeds from the assumption that sovereign nations which are in breach of norms set by the *Proclamation of Human Rights* or other international agreements have forfeited their right to sovereignty and that the 'international community' is entitled to intervene. If the institutions of the 'international community' turn out to be incapable to act, then the 'Western states' have to act as, for example, in the

Kosovo crisis.[51] Such a position poses several serious problems which, among others, include a new definition of state sovereignty as a matter of principle and the more specific question under which conditions an intervention should take place.

"Kosovo, for all its problems," writes Kampfner, "was the high point in liberal intervention, when Blair enjoyed the support of most of the party and country not just for the moral justification of war but the means by which it was being prosecuted."[52] Blair himself left no doubt concerning the moral righteousness of the military intervention:

> We cannot rest until the refugees are home. Then, truly, we will be able to say that Good has triumphed over evil
> Justice has overcome barbarism
> And the values of civilisation have prevailed.[53]

During his visit to the NATO summit to celebrate the 50th anniversary of the organisation in the USA in 1999, Blair justified the intervention of NATO in the affairs of the sovereign Federal Republic of Yugoslavia as a 'new moral crusade'. While conceding strategic interests in the stability of the Balkans, the intervention was 'a moral cause with a moral purpose':

> I make no apology for saying so, it is a moral cause with a moral purpose. [...] whatever different views were expressed on how we achieve our aims [in Kosovo], there was complete unity in the sense of purpose, that the values of democracy and justice and basic civilisation and decency have to be upheld.[54]

The moral dimension was again stressed by Blair in an article written by himself for *Newsweek* which not only carried the title "A New Moral Crusade" but explained the success of the military campaign in Kosovo and its justification with explicit references to its morality:

> We are succeeding in Kosovo because this was a moral cause which was backed by the great majority of our citizens. When they saw horrors reminiscent of Nazi Germany being revisited on the continent of Europe at the end of the 20th century, our peoples understood that we had to use our forces and money to stop it. They understood that we had to reverse the ethnic cleansing. Now we have a new moral cause. Once we have

pinned down the details of this deal, we must rebuild the Balkans and remove the cancer of ethnic conflict from it forever.[55]

Riddel argues that moral and ethical concerns have been more relevant than ideology for Blair's approach to politics and that this could be seen in repeated references to the importance of the family but also in the context of the Kosovo conflict: "In an echo of Gladstone, and unlike his recent predecessors in Downing Street, Mr Blair's approach to politics has deep moral and ethical rather than ideological roots."[56]

But it was not only Blair who repeatedly used moral arguments. Cook, for example, declared in an interview on 27 April 1999:

> I am absolutely robust that we are right to be fighting this evil. There is no conflict between the traditional values of the left and being against this. What we are witnessing is the resurgence of fascism in Europe [...]. We have not seen trains used to take men, women and children from their homes since the days of Hitler and Stalin. I do not think that anyone on the left should have any reservations about fighting this evil.[57]

One might assume that such a presentation of an international conflict in terms of 'good' and 'evil' helps to get the public support definitely needed for putting at risks one's soldiers and spending taxpayers' money in the conflicts of distant countries in the absence of any immediate threats to one's own well-being. The 'good' versus 'evil' approach is, however, far from unproblematic, because, argues Brittan, the moralistic approach

> tends to deprive diplomacy of its normal function of attempting to ease disputes without recourse to war and of negotiating a settlement when war has broken out. For once a dispute is seen, not as a conflict of interest, but of struggle between good and evil, then bargaining with the other side is seen as at best an odious expedient, and at worst a betrayal of all that is sacred.[58]

Vickers, specifically referring to Blair and the Kosovo crisis, points out that there is a problem involved in 'moral crusades': "Having presented intervention as a moral imperative, he [Blair] could not then back out when it became apparent that the military campaign would not be over in a few days."[59]

171

7. Conclusion

The particular way in which first the crisis and then the decision to intervene militarily in Kosovo were discursively represented and conceptually framed clearly aimed at those who were initially hesitant to follow the British lead: the newly united Germany, arguably being the main problem among the NATO members and the European Union, the Americans, who were hesitant to become involved at the beginning, and, of course, also sizeable sections of the Labour Party and the British public at large. The main emphasis *had* to be on the fate of the Kosovar Albanians and the similarities between World War II and the events in Kosovo. National and strategic interests were admitted – but only as secondary factors. The inactivity in similar or worse crises before, but more importantly also *after* Kosovo suggests that the wish to avoid or mitigate humanitarian catastrophes may only lead to an involvement if national interests are affected to a sufficient degree. With regard to the concrete decision to intervene (or not to), Dunne and Wheeler point out that "[g]iven the proximity of the FRY and the presence of NATO, this was a crisis that the government *could* do something about".[60] It should be emphasised, however, that *any* major engagement which might involve heavy casualties for the intervening states but no national interests at all is most unlikely. The avoidance of the deployment of ground forces in the early stages of the Kosovo War, which would have been much more effective in avoiding further ethnic cleansing, rape, murder and torture than the large-scale bombing campaign, is a point in case. But, following Etzioni, I strongly reject the view that mixed motives undermine the legitimacy of humanitarian interventions:

> Critics have no case when they reveal that humanitarian interventions draw on a variety of motives and that not all of them are noble or altruistic ones, as the term 'humanitarian' implies. [...] So long as intervening forces help to prevent or at least stop genocides once they have started, their actions are highly legitimate in terms of what most people value highly – a life free from the threat of displacement, annihilation, torture and rape.[61]

Dunne and Wheeler argue – in contrast to some critics of the intervention in Kosovo – that "intervention must be motivated by humanitarian goals" but they do not claim "that the humanitarian rationale must be the sole or even the over-riding motive". They insist, however, that "what must be ruled out is the invocation of just cause in order to cover the pursuit of self-interest, and that any non-humanitarian reasons for action do not undermine the humanitarian purpose of the mission".[62] Higgins, a former member of Britain's diplomatic service, wrote in 2000 that

> [t]he conclusion to which all this points is that foreign policy cannot be built entirely from either an absolute 'ethical' or an unqualified 'national interest' foundation. The choice is simply not between the saintly and the cynical.[63]

The new definition of sovereignty in the context of the Kosovo intervention could be a good thing – dictators should not expect to get away with mass killings, ethnic cleansing and the like. But it does also pose extremely difficult questions, questions which have not been conclusively answered by Blair and his five criteria for interventions in sovereign states. Blair's common reference to the 'international community' does not really solve any problem either because the concept itself is too fuzzy to be employed consistently. Chandler holds that the term 'international community' "is a politically loaded one which attempts to minimise the importance of the opposition to the war from Russia, China, India and many other members of the 'international community'".[64] For many observers outside Europe and NATO, the term 'international community' is only a euphemism for the power politics – however well-intended it may be in a particular case – of the major western powers, most notably the USA. This is especially true if the acting parties, as in the Kosovo War, cannot get the full support of the United Nations – the institution that, at least in theory, represents the 'international community'. Dunne and Wheeler hold that in a case like that of Kosovo where only a few states are opposing military intervention in order to stop exceptional human suffering:

> Blair was right to argue that the veto power of Russia and China must not be allowed to block the defence of human rights. But one of the consequences of eroding compliance with international law is that the doctrine of international community begins to look like an instrument for maintaining Western dominance. In the absence of a consensus on 'new rules' backed by the threat of enforcement, the view from the non-Western world is that these are a cover for a group of liberal-democratic

173

states prepared to defend liberalism by force in their relations with non-liberal states. As we emerge out of the latest phase of the Balkan crisis, the challenge for the new doctrine is to put into practice the Third Way commitment to dialogue in the course of securing legitimacy for these 'new rules' of the international community.[65]

As long as this legitimacy for the 'new rules' has not been established, it may be argued, any disregard of the international legal system and any challenge to the principle that the Security Council, and only the Security Council can authorise the use of force against sovereign states, however well-intended, not only severely undermines the effectiveness of international institutions and agreements but also invites disregard of other nation-states for the international legal order. The concept of pre-emption, as embodied in the American *National Security Strategy* (*NSS*) of 2002 could be considered as the extreme end of the belief that intervention in sovereign states is justified. The *NSS* demands that the United States "must be prepared to stop rogue states and their terrorist clients before they are able to threaten or use weapons of mass destruction against the United States and our allies and friends".[66] Although the support of other nations for the United States in their efforts to prevent terrorist attacks is appreciated, it is ultimately the independent decision of the US administration to choose what action is appropriate:

> All free nations have a stake in preventing sudden and catastrophic attacks. And we're asking them to join us, and many are doing so. Yet the course of this nation does not depend on the decisions of others. (Applause.) Whatever action is required, whenever action is necessary, I [George W. Bush] will defend the freedom and security of the American people.[67]

With hindsight, the significance of the war in Kosovo as a defining moment for the move towards a new world order cannot be overestimated. The war not only provided a new example of international institutions like the United Nations being ignored but also of a revolutionary re-definition of the concept of sovereignty: military intervention, agreed upon by a coalition of *democratically elected* governments, was justified in terms of community, responsibility for the fate of others, values, ethics and morality. The re-definition of the concept of sovereignty was potentially more

174

important for the future course of international relations than the ignoring of the United Nations in particular circumstances.

Notes

1 John Kampfner: *Blair's Wars*, London, 2003, p. 349.
2 Tony Blair: "Speech at the Lord Mayor's Banquet, 22 November 1999", 1999i <http://www.number-10.gov.uk – 23 June 2002>.
3 Labour Party: "Britain Will Be Better with New Labour", 1997 <http://www.labour.org.uk/views/manifesto/text_versions/britain.doc – 15 August 1997>.
4 *Ibid.*
5 Robin Cook: "British Foreign Policy Statement, 12 May 1997", 1997 <http://www.guardian.co.uk/indonesia/Story/0,2763,190889,00.html – 12 May 2005>.
6 *Ibid.*
7 For a discussion of this problem in the context of the Suez Crisis and other parallels see Schmitt-Kilb's paper in this volume.
8 Tim Dunne & Nicholas J. Wheeler: "The Blair Doctrine: Advancing the Third Way in the World". – In Richard Little & Mark Wickham-Jones (Eds.): *New Labour's Foreign Policy. A New Moral Crusade?*, Manchester & New York, 2000, p. 67.
9 *Ibid.*, 62.
10 Tony Blair: "Doctrine of the International Community, 23 April 1999", 1999a <http://www.number-10.gov.uk/ – 22 June 1999>.
11 Cook (1997: n.a.).
12 Peter Riddell: "Blair as Prime Minister". – In Anthony Seldon (Ed.): *The Blair Effect. The Blair Government 1997-2001*, London, p. 32.
13 Bill Emmott: "Survey 20th Century. On the Yellow Brick Road", *The Economist*, 1999 <http://www.economist.com – 22 February 2000>.
14 Elizabeth Pond: "Kosovo: Catalyst for Europe", *The Washington Quarterly* 22:4, 1999, 77.
15 Kampfner (2003: 39).
16 Blair (1999a: n.a.).
17 Kampfner (2003: 44).
18 Rhiannon Vickers: "Blair's Kosovo Campaign. Political Communications, the Battle of Public Opinion and Foreign Policy", *Civil Wars* 3:1, 2000, 59.
19 *Ibid.*, 60.
20 *War in Europe* 2000, quoted in Vickers (2000: 60); for a more detailed discussion of the media aspects of the war see, Kampfner (2003: 45ff).

21 Javier Solana: "Nato's Success in Kosovo", *Foreign Affairs* 78:6, 1999, 118.

22 Blair (1999a: n.a.).

23 Interview of Tony Blair & Kofi Annan: "Doorstep Interview with Kofi Annan, 21 April 1999", 1999 <http://www.number-10.gov.uk/ – 20 February 2000>.

24 Blair (1999a: n.a.).

25 *Ibid.*

26 *Ibid.*

27 *Ibid.*

28 *Ibid.*

29 *Ibid.*

30 Dunne & Wheeler (2000: 72).

31 MoD: *Kosovo: Lessons from the Crisis*, Presented to Parliament by the Secretary of State for Defence by Command of Her Majesty, June 2000 <http://www.mod.uk/publications/kosovo_lessons/contents.htm – 02 July 2003>.

32 Dunne & Wheeler (2000: 72).

33 *Ibid.*, 73.

34 Brian Beedham: "The Empire of Democracy", *The Economist*, 2000 <http://www.theworldin.com/ 1999/arts/lea/lea3.htm – 19 January 2000>.

35 Blair (1999a: n.a.).

36 Tony Blair: "A New Moral Crusade", *Newsweek* 14 June 1999, 1999h, 38.

37 Tony Blair & Javier Solana: "Press Conference NATO, NATO Headquarters, 21 April 1999", 1999 <http://www.number-10.gov.uk/ – 19 January 2000>.

38 Tony Blair: "Today Programme Interview, 04 May 1999", 1999e <http://www.number-10.gov.uk/ – 10 February 2000>.

39 Tony Blair: "Interview with NBC Today, 04 May 1999", 1999d <http://www.number-10.gov.uk/ – 15 February 2000>.

40 MoD: *Strategic Defence Review*, July 1998 <http://www.mod.uk – 03 August 2006>.

41 Blair (1999a: n.a.).

42 Tony Blair: "Prime Minister's Speech on a New Beginning for Kosovo, 10 June 1999", 1999b <http://www.number-10.gov.uk/ – 12 January 2000>.

43 Tony Blair: "Speech at the World Economic Forum at Davos, Switzerland, 18 January 2000", 2000 <http://www.number-10.gov.uk/ – 24 February 2000>.

44 MoD (1998: n.a.).

45 Margarita Mathiopoulos & István Gyarmati: "Saint Malo and Beyond: Toward European Defense", *The Washington Quarterly* 22:4, 1999, 73.

46 David Chandler: "Rhetoric without Responsibility: The Attraction of 'Ethical' Foreign Policy", *The British Journal of Politics & International Relations* 5:3, 2003, 300-1.

47 Blair (1999a: n.a.).

48 Tony Blair: "Statement on NATO Summit in Washington, House of Commons, 26 April 1999", 1999g <http://www.number-10.gov.uk/ – 15 January 2000>.

49 Brian Beedham: "All Eyes on Turkey", *The Economist*, 1998 <http://www.theworldin.com/1998/in002.html – 12 September 1999>.

50 Mark Wickham-Jones: "Labour's Trajectory in Foreign Affairs: the Moral Crusade of a Pivotal Power". – In Richard Little & Mark Wickham-Jones (Eds.): *New Labour's Foreign Policy. A New Moral Crusade?*, Manchester & New York, 2000, p. 4.

51 Jürgen Krönig: "Britische Solidarität. Auch dem Juniorpartner kommen Zweifel am Sinn eines Krieges", *Die Zeit* 04, 2003 <http://hermes.zeit.de/ pdf/archiv/2003/04/Kr_9anig-Kasten.pdf – 20 October 2005>.

52 Kampfner (2003: 47).

53 Blair (1999b: n.a.).

54 Tony Blair: "On Kosovo in the USA, Doorstep on Capitol Hill, 4 May 1999", 1999f <http://www.number-10.gov.uk/ – 14 February 2000>.

55 Blair (1999h: 38).

56 Riddell (2001: 24).

57 Robin Cook, quoted in: Vickers (2000: 62).

58 Samuel Brittan: "An Ethical Foreign Policy?" *Hinton Lecture*, 24 November 1999 <http://www.samuelbrittan.co.uk/spee6_p.html – 4 November 2005>.

59 Vickers (2000: 60).

60 Dunne & Wheeler (2000: 74).

61 Amitai Etzioni: "Genocide Prevention in the New Global Architecture", *The British Journal of Politics & International Relations* 7:4, 2005, 478.

62 Dunne & Wheeler (2000: 68).

63 Ronald Higgins: "Saintly or Cynical: An Ethical Dimension to Foreign Policy?", *ISIS Briefing Paper* No. 77, June 2000 <http://www.isisuk.demon.co.uk/0811/isis/uk/ regpapers/no77_paper.html – 12 October 2005>.

64 Chandler (2003: 311).

65 Dunne & Wheeler (2000: 74-75).

66 *The National Security Strategy of the United States of America*, 2002, p. 14, <http://www.whitehouse.gov/nsc/nss.pdf – 12 February 2003>.

67 George W. Bush: "State of the Union, 28 January 2003", 2003 <http://www.whitehouse.gov/news/releases/2003/09/20030923-4.html – 23 March 2003>.

Bibliography

Beedham, Brian: "All Eyes on Turkey", *The Economist*, 1998 <http://www.theworldin.com/1998/in002.html – 12 September 1999>.

---: "The Empire of Democracy", *The Economist*, 2000 <http://www.theworldin.com/ 1999/arts/lea/lea3.htm – 19 January 2000>.

Blair, Tony: "Doctrine of the International Community, 23 April 1999", 1999a <http://www.number-10.gov.uk/ – 22 June 1999>.

Blair, Tony: "Prime Minister's Speech on a New Beginning for Kosovo, 10 June 1999", 1999b <http://www.number-10.gov.uk/ – 12 January 2000>.

Blair, Tony: "Speech to the Atlantic Club of Bulgaria, 17 May 1999", 1999c <http://www.number-10.gov.uk/ – 13 February 2000>.

Blair, Tony: "Interview with NBC Today, 04 May 1999", 1999d <http://www.number-10.gov.uk/ – 15 February 2000>.

Blair, Tony: "Today Programme Interview, 04 May 1999", 1999e <http://www.number-10.gov.uk/ – 10 February 2000>.

Blair, Tony: "On Kosovo in the USA, Doorstep on Capitol Hill, 4 May 1999", 1999f <http://www.number-10.gov.uk/ – 14 February 2000>.

Blair, Tony: "Statement on NATO Summit in Washington, House of Commons, 26 April 1999", 1999g <http://www.number-10.gov.uk/ – 15 January 2000>.

Blair, Tony: "A New Moral Crusade", *Newsweek* 14 June 1999, 1999h.

Blair, Tony: "Speech at the Lord Mayor's Banquet, 22 November 1999", 1999i <http://www.number-10.gov.uk – 23 June 2002>.

Blair, Tony: "Speech at the World Economic Forum at Davos, Switzerland, 18 January 2000", 2000 <http://www.number-10.gov.uk/ – 24 February 2000>.

Blair, Tony & Javier Solana: "Press Conference NATO, NATO Headquarters, 21 April 1999", 1999 <http://www.number-10.gov.uk/ – 19 January .2000>.

Blair, Tony & Kofi Annan: "Doorstep Interview with Kofi Annan, 21 April 1999", 1999 <http://www.number-10.gov.uk/ – 20 February 2000>.

Brittan, Samuel: "An Ethical Foreign Policy?" *Hinton Lecture*, 24 November 1999 <http://www.samuelbrittan.co.uk/spee6_p.html – 4 November 2005>.

Bush, George W.: "State of the Union, 28 January 2003", 2003 [http://www.whitehouse.gov/news/releases/2003/09/20030923-4.html – 23 March 2003>.

Chandler, David: "Rhetoric without Responsibility: The Attraction of 'Ethical' Foreign Policy", *The British Journal of Politics & International Relations* 5:3, 2003, 295-316.

Cook, Robin: "British Foreign Policy Statement, 12 May 1997", 1997 <http://www.guardian.co.uk/indonesia/Story/0,2763,190889,00.html – 12 May 2005>.

Dunne, Tim & Nicholas J. Wheeler: "The Blair Doctrine: Advancing the Third Way in the World". – In Richard Little & Mark Wickham-Jones (Eds.): *New Labour's Foreign Policy. A New Moral Crusade?*, Manchester & New York, 2000, pp. 61-76.

Emmott, Bill: "Survey 20th Century. On the Yellow Brick Road", *The Economist*, 1999 <http://www.economist.com – 22 February 2000>.

Etzioni, Amitai: "Genocide Prevention in the New Global Architecture", *The British Journal of Politics & International Relations* 7:4, 2005 469-484.

Freedman, Lawrence: "Defence". – In Anthony Seldon (Ed.): *The Blair Effect. The Blair Government 1997-2001*, London, 2001, pp. 289-305.

Higgins, Ronald: "Saintly or Cynical: An Ethical Dimension to Foreign Policy?", *ISIS Briefing Paper* No. 77, June 2000 <http://www.isisuk.demon.co.uk/ 0811/isis/uk/ regpapers/no77_paper.html – 12 October 2005>.

Kampfner, John: *Blair's Wars*, London, 2003.

Krönig, Jürgen: "Britische Solidarität. Auch dem Juniorpartner kommen Zweifel am Sinn eines Krieges", *Die Zeit* 04, 2003 <http://hermes.zeit.de/pdf/archiv/ 2003/04/Kr_9anig-Kasten.pdf – 20 October 2005>.

Little, Richard & Mark Wickham-Jones (Eds.): *New Labour's Foreign Policy. A New Moral Crusade?*, Manchester & New York, 2000.

Labour Party: "Britain Will Be Better with New Labour", 1997 <http://www.labour.org.uk/views/manifesto/text_versions/britain.doc – 15 August 1997>.

Mathiopoulos, Margarita & István Gyarmati: "Saint Malo and Beyond: Toward European Defense", *The Washington Quarterly* 22:4, 1999, 65-76.

MoD: *Kosovo: Lessons from the Crisis*, Presented to Parliament by the Secretary of State for Defence by Command of Her Majesty, June 2000 <http://www.mod.uk/publications/kosovo_lessons/contents.htm – 02 July 2003>.

MoD: *Ministry of Defence Policy Paper. Paper No. 3: European Defence*, November 2001 <http://www.mod.uk/linked_files/european_def.pdf – 13 April 2002>.

Pond, Elizabeth: "Kosovo: Catalyst for Europe", *The Washington Quarterly* 22:4, 1999, 77-92.

Riddell, Peter: "Blair as Prime Minister". – In Anthony Seldon (Ed.): *The Blair Effect. The Blair Government 1997-2001*, London, 2001, pp. 21-40.

Solana, Javier: "Nato's Success in Kosovo", *Foreign Affairs* 78:6, 1999, 114-120.

UKSCD: *Eighth Report, Session 1997-1998, United Kingdom House of Commons Select Committee on Defence*, 10 September 1998 <http://www.parliament.the-stationary-off…cm199798/cmselect/cmdfence/ 138/23809 – 24 July 1999>.

Vickers, Rhiannon: "Blair's Kosovo Campaign. Political Communications, the Battle of Public Opinion and Foreign Policy", *Civil Wars* 3:1, 2000, 55-70.

War in Europe, written and presented by Michael Elliot, Channel 4, Episode 2 (6 February 2000), quoted in Rhiannon Vickers: "Blair's Kosovo Campaign. Political Communications, the Battle of Public Opinion and Foreign Policy", *Civil Wars* 3:1, 2000, 60.

Wickham-Jones, Mark: "Labour's Trajectory in Foreign Affairs: the Moral Crusade of a Pivotal Power". – In Richard Little & Mark Wickham-Jones (Eds.): *New Labour's Foreign Policy. A New Moral Crusade?*, Manchester & New York, 2000, pp. 3-32.

*Kathleen Starck (*Bremen*)*

Up against a Brick Wall? – Understanding the Ritual Qualities of Northern Irish Murals

1. Introduction

The first time I saw Northern Irish murals was as a tourist on a 'Black Cab Tour' through Belfast in 2001 – and it was not without apprehension.

We were taken on a tour of the Protestant and Catholic residential areas. The taxi company employed ten drivers, five of them Protestant and five Catholic. I never got to know the denomination of our driver, which was probably part of the taxi company's politics. I do remember, though, asking the driver what he thought would happen if the British troops were withdrawn. His answer was: civil war.

So we toured the murals on both 'sides' and were encouraged to write a wish onto the so-called peace wall which separates Protestant and Catholic areas from each other (it was being built higher at the time). Although our driver assured us that it was perfectly safe to get out of the taxi and take photos, I still felt uneasy and somewhat intimidated by some of the murals, especially the militaristic ones. They seemed to propagate unlimited violence. Apart from feeling intimidated, my main reactions were confusion and anger. I could not stop asking myself: why do people turn members of terrorist paramilitary organisations into martyrs, why would anyone want to paint the gables of their houses with hooded people with guns and grenades?

The point I am trying to make is that the Northern Irish Troubles and thus their cultural representations are very complex and at first glance, and even at second glance very confusing to the outsider. A myriad of political and paramilitary splinter groups often make it hard to understand who is fighting whom and for what reason.

Although a peace process has been in existence for many years and the IRA decommissioned their weapons in September 2005 (though Ian Paisley, the leader of the Democratic Unionist Party, keeps demanding photographs as a proof), the Troubles have not come to an end yet. Whether programmes such as *Facing the Truth*, aired by the BBC in March 2006, where victims and perpetrators of Northern Ireland's conflict were brought together in the presence of Archbishop Desmond Tutu, will be successful in initiating a process of reconciliation and healing remains to be seen.

A vital part of the peace process, I would like to argue, is an understanding of the historical and contemporary complexities of the Troubles. One way of gaining this insight can be the study of cultural representations of the Troubles – such as the murals which can be found all over Northern Ireland.

Of course, murals are also popular in other parts of the world, for example in South America, in California or also in Berlin. Yet, Northern Irish murals are very specific in their forms and functions. In order to understand them or, at least, come a bit closer to understanding them, I tried to identify what functions they fulfil in the Northern Irish conflict. The functions and purposes I found, however, turned out to be very heterogeneous. Therefore, I consider it useful to find an approach which might cover all of them. Thus I suggest analysing what these murals share: their ritual qualities.

Yet, the murals' functions cannot be understood without some knowledge of their history. Hence, before I give an overview of the murals' functions and explain how and why they lend themselves to a reading of their ritual qualities. I will first give a brief account of their origins and historical development.

2. History

Murals in Northern Ireland are not a phenomenon of the recent Troubles. Instead, they have a history which goes back to the beginning of the twentieth century. The annual celebrations of the Battle of the Boyne (the defeat of Catholic King James II by Protestant Prince William of Orange), which became known as 'The Twelfth' (taking place on 12 July) involved marches, flags, banners and murals.

Conflict researcher Neil Jarman even sees the murals' origin in the early years of the nineteenth century with their

> elaborate displays of flags, flowers and bunting [which] were hung from houses and across streets for the July commemorations of the Battle of the Boyne. Each year wooden, metal or floral arches were installed in the centres of many towns and villages and in staunchly Protestant residential areas. [...] But they were short-lived. Most lasted no longer than a few days and then the streets and buildings returned to their everyday appearance [...]. However the introduction of mural paintings in working-class areas of Belfast changed all this, making these hitherto temporary and seasonal affirmations of loyalty much more permanent.[1]

This beginning of mural painting is traced by mural researcher Bill Rolston to the year 1908, when "loyalist artisans – coach painters, house painters, etc. – began to paint large outdoor murals each July".[2]

In accordance with the occasion, these early murals mostly depicted William of Orange – King Billy – who for many decades to come was turned into the main icon of loyalist murals. He became the symbol of consolidated British rule in Ireland with the 'Protestant Ascendancy' discriminating against and containing the Catholic population.

After the partition in 1920 and the establishment of the Northern Irish State, the annual celebration of the Twelfth clearly became a state ritual. Unionist identity was reaffirmed and, according to Rolston, the celebrations, including the murals "became in effect a civic duty, recognised and legitimised as such by the state and its governing party."[3] All differences within unionism were glossed over and the myth of a Protestant unity was created, a myth which has not lost its relevance until today.

However, in the light of political unrest and changes from the late 1960s on, a splintering occurred within unionism and this started to be mirrored in the murals. Thus, King Billy became less frequent and loyalist murals now displayed a vast variety of symbols, such as the red hand of Ulster, the Union Jack, emblems, insignia and shields. Rolston notices a striking absence of humans and an emphasis on inanimate symbols.

After the Anglo-Irish Agreement of 1985, there was a remarkable increase in the use of paramilitary motives which can be seen as reflecting the rearmament of loyalist groups in the 1980s.

"Younger men with militant views thought the Anglo-Irish Agreement was a sell-out and began to paint more militant and intimidating murals [...]"[4] as a show of strength and a statement of authority. These murals show members of loyalist military organisations such as the Ulster Freedom Fighters (UFF), the Ulster Voluntary Force (UVF) and the Red Hand Commando (RHC). In addition, there has been a tradition of painting memorial murals, commemorating the 'comrades' who 'died in action'.

By the early nineteen nineties, there were, according to Rolston, more killings by loyalists than by republicans and military images in the murals now became most common, sometimes they even espoused ethnic cleansing. Examples are cited by Rolston: "There is no such thing as a nationalist area of Ulster, only areas temporarily occupied by nationalists" or "In remembrance of all those who have given their lives and their freedom in the struggle to keep Ulster Protestant."[5]

Although the depiction of historical events continued, no new events were added, which is in stark contrast to republican murals. Recently, there have also been humorous loyalist murals, which draw on techniques and motives of cartoons and pop culture.

Interestingly, after the ceasefire of 1994, loyalist murals only rarely referred to political developments. Rolston states that, surprisingly, there is a lack of murals demanding decommissioning by the IRA or in support of loyalist candidates. Instead, the prevailing images remained militaristic, masked and armed men in action. This might be attributed to the loyalists' holding on to something in existence, i.e. Northern Ireland as part of the UK, whereas republican muralists started including other motives, celebrating their vision of a future: "Loyalist muralists cannot put into visual form aspirations that are not there, hence the continuing popularity in loyalist areas of paramilitary images even in the midst of a peace process."[6]

Comparing loyalist and republican muralists' reactions to the ceasefire, Rolston comes to the following conclusion:

> The difficulty of representing a ceasefire without showing signs of capitulation was a particularly profound [problem] for loyalist murals. The original solution was to acknowledge simply that the capitulation was one-sided, that it was the IRA which had surrendered [...], while at the same time stressing that the paramilitary potential of the loyalist groups was in no way diminished.[7]

The emergence of republican murals is a much more recent phenomenon than that of their loyalist counterparts. This results from the fact that for the duration of the unionist state, censorship and policing were in place.

Their [Catholic] culture was marginalized, relegated to the private spaces of Catholic church halls, Gaelic sports fields, and private clubs. Nationalist opposition to partition took a number of forms, most obviously the sporadic military campaign of the Irish Republican Army (IRA). But the streets and public places were unionist.[8] Nationalists were confined to ghettos, where they had a vibrant culture, but one which was virtually invisible to the rest of society.[9]

This situation changed with the civil rights movement of the nineteen seventies and particularly with the hunger strike of 1981. Republican prisoners protested in order to be granted prisoner-of-war status. Ten of them died and became commemorated in numerous murals as martyrs, with Bobby Sands probably the most popular. After the hunger strike, other subjects became prominent such as current political events or police and army repression of the Catholic population. Other popular topics were Irish history and mythology and international political struggles, which republicans were encouraged to see paralleling their own struggle for freedom. Thus, republican murals borrowed images from political struggles around the world such as the ones in Palestine and Nicaragua. Although some murals depicted the 'armed struggle', as the IRA called it, this subject was never as predominant as in loyalist murals where the paramilitary images constituted 70 % of the paintings.[10]

Following the IRA ceasefire of 1994, these images disappeared or were used only in commemoration of 'real people', not masked ciphers. They were replaced by demands to disband the mainly Protestant Northern Irish police force, the Royal Ulster Constabulary (RUC), the release of political prisoners (called POWs, which again highlights a particular rhetoric of war), or the withdrawal of the British army. One prevailing slogan referring to the latter became "Time to go".

Republican muralists have, however, recently also turned to very different themes such as violence against women, the murder of nationalist black taxi drivers by loyalists, media censorship, the revival of the Irish language and the Travelling community.[11] Stylistically, they borrow from many sources such as commercial film posters, anti-fascist graphics from the nineteen thirties, socialist newspaper cartoons, murals and posters from other anti-imperialist struggles, and elaborate Celtic designs reminiscent of ancient Irish manuscripts.[12]

Most recently, though, loyalist murals have likewise started to explore historical themes such as the opposition to Home Rule, Oliver Cromwell's campaign, the events of the Williamite wars, as well as the exploration of the Ulster-Scots ancestry of US history.

This is a trend which was also confirmed in a historic discussion between republican and loyalist muralists at the Ulster Museum in May 2000. Here, for the first time, painters from both traditions shared a platform. During the discussion, it emerged that republican muralists belong to a far younger tradition, which is far more spontaneous and independent than that of the loyalists. Although most muralists on both sides are children of the hunger strike era, loyalist murals tend to be more timeless, whereas republican murals respond to more specific political events. This might also be due to the fact that loyalist murals are mostly commissioned whereas republican murals often appear spontaneously. Republican muralists work within a movement, whereas loyalist painters work within a group, with the former being open and the latter closed. As well as this, on the loyalist side it is particularly the UVF muralists who portray a more definite institutional and exclusive history to refer to the Ulster Volunteers of the early twentieth century. "This narrowly organisational approach to murals," Prof. Rolston suggests, "can be traced both to the division within loyalism, and also to a crisis in formal education in Protestant areas, which leads to an ignorance of history, a narrowly sectarian vision of history."[13]

One of the most renowned republican muralists, Denny Devenny, sees republican murals as a way of overcoming censorship and calls them "storybooks of events".[14] This functioning of republican murals as editorials of current affairs is confirmed by Belfast muralist Mo Chara who states that the murals "give people of the immediate area a sense of pride ... (*sic*) people would stand and look at a mural before they would read a paper".[15] Republican activist Baibre de Brun points to yet another reason for the murals' response to specific political events when he says that republican murals are part of the recognition that "our culture, our heritage isn't going to be reflected in the television, in the mass media [...] if we want to see it, to make it visible, then we have to do it ourselves".[16]

Emphasising an increased turn to historical themes, republican muralist Devenny describes his more recent murals as "a pathway to the future with an angle to the past".[17] Republicanism can present itself as visionary since time and change seem to be on their side, whereas the loyalist message is a narrow one of maintaining the status quo in the North.[18]

Concerning loyalist murals, Devenny goes as far as saying that loyalist politicians are embarrassed by the loyalist paramilitary images since they reflect insecurity. In line with this, in a press release of the University of Ulster, Rolston is quoted saying: "For all that they are threatening, the loyalist murals also speak of a deep inferiority complex, a defensiveness and a fear that the writing is literally on the wall for loyalists. There are many deep problems facing them."[19] This opinion is not shared by loyalist painter Noel Large, who, however, thinks "there are other things they [the murals] should diversify into now."[20]

Although Devenny and Large agree that it would be much too early for republican and loyal muralists to come together to paint, cross-community projects are, in fact, in existence. New types of murals appeared for example by BlazeFX, who are graffiti artists. For them it is important to get involved with the community, to work with young people and produce (cross-community) murals in their own areas with positive and educational messages.[21] Likewise, the artist George Newell has created a 'hope-wall' depicting cross-community murals which were painted by children.

Against this historical background, I would now like to highlight some of the most prevalent functions of murals in Northern Ireland and analyse their ritual qualities.

3. Functions

The most recurrent argument in explanation of the murals is that of the demarcation of territory. The murals are part of what Bourdieu calls "the labour of representation",[22] the work to represent a diverse community through the use of symbols. Murals effect a transformation of public space through political imagery. Thus, Neil Jarman highlights their historic role in the construction of sectarian space. With regard to Protestant murals, he argues, "[m]urals helped to transform 'areas where Protestants lived' into 'Protestant areas'".[23] On the other hand, in Catholic areas, they expressed people's control over their own areas, places in which the community could redefine themselves on their own terms, marking loci of cultural and ideological resistance. All murals, Jarman continues, "create a new type of space, they redefine mundane public space as politicised place and can thereby help to reclaim it for the community".[24]

Thus, although mainly aimed at their own community, murals at the same time deliver a message to society outside these communities. Some paintings, in fact, are positioned in such a way that they are visible from main thoroughfares. They constitute a warning to members of other communities. Tony Tayler, the director of Australia's National Centre for History Education, classifies murals as a form of graffiti which can "act as a warning to passers-by and to 'enemies' that they are entering special territory".[25] Rolston agrees with this when he comments on paramilitary loyalist murals: "If you're a nationalist, say, whose brother has been shot dead by a squad of UVF men, then that image is not a neutral image [...]" and that "they [the murals] also say to me 'Stay out, do not come in here, whatever you do'".[26]

In addition to warning, murals, of course, function as political propaganda, 'spreading the word' to a wider society. This last function is particularly well illustrated in the Northern Irish and world media's use of murals as a kind of short hand for the Troubles, a phenomenon which has recently been increasingly used by mural painters.

Jarman goes even further when he claims that murals have become news items themselves, with the local media reporting the appearance of new murals. This might be related to another rather recent development: murals have been turned into a commodity. They are sold as postcards, t-shirts, etc. and are marketed as sights to tourists. A whole industry seems to have developed with several taxi and bus companies offering guided tours (see for example the official Belfast tourism website).

Another function of murals is their use as memorials. They transform unmarked space into places at which to honour and remember the dead. In this they do hardly differ from other kinds of memorials. What is remarkable, though, is described by Jarman as follows:

> [...] the murals are probably the most assertive [memorials] in demanding acknowledgement of their presence. Most formal memorials are self-effacing objects which, while they remain as permanent reminders to death, rarely confront or challenge the passer by. It is usually considered inappropriate for memorials to be colourful. [...] For most of the year the memorials merge into the background, forgotten and ignored at the fringe of social consciousness.[27]

Murals, on the other hand, are mostly much more visible and thus more likely to have an impact on their onlookers. This is amplified by their location. Whereas memorials exist in what Jarman calls liminal spaces "carved out and set aside from daily routine,"[28] commemorative murals are placed on main thoroughfares in residential and shopping areas.

This, in spite of the changing and extending functions of murals, is in accordance with Rolston's statement that

> [m]urals are always the backdrop to news reports. But who are they painted for? Not for tourists or the media; not against the other side; but to the community. The vast bulk of murals are painted not at the but in the centre of communities (sic).[29]

Being in the centre of communities, murals fulfil yet another function which is decisive for my analysis: they help to create and sustain imagined communities.

In line with this and Rolston's statement above is historian David Welch's view that

> individuals seek out opinion formers from within their own class or sex for confirmation of their own ideas and attitudes. Most writers today argue that propaganda confirms rather than converts, and is most effective when its message is in line with existing opinions and beliefs of those it is aimed at.[30]

Analysing loyalist murals, Lyell Davies claims that the process of 'community making' has been institutionalised: "Thus, painting Loyalist murals is in a sense a quasi-state activity since these murals have historically articulated the values of Unionist rulers."[31]

189

4. Ritual Qualities

Before I can now turn to my suggestion to analyse the ritual qualities of Northern Irish murals, it is necessary to briefly introduce some methodological concepts for the analysis of visuals. In her introduction to visual methodologies, cultural geographer Gillian Rose stresses the embeddedness of visual images in a wider culture such as historically specific producers, mediators and consumers of visual images.[32] She further identifies three sites of visual images. First, the sites of production, which include the technical side, the genre, contemporary economic processes, the social and political identities which are mobilised in the making of the image and the question of who is the author. The second site is the image itself with its formal components depending on technologies and social practices. The third site(s), the image's audiences, raises questions concerning the effects the image has on its viewers, how it is looked at differently within different contexts, the social practices which structure the viewing of particular images in particular places and the social identities of those doing the watching.[33]

Applying these ideas to Northern Irish murals, it needs to be said that the ritual qualities are particularly evident for the sites of the production and the audiences of murals. However, also the site of the images themselves displays at least one ritual feature: the symbols and motives that are used (see below for details). Thus, taking into account that a visual consists of *all three* – the sites of production, the image itself and the audience – I consider the concept of ritual for reading the murals a viable one, which I will prove in the following.

Sally Moore and Barbara Myerhoff have developed a list of six points in their attempt to define a minimal consensus with regard to the term 'ritual'.[34] These points are:

1. Recursiveness of occasion content or form;
2. Conscious experiencing as opposed to spontaneous acting;
3. Special and stylised behaviour;
4. Obsessiveness;
5. Heightened receptiveness;
6. Collective dimension.

With regard to points 2, 3 and 5, I would like to point to the preparation it takes to paint a mural. The minimum conditions would require the provision of paint, sometimes scaffolding, and a site, which makes spontaneous acting impossible. In addition, the painters are not free as to their choice of a site. They are restricted to 'their own side', or to integrated or disputed areas and even within their own territory they may face problems. Bryan, for example, stresses the class division evident in the Northern Irish conflict which, by implication, equals loyalism with being working-class.[35] He underlines his statement by drawing attention to the higher number of mixed marriages amongst the middle classes who are also more likely to attempt to set up integrated education. As well as this, "[l]eisure pursuits with a more middle-class basis tend to show less concern over ethnic identity".[36] Dixon likewise points out the disproportionate working-class support of extreme political parties[37] and the fact that the peace process has largely been pursued by elites.[38] As a result of this class division, there are far less murals to be found in middle-class residential areas.

Moreover, although the symbols used in murals are not static (see below), they are not spontaneous inventions of the muralists either, but regulated by conventions. These determine the use of motives with different parties laying claim to particular symbols. So, Celtic designs, the use of the Irish language, the Harp, the Easter Lily and the Irish Tricolour are used by nationalist muralists, whereas the Union Jack, the Crown, the Star of David as well as the colours red, white and blue are typical of loyalist murals, to name but a few. Their meaning, in turn, is part of a collective knowledge and the murals' spectators possess a heightened sensitivity to these symbols. The most overt examples of a 'special behaviour' that the murals produce in their viewers are a result of the murals' function of demarcating one's own territory and warning members of the other side of violating this "topographic-ideological boundary".[39] This behaviour might include avoiding those areas, entering them with increased caution, or provocatively/violently transgressing the boundaries. Thus, the precondition for ensuring unharmed daily 'survival' (or a successful attack on the other side) is a heightened sensitivity to the murals' symbols, motives, 'messages' and the paintings' positioning.

Another group of mural recipients should be mentioned at this point. When tourists go on a 'tour of the political murals', they might not share the conventional knowledge of the murals' symbols and motives, yet they likewise display a 'special behaviour'. Most of them will take photos of the paintings, wonder at their meaning, listen to their guides' explanations and might even feel intimidated by the idea of being in a 'fundamentalist' residential area.

Concerning point 4 of the definition of rituals, obsessiveness, I would like to draw attention to the sheer number of murals in Northern Ireland.

In the following, my focus will be on rituals' collective dimension and on their recursiveness. One of the first questions that arises is: How can murals be rituals if they are fixed in time and space, rather objects than processes? An answer with regard to symbols is provided by social anthropologist Dominic Bryan, who claims that symbols in general – and I suggest symbols used in murals in particular – communicate a collection of meanings and therefore *are not static*. They are invented and their political importance and value can rise and diminish over time, different groups can compete over their ownership and they can go out of existence.[40] For example, the Celtic hero Cuchulain, the central figure of the Ulster Cycle, has traditionally been a republican symbol. However, recently this mythic figure has also been appropriated by loyalist muralists. They make use of one particular saga, Tain Bo Cuailnge (Cattle Raid of Cooley).[41] At times depicted as a loyalist Pict, Cuchulain is shown fighting off the armies of Queen Maeve of Connacht, thus symbolising the defeat of Irish/republican invaders by an Ulster hero:

> [S]ometimes the [loyalist] muralists have actually used the statue of him in the GPO [General Post Office, often itself seen as a symbol of Irish Republicanism] in Dublin, commissioned by de Valera, as the model for their images.[42]

Consequently, the symbols used in murals are not fixed in time and space, but are subject to changes.

The aspect of the murals' processuality is most commonly described as the collective dimension of rituals[43], they are *publicly* reproduced texts.[44] My claim is that murals produce and are produced by interactions and interplays between a number of social phenomena. Apart from the actual process of painting murals, which is of course, an interaction, murals help create and sustain communities, group identities. People interact with the murals, they invest them with meaning, but simultaneously the murals 'act upon' people and change the individual by constituting him or her as part of a community.

According to Bryan, a ritual can create solidarity in a group, even in the absence of consensus. It also provides access to political legitimacy and shapes people's understanding of the world. Likewise, rituals objectify a group to the outside world, they "mark boundaries and give an outward appearance of group consciousness".[45] In addition, and this might be particularly visible for loyalist murals if the continuing prevalence of paramilitary symbolism is considered, rituals can give the impression of unity and continuity during periods of change and thus provide resources in power relations.

Anthropologist and historian David Kertzer explains the creation of group identity through symbolic dramatizations (i.e. rituals) as follows:

> The struggle between political forces is exceedingly abstract and distant from the everyday experience of most people. One of the primary ways it can be made palpable is through the symbolic dramatizations of conflict [...]. Individuals can then identify political positions with tangible symbols.[46]

Interconnected and interacting with the murals' 'community making' is their transformation of space. Space, as has been agreed upon by many social scientists, is always socially constructed and it always means different things to different people. Sociologist Regina Bormann describes spatial phenomena as carrying symbolic meaning and thus functioning as a medium of communication.[47] Through this medium, then, not only ideas of a shared identity, but also power structures are communicated. This is in line with social geographers Russell Murray and F.W. Boal who view spatial constructs as mediating economic structures, class formations, and nationalist and sectarian ideologies: "[...] they [Murray and Boal] identify politicised space in Northern Ireland as a long-term historical structure with a determining impact comparable to economic or ideological structures".[48]

Murals are one 'agent' in this construction of space. Thus, ordinary residential areas are transformed through murals into segregated republican or loyalist areas and what is communicated is ownership. At the same time, these murals form what Boal and Murray call 'interfaces', topographic-ideological boundary sectors which physically demarcate ethnic communities.[49] They continue to explain that

> [t]his conversion of communities into 'no-go' areas automatically codified the other side of the barricade as an immanent source of transgression. [...] Spatial formation was reorganized into a mirror relation that had a profound ideological impact [...].[50]

As a consequence, residential areas are infused with yet another meaning, i.e. that of a sanctuary of 'one's own group' separated by an interface/mural from the sanctuary of the 'others' group'.[51] By warning 'the others' about entering the territory and these 'others' abiding, ignoring or visibly/symbolically resisting the message, there is a whole cluster of agents interacting with each other and the murals.

In addition to their processuality, murals' functions as a site of community formation, of political struggle and as transformers of space all point to another ritual quality: power. Power as a main characteristic of rituals has been stressed by Jan Platvoet's analysis of the history of ritual theories. He notices an increased turn towards 'rituals of power' and a tendency to understand rituals as strategies of the symbolic construction of power relationships.[52] Underlining this point is Dominic Bryan's definition of the attempt to control the meaning of symbols as one of the main issues of the Northern Irish Troubles.[53] Political scientist Paul Dixon makes this particularly clear when he analyses what he calls the 'propaganda war' in Northern Ireland. Dixon identifies three distinct aims of propaganda:[54]

Firstly, it is directed directly against the enemy to undermine their will, secondly, it is directed at the international community to win support and sympathy and thirdly, it is an attempt to break the opponent's will to resist in the propaganda war by showing determination (e.g. demonising the opponent).

Murals are part of this 'propaganda war' and as such are sites of the production, reproduction and contestation of power. They are used by a number of groups in their attempt to control the discourse on the Northern Irish Troubles. Some such strategies for the control

194

of discourses are suggested by Foucault. One of these is the limitation of 'speaking subjects'.[55] This, he explains, can be achieved through rituals, since rituals define the qualities which the speaking subject is required to possess, such as gestures, ways of behaviour, circumstances and all signs which accompany the discourse.[56] Anthropologists Caroline Humphrey and James Laidlaw express this similarly when they say that "in ritual one both is, and is not, the author of one's acts".[57] Bryan argues that

> [t]he actor is effectively buying in to something that 'exists'. Ritual [...] becomes comprehended by the actors as external, objectified, and thus 'apprehensible' – it can be understood, perceived and seized or appropriated.[58]

I argue that the ritual of mural painting is a limitation of speaking subjects. Although there might not be legal restrictions as to who can how and where paint murals, there certainly are shared assumptions concerning symbols and sites of murals. However, the latter are not necessarily shared by all members of the community. Yet, dissent is hard to voice since not everyone is allowed to speak. Thus, according to Jarman,

> some of the murals are too closely identified with the paramilitary culture and paintings are therefore not welcome. It is difficult to gauge how widespread opposition might be since few people have been prepared to [...] declare their objections. The acknowledged close association between the murals and paramilitary groups is both a reason to oppose the paintings and also a reason not to speak out publicly.[59]

This limitation of 'who is allowed to speak' is likewise pointed out by Rolston for the example of loyalist murals when he writes that

> [f]or too many years unionism has been portrayed as a monolith with a very narrow range of voices. The nuances have been lost. There are a thousand unionist voices to be heard, and they will not be heard until unionists are forced to say what they want and not what they don't want. If and when that day comes, there will be many themes for loyalist muralists too.[60]

The unity of the community, which is proclaimed by murals, does not exist. This is in line with Bryan's observation that "[i]t is part of an effort by an elite to represent unified community in contrast to other possible representations, such as those of class, denomination or perhaps generation, and in doing so sustain its own political position".[61] Hence, the discourse of the Troubles is, among other phenomena, regulated by the ritual of mural painting and the ritual qualities of the murals themselves and thus allows merely selected members of the community to publicly speak.

A further quality which allows for a reading of Northern Irish murals as rituals is their recursiveness. As described in the first part of the article, they have been painted since the early nineteen hundreds. Many existing murals are being repainted on a regular basis to preserve them, sometimes they are even moved from one site to another, such as in the case of construction works. The probably most famous example is the free-standing gable at an intersection in (London)Derry, which proclaims that "You Are Now Entering Free Derry". The mural goes back to the civil rights movement and its demonstrations, including Bloody Sunday, of the nineteen seventies. The gable is not attached to a house anymore and the writing is regularly repainted.

Moreover, after a certain period of time, murals are sometimes painted over with a new, possibly more current, motive by the same muralists who painted the original. In addition, there is a clear repetition of particular motives and symbols over decades. Therefore, to briefly return to Rose's visual methodology, it is not only the site of the image's production which is repeated, but the site of the image itself likewise proves to display a highly repetitive content.

One of the functions of this recursiveness is the creation of an apparent historical continuity and stability. This might be most obvious in historical murals which emphasise the origin myths of republicans and loyalists, such as Irish mythology, particularly the heroism of Coechulain for the former and historic events such as the Battle of the Boyne or the Siege of Derry for the latter. I argue with Allen Feldman that

> [Loyalist and Republican origin myths] fulfil identical purposes: the origin guarantees the recursive character of history through spatial metaphor. The mimesis of the origin in present events endows the latter with coherence. Linearity and repetition, metaphorized as history, are deployed [...] to repress historicity – the anthropological capacity to generate dispersal, difference, and alterity in time and space. The use of history to repress historicity is a central ideological mechanism in the

political culture of Northern Ireland. And where this occurs, the recursive character of the historical is often expressed and always legitimated by geographical metaphor.[62]

Recursiveness creates, on the site of the image's audience, an assumption of unchanging social relationships, which, in turn, aims once more at the unification of a community.

It is likewise recursiveness which marks the murals' use by the media. Time and again, they accompany Northern Irish news items. Through this rather inflationary utilization of murals, often regardless of their content, they have come to symbolise the Northern Irish Troubles as such. Jarman even cites examples of film companies initiating the painting of murals in Cardiff, Manchester and Dublin in order to authenticate these places for the filming of dramas about the Troubles.[63]

Yet another characteristic of rituals is expressed by Victor Turner, the 'father' of theories of rituals. He argues that rituals possess a reflexive potential in the sense that they often express direct or encoded criticism.[64] This idea resonates in a number of writings on rituals:[65] They have been described as a site of problem solving, as carrying out important societal work, and are seen as the condensed expression of values and ideas of groups.[66] I argue that Northern Irish murals display reflexive potential. Not only do they constitute a permanent visual and physical/spatial presence of Northern Irish segregationism. They also directly react to and comment on current political events and thereby enter the discourse on Northern Irish politics.

Furthermore, the Northern Irish Troubles are typical as a context which engenders rituals. According to Max Gluckman and Victor Turner, the values emphasised by rituals are often those which are currently not ensured in a particular society. As a result, ritual behaviour often occurs in contexts where the social structure displays strong contradictions.[67] In Northern Ireland, this clearly is the case, since the values of neither side are ensured. Nationalist murals propagate the visionary values of a united Ireland, whereas their loyalist counterparts attempt to defend those values which, although still legally in place, are very much threatened by recent political developments.

Within such a context, the ritual serves as an orientation and compensates for or balances shortcomings of the social structure and at the same time provides an analysis of social differentiation. It produces a ritual catharsis through the symbolic expression of social conflicts. This ritual catharsis, in turn, engenders a strengthening of social cohesion.[68]

Thus, I have come full circle. The main quality, which allows a reading of the ritual qualities of Northern Irish murals and which in fact might be the most important aspect of rituals in general, is their 'community making' and the strategies by which 'unity' is achieved. This is in accordance with ethnologist Ivo Strecker, who emphasises that the aim of rituals is persuasion.[69] Reading these murals as community making rituals may help understand their complexity and open up possibilities of exploring them beyond their symbols.

Notes

1 Neil Jarman: "Painting Landscapes: The Place of Murals in the Symbolic Construction of Urban Space" <www.cain.ulst.ac.uk/bibdbs/murals/jarman.htm – 26 September 2005>.

2 Bill Rolston: *Drawing Support 2. Murals of War and Peace*, Belfast, 1998, p. i.

3 *Ibid.*

4 "War on the Walls" <www.northernireland.ideasfactory.com/art_design/features/ni_fea... – 28 September 2005>.

5 Rolston (1998: 12).

6 Bill Rolston: "Visions or Nightmares?" <www.Columbia.edu/cu/seminars (IrishStudies/Nov_2003_min... – 3 January 2005>.

7 Rolston (1998: vii).

8 *Ibid.*, i.

9 Bill Rolston: *Drawing Support 3. Murals and Transition in the North of Ireland*, Belfast, 2003, p. v.

10 Rolston: "Visions or Nightmares?", 2005.

11 Rolston (2003: x).

12 Lyell Davis: "Republican Murals, Identity, and Communication in Northern Ireland", *Public Culture* 13:1, 2001, 156.

13 Rolston: "Visions or Nightmares?", 2005.

14 "War on the Walls."

15 Davis (2001: 157).

16 *Ibid.*

17 "War on the Walls."

18 Rolston: "Visions or Nightmares?", 2005.

19 "Ulster's Ever-Changing Murals", University of Ulster News Releases on 30 July 2003 <www.ulster.ac.uk/news/releases/2003/872.html – 3 January 2005>.

20 Noel Large, quoted in William Cook: "The Long Drawn-out Struggle – Northern Ireland" <www.findarticles/p/articles/mi_m0FQP/is_4492_129/ai_... – 28 September 2005>.

21 "War on the Walls."

22 Pierre Bourdieu: *On Language and Symbolic Power*, Cambridge, 1991, p. 130.

23 Jarman (2005).

24 *Ibid.*

25 Tony Taylor: "Seeing the Writing on the Wall. Graffiti in History – from Pompeii to Belfast", The National Centre for History Education <www.hyperhistory.org/site/index14php?option=displaypage... – 3 January 2005>.

26 Cook (2005).

27 Jarman (2005).

28 *Ibid.*

29 Rolston: "Visions or Nightmares?", 2005.

30 David Welch: "Power of Propaganda", *History Today* 8, 1999, 26.

31 Davis (2001: 156).

32 Gillian Rose: *Visual Methodologies An Introduction to Visual Materials*, London, 2001, p. 11.

33 *Ibid.*, pp. 19-20.

34 Gerrit Herlyn: *Ritual und Übergangsritual in komplexen Gesellschaften. Sinn- und Bedeutungszuschreibungen zu Begriff und Theorie*, Hamburg, 2002, p. 41.

35 Dominic Bryan: *Orange Parades. The Politics of Ritual, Tradition and Control*, London, 2000, p. 14.

36 *Ibid.*

37 Paul Dixon: *Northern Ireland. The Politics of War and Peace*, Houndmills, Basingstoke, 2001, p. 40.

38 *Ibid.*, 42.

39 F.W. Boal and Russel Murry, quoted in Allen Feldman: *Formations of Violence. The Narrative of the Body and Political Terror in Northern Ireland*, Chicago, 1991, p. 35.

40 Bryan (2000: 20).

41 "Local Legends. The Hound of Ulster" <www.bbc.co.uk/legacies/myths_legends/northern_ireland/ni_7/article_1.shtml – 25 April 2006>.

42 Rolston: "Visions or Nightmares?", 2005.

43 E.g. Hans-Georg Soeffner, quoted in Herlyn (2002: 42); Sally Moore & Barbara Myerhoff, quoted in *Ibid.*, 41.

44 Catherine Bell: *Ritual: Perspectives and Dimensions*, New York, 1997, p. 45.
45 Bryan (2000: 27).
46 David I. Kertzer: *Ritual, Politics and Power*; New Haven, 1988, pp. 120-21.
47 Regina Bormann: *Raum, Zeit, Identität*, Opladen, 2001, p. 290.
48 Russell Murray and F.W. Boal quoted in Feldman (1991: 26).
49 *Ibid.*, 28.
50 *Ibid.*, 35.
51 *Ibid.*
52 Herlyn (2002: 37).
53 Bryan (2000: 8).
54 Dixon (2001: 34).
55 Foucault (1999: 68).
56 *Ibid.*, 70.
57 Caroline Humphrey & James Laidlaw: *The Archetypical Actions of Ritual: A Theory of Ritual*, Oxford, 1994, pp. 99, 106.
58 Bryan (2000: 18-19).
59 Jarman (2005).
60 Bill Rolston: "Culture, Conflict and Murals: The Irish Case" <www.zonezero.com/magazine/essays/distant/zcultu2.html – 3 January 2005>.
61 Bryan (2000: 8).
62 Feldman (1991: 18).
63 Jarman (2005).
64 Herlyn (2002: 30).
65 Catherine Bell, Thomas Gerholm, Rainer Wiedemann, quoted in *Ibid.*, 39.
66 Cf. also Ivo Strecker: "Auf dem Weg zu einer rhetorischen Ritualtheorie". – Alfred Schäfer & Michael Wimmer (Eds.): *Rituale und Ritualisierungen*, Opladen, 1998, p. 65.
67 *Ibid.*, 66.
68 Max Gluckman & Victor Turner quoted in *Ibid.*
69 *Ibid.*, 68.

Bibliography

Bell, Catherine: *Ritual: Perspectives and Dimensions*, New York, 1997.
Bormann, Regina: *Raum, Zeit, Identität*, Opladen, 2001.
Bourdieu, Pierre: *On Language and Symbolic Power*, Cambridge, 1991.
Bryan, Dominic: *Orange Parades. The Politics of Ritual, Tradition and Control*, London, 2000.

Davis, Lyell: "Republican Murals, Identity, and Communication in Northern Ireland", *Public Culture* 13:1, 2001, 155-158.

Dixon, Paul: *Northern Ireland. The Politics of War and Peace*, Houndmills, Basingstoke, 2001.

Feldman, Allen: *Formations of Violence. The Narrative of the Body and Political Terror in Northern Ireland*, Chicago, 1991.

Foucault, Michel: *Botschaften der Macht. Der Foucault-Reader Diskurs und Medien*. Ed.. Jan Engelmann, Stuttgart, 1999.

Herlyn, Gerrit: *Ritual und Übergangsritual in komplexen Gesellschaften. Sinn- und Bedeutungszuschreibungen zu Begriff und Theorie*, Hamburg, 2002.

Humphrey, Caroline & James Laidlaw: *The Archetypical Actions of Ritual: A Theory of Ritual*, Oxford, 1994.

Kertzer, David I.: *Ritual, Politics and Power*, New Haven, 1988.

Rose, Gillian: *Visual Methodologies An Introduction to Visual Materials*, London, 2001.

Rolston, Bill: *Drawing Support 2. Murals of War and Peace*, Belfast, 1998.

---: *Drawing Support 3. Murals and Transition in the North of Ireland*, Belfast, 2003.

Schäfer, Alfred & Michael Wimmer (Eds.): *Rituale und Ritualisierungen*, Opladen, 1998.

Strecker, Ivo: "Auf dem Weg zu einer rhetorischen Ritualtheorie". – Alfred Schäfer & Michael Wimmer (Eds.): *Rituale und Ritualisierungen*, Opladen, 1998, pp. 61-93.

Welch, David: "Power of Propaganda", *History Today*, 8, 1999, 24-26.

Wulf, Christoph *et al.*: *Das Soziale als Ritual*, Opladen, 2001.

Internet Resources

"Black Cab Tours Northern Ireland" <www.blackcabtoursni.com/belfast.html – 27 September 2005>.

Cook, William: "The Long Drawn-out Struggle – Northern Ireland" <www.findarticles.com/p/articles/mi_m0FQP/is_4492_129/ai_... – 28 September 2005>.

Cunningham, Stephen: "Alamo Hero Hailed by Ulster Kinfolk", Aljazeera.net on <www.english.aljazeera.net/english/templates/GAArchive.aspx?GUI... – 26 September 2005>.

"Go to Belfast", Belfast's Official Tourism Website <www.gotobelfast.com/localtours/viewdetail.cfm/Localtour_K – 27 September 2005>.

Jarman, Neil: "Painting Landscapes: The Place of Murals in the Symbolic Construction of Urban Space" <www.cain.ulst.ac.uk/bibdbs/murals/jarman.htm – 26 September 2005>.

"Local Legends. The Hound of Ulster" <www.bbc.co.uk/legacies/myths_legends/northern_ireland/ni_7/article_1.shtml – 25 April 2006>.

Rolston, Bill: "Culture, Conflict and Murals: The Irish Case" <www.zonezero.com/magazine/essays/distant/zcultu2.html – 3 January 2005>.

---: "Visions or Nightmares? Murals and Imagining the Future in Northern Ireland" (7 November 2003). Irish Studies Seminar at Columbia University. <www.columbia.edu/cu/seminars(IrishStudies/Nov_2003_min... – 3 January 2005>.

Taylor, Tony: "Seeing the Writing on the Wall. Graffiti in History – from Pompeii to Belfast", The National Centre for History Education <www.hyperhistory.org/site/index14php?option=displaypage... – 3 January 2005>.

"Ulster's Ever-Changing Murals", University of Ulster News Releases on 30 July 2003 <www.ulster.ac.uk/news/releases/2003/872.html – 3 January 2005>.

"War on the Walls" <www.northernireland.ideasfactory.com/art_design/ features/ni_fea... – 28 September 2005>.

Sebastian Berg (Chemnitz)

Multiculturalism, British Muslims and War[1]

1. A New Evil Empire

In his autobiographical book, *Desperately Seeking Paradise. Journeys of a Sceptical Muslim*, the British author and intellectual Ziauddin Sardar describes how, together with a number of friends, he experienced the events that ended the Cold War. After initial elation and a nightlong celebration when the Berlin wall was opened in November, 1989, they eventually began to think about the consequences for Muslim people in Europe. They feared the continent would turn again on its original 'other', making it the new 'evil empire' and predicted, as a reaction, Muslim retreats into conservatism and isolation. Or, as one of the friends summarized: "We'll be back to square one."[2] Seventeen years later, these prophecies seem to be not too far off the mark, especially after the war against Iraq in 2003 and the terrorist attacks on the London tube in 2005. Hence, in this article I analyse in how far the experience of war has influenced the perceptions mainstream British society (Britain's mostly white, Christian or post-Christian secular people) and British Muslims have of each other – at least as far as this is expressed in published discourse.

It is often claimed that the wars of the post-Cold War era have not been fought between Muslims and the West. There are, however, numerous and outspoken people who suggest to understand them along the lines of Samuel Huntington's 'clash of civilisations' thesis and, who, obviously, influence public opinion:[3] the pervasiveness and growth of 'Islamophobia' has been proven, for example, by two research projects carried out by the Runnymede Trust and published in 1997 and 2004.[4] The existence of 'Westophobia' needs no further proof after the tube attacks in London. And there were, of course, in the last fifteen years, a considerable number of wars in which Muslim civilians were killed by non-Muslim soldiers (in the first Gulf War, in Bosnia and Kosovo, and, under the heading of the 'war against terrorism', in Afghanistan and Iraq). We saw other conflicts, in which the West in general, or Britain in particular, stood accused of colluding with anti-Muslim forces, for example, in Palestine. Additionally, the recent past witnessed domestic conflicts in Britain – from the Rushdie affair in 1989 to the uprisings of predominantly Muslim youngsters in several cities of the North in 2001.

In the following, I will argue that in this context of war and conflict British perceptions of multiculturalism have changed too. Although multiculturalism has never been an uncontroversial concept in British politics, it has been supported, in a moderate version, by many on the centre-left. Most New Labour politicians, liberal academics, and 'race' specialists would have subscribed to a model like the following formulated by Floya Anthias and Nira Yuval-Davis in the early 1990s:

> Multiculturalism constructs society as composed of a hegemonic homogeneous majority and small unmeltable minorities with their own essentially different communities and cultures which have to be understood, accepted and basically left alone – since their differences are compatible with the hegemonic culture – in order for society to have harmonious relations.[5]

This belief in a peaceful compatibility has been shattered among people like the former Home Secretary, David Blunkett, or even Trevor Phillips, chair of the Commission for Racial Equality. In April 2004, Phillips characterised multiculturalism as an "outdated idea" and declared: "[T]here are some common values – democracy rather than violence, the common currency of the English language, honouring the culture of these islands, like Shakespeare and Dickens".[6] The new insistence on the necessity to embrace so-called British values responds to the alleged failure of British Muslims to integrate into mainstream society – which, allegedly, constitutes a threat to its cohesion and internal peace. The Muslim population, correspondingly, discuss whether they will have a future as British Muslims or just as Muslims in Britain – a fine distinction with consequences for their self-images, political activities, and educational efforts.

The transformation of the 'war against terror' into a war against territorial states, the debates on 'clashes of civilisations' and the questioning of British Muslim loyalties to the British state have contributed to an incremental abolition of multiculturalism and the rehabilitation of assimilation as the guiding principle of integration policies. This will be shown through an evaluation of published discourse – statements by politicians, comments in the mainstream press, and opinions expressed in the Muslim papers over the last couple of years.[7] The main focus will be on three questions:

- How do specialists, politicians, mainstream press editorials and opinion pages view British Muslims?
- How do specialists, politicians, mainstream press editorials and opinion pages judge multiculturalism?
- How do British Muslims, in some of their periodicals, view British society, politics, and demands for integration?

2. Enemy Within?

In the immediate aftermath of 9/11, politicians, fearing a backlash against the Muslim population of the UK, explicitly differentiated between terrorists and Muslims. In late September, 2001, Foreign Secretary Jack Straw declared: "Blaming Islam for what happened would be as wrong as blaming Christianity for sectarian attacks in Northern Ireland."[8] And Tony Blair explained: "What happened in America was not the work of Islamic terrorists. It was not the work of Muslim terrorists. It was the work of terrorists pure and simple."[9] Soon, however, the tone began to change. British Muslims' annoyance about the wars in Afghanistan and Iraq provoked questions about their loyalty. In particular, the government was concerned that the Muslim Council of Britain – very much a creation of New Labour – only reluctantly supported the war in Afghanistan.[10] Even for this lukewarm backing, the organisation was severely criticised by Muslim groups,[11] and it later declared its unambiguous opposition to the war in Iraq. This lack of enthusiasm of what the government considered to be mainstream Muslim Britain, combined with revelations that obviously also the UK accommodated people involved in global terrorism led to appeals to British Muslims to do more – more to condemn Islamist violence and more to integrate. In May 2002, for example, the Labour politician and minister for Europe, Peter Hain, pointed out:

> We very much welcome the contribution the Moslem community makes to British culture. They enrich our culture, they are welcome here. But there is a tendency among a minority to isolate themselves and that leaves them vulnerable to either exploitation by Osama-bin-Laden type extremists and fanatics on the one hand or targeting by racists and Nazis on the other. That is where we need to work together to confront this problem.[12]

Hain's statement, met by widespread approval in the press, still spoke about a minority of isolated people and the need to work together. Two years later, Trevor Phillips, chair of the Commission for Racial Equality, had moved on. He declared:

> Muslim protestations that the faith is opposed to the crimes being carried out in its name, that it embodies diversity, and that it regards equality of women as intrinsic to Islam, can only be taken seriously if we see those assertions in our own communities.[13]

This statement reveals serious doubts about the values of *all* British Muslims and is symptomatic for the increasing distance between even moderate Muslims and the British centre-left. Because this alienation was likely to cost the Labour Party important votes, the Chancellor, Gordon Brown, tried to identify new common ground shortly before the 2005 general elections. He emphasised Muslims' contribution to the British economy and the existence of common values such as a belief in fair play, social justice, and equality.[14] In electoral terms at least, Brown's initiative was of limited success. Two months later, of course, the climate deteriorated with the suicide attacks on the London tube. Tony Blair, in his speeches, substituted 'the war against extremism' for 'the war against terrorism'.[15] This is more than a simple change of words. Terrorism is a crime while extremism is a way of thinking that is supposed to prepare and legitimise such crime. Thus, the war against extremism has more ambitious goals.

The media had already started denouncing Muslim militancy and radicalism during the Rushdie affair and, shortly after, questioned Muslim loyalties in the 1991 Gulf War.[16] London was reported as being the "Middle East's intellectual capital" as early as the mid-1990s,[17] and former anti-communist freedom fighters in exile incrementally mutated into "fanatics with refugee status" and "mad mullahs".[18] After 2001, even liberal papers like the *Guardian* offered people such as David Coleman, from Migrationwatch UK, the opportunity to claim the non-assimilability of Muslims and to call for immigration policies that explicitly excluded them.[19] Also liberal journalists, such as the *Guardian's* Polly Toynbee, were alarmed because they saw it as increasingly difficult to criticise Islam as a religion without being accused of Islamophobia, i.e. of hating Muslims.[20] However, in several cases even the quality media were not able or willing to distinguish between terrorists and Muslims, let alone between Islam and Muslims. Or how else should one explain the following anecdote, told by Shagufta Yaqub, editor of the British Muslim monthly *Q-News*, shortly after 9/11: "BBC 5 wanted me on a show to tell them what's going through Osama bin-Laden's mind. How on earth should I know? I told them to find a psychiatrist."[21]

3. Return of a Bogey?

Not only discourses on Muslims have hardened but also the views on multiculturalism. A new appreciation of assimilation goes along with a revival of renunciations of multiculturalism as they were all too familiar in large sections of the British press in the 1980s. David Blunkett, when Home Secretary, became the leading government critic of multiculturalism. His interventions took account of the experiences of 9/11 but also of the uprisings in the northern cities of Oldham, Burnley and Bradford earlier in 2001.[22] He argued that multicultural policies had supported tendencies towards self-segregation which, in turn, had produced alienation, violence, and even terror. For him, multiculturalism became an "excess of cultural diversity and moral relativism".[23] He urged: "We need to say that we will not tolerate what we would not accept ourselves under the guise of accepting a different culture."[24] He criticised the practice of 'forced marriages' which, obviously, he seemed to conflate with 'arranged marriages', demanded an oath of allegiance as precondition for gaining British citizenship (a move for which *The Sun* called him a "brave man"[25]) and generally pleaded for "a sense of identity and belonging".[26] This should be built on an embrace of British values and on the duty to learn the English language. Command of the language, according to him, prevented cultural schizophrenia and allowed "participation in wider modern culture".[27] More surprising, perhaps, than Blunkett's positions were opinions among professionals from the 'race relations industry'. Again, it was Trevor Phillips, chair of the Commission for Racial Equality, who tried to define British core values and characteristics. Apart from the bow to high culture mentioned above (Shakespeare and Dickens), he offered, in 2004, a surprisingly eclectic mix: tolerance, eccentricity, parliamentary democracy, energy in the big cities.[28] Raminder Singh, a former vice-chair of the Commission for Racial Equality and author of a report investigating the 2001 uprisings in Bradford, complained about two separate worlds in the city. Furthermore, using Thatcherite terminology, he argued that the high visibility of British Muslims would leave white people with a feeling of being "swamped".[29]

Such statements were welcomed by most of the press. The *Daily Mail* applauded Trevor Phillips: "How right he is. How sad that *bien pensant* opinion has taken so long to wake up to the importance of integration, patriotism and pride in this great nation."[30] The *Sun* recycled its 1980s allegations but added a specific anti-Muslim spin:

> Multiculturalism means celebrating Diwali but banning Christmas. It means tolerating a mosque named after Saddam Hussein in the middle of our second biggest city but banning the Union Jack on the ground that it is offensive to minorities. It means free speech for mad Mullahs burning our flag in Regent's Park and vowing death to Britain, America and the Jews, but 'No Platform For Racists' for those who beg to differ. It means the BBC banning Land of Hope and Glory and Rule Britannia from the Proms and the World Service TV ruling that it is 'inappropriate' for presenters to wear poppies. Multiculturalism means worshipping all cultures and traditions, other than those of the majority. It means teaching African Studies but ignoring British history in schools. It means denigrating our ancestors' achievements and making our children ashamed of their country's past.[31]

From the *Sun*, such a statement was not too surprising. But the scepticism about multiculturalism was shared by more sophisticated papers. They often took up the issue of war and the fear of retaliation. Nicholas Frazer, a specialist on Europe's New Right, expressed his apprehensions in the following way:

> How much difference is acceptable when 13 per cent of British Muslims declare themselves in agreement with the aims of al-Quaeda? [...] Shakespeare, Dickens and civic education are not to be sneered at under any circumstances, but by themselves they may not help much. [...] How do we preserve the place of mixed loyalties that Britain has become? How do we protect ourselves? Can anyone begin to guess where we will be if someone sneaks a briefcase with a dirty bomb into central London?[32]

One day after the actual explosion of bombs in London, the *Daily Express* returned to the question of values and loyalties:

> We may now be entering an era in which the slow-to-anger British people will become more militant about defending the traditional tenets of their society. They will be less ready to indulge those who refuse to abide by these values; [...] how to ask more from some ethnic minority communities, while reassuring them they are valued and respected.[33]

4. "British Muslims or Muslims in Britain"?

The last two quotes reveal a fear that, in times of war, is understandable enough. However, over the last couple of years, fear has become a widespread feeling among the British Muslim population, too. They fear to be asked for ever more, while being accepted and valued increasingly less. This perception is accompanied by a deep anger and frustration about the fact that the British government denies any possible link between the positions it takes in international politics and the growing radicalism among sections of British Muslims. The stances taken and strategies chosen by British Muslims to deal with their increasingly vulnerable position in society varied widely. They reached from Muslim Labour MPs supporting the Iraq war via activists participating in the Stop the War Coalition to those who claimed that Muslim political activity should be limited to the creation of a pan-Muslim caliphate. The Islamist group Hizb-ut-Tahrir, for example, which has followers especially among university students and professionals, held a conference in 2003 with the title: "Are you British or are you Muslim?" According to internal estimates, this event was attended by 6,000 to 7,000 persons.[34] The huge majority of Muslim people, however, seem to believe in some form of integration and in a general compatibility of Islamic and British values. This was the result of a poll by the Commission for Racial Equality in 2004.[35] Nevertheless, most are strongly opposed to Britain's role in the 'war on terrorism', a fact repeatedly emphasised by the monthly publication *Muslim News*. The consequence seems to be the declining wish 'to integrate'. According to an *ICM-Guardian* poll, also published in 2004, the number of those who thought they should do more to ingrate went down from 41 to 33 per cent between 2002 and 2004. The number of those suspecting they had already done too much simultaneously rose from 17 to 26 per cent.[36]

Mohammad Siddique Seddon, a research fellow at the Islamic Foundation in Leicester, explained in *Q-News* in spring 2004 that a lot of Muslims faced a dilemma: "Whilst the reality of an emerging identity that is increasingly British is experienced, finding a voice to express it is increasingly difficult."[37] This is exacerbated by the pressure to assimilate. The difference between the two concepts of assimilation and integration is implicitly explained by the young editor of a life style magazine in the *Guardian* in late 2004: "Integration does not mean 'become'. It means being involved, and the changing face of Britain means that there are a lot of different types of Britishness."[38] 'Being involved' for numerous Muslims includes a critique of Britain's, and the West's, role in international politics. Shortly, they blame them for not living up to their own standards, recounting the many examples of wars, state coups, implanted dictatorships, incidences of torture and murder in which western states, militaries, and secret services have been involved. The *Muslim News'* August 2005 issue criticized the "complete lack of consideration of British foreign policy to breeding extremists".[39] And Fuad Nahdi, chief editor of *Q-News*, emphasised the mixture of strong feelings on the war in Iraq and the daily experience of socio-economic marginalisation.[40] After meetings organised by the Home Office to consult (or, as some claimed, rather to instruct) Muslim communities in the aftermath of the attacks of July 2005, some participants expressed a bleak picture of their position in British society:

> The echoing questions following the meeting were: Are we the new Irish in our treatment by the British government? Are we the new blacks due to the colour of our skin? Are we the new Jews due to our faith? With the collective numbers of Muslims in Britain amounting to some

1.8 million, that would create social instability like never before witnessed within our society.[41]

This does not mean that British Muslims consider themselves to be passive victims. In particular, a growing number of Muslim 'organic intellectuals' has gone public with calls for a critical engagement with British politics, for analyses of the situation of Muslims in British society, or of internal community problems. Occasionally, they demand a reinterpretation of Islamic theology that must be

> independent from the Arab or South Asian socio-cultural influences and must be an attempt to bring Britain's existential experiences to the text, what is typical Britain and searching for a British Muslim intellectual self-definition.[42]

However, doubts remain in how far British society and politics will be able and willing to notice such innovative efforts in times of war. This point was made in a different context by Ahdaf Soueif, commenting on reactions to the Abu Ghraib torture photographs in the Guardian:

> The media are fearful that these images will go down badly in the Arab world because 'they show Muslim men being humiliated by American women'. Again, the not-so-subtle reduction of the Arab world to an entity that reacts only to religious prodding. Actually the photographs have confirmed people's belief that the US and Britain are not in Iraq as an act of goodwill. They have strengthened the feeling that there is a deep racism underlying the occupiers' attitudes to Arabs, Muslims and the third world generally.[43]

Neither the crimes at Abu Ghraib nor these reactions to them, of course, acted as incentives for Muslims to 'integrate' into British society.

5. Fruits of War

British debates about multiculturalism, integration, and identities have become polarised in recent times. The belief in the compatibility of different cultural identities and practices (which, nevertheless, share a number of universal values) has been weakened and replaced – at least partly – by essentialist sets of ideas whose most extreme forms are Islamophobia and Westophobia. In his 2002 article "Muslims and the Politics of Multiculturalism in Britain", the British sociologist Tariq Modood defines this process as a discursive operation that equates terror with Islamism and Islamism with Islam.[44] A complementary, though weaker and arguably reactive, counter-discursive operation associates, I think, the 'war on terror' with the West, and the West as a whole with a racist, orientalist enemy of the Muslim world. In other words, the experience of war suggests a logic of homogenisation and dichotomies.

This has consequences. It invites to demand assimilation from British Muslims, to explain socio-economic and political conflicts (such as the uprisings in the northern cities in 2001) with cultural differences, to declare war not just on 'terrorism' but also on 'extremism'. And it leads to a re-conceptualisation of widely-held values as British ones – a process in which hierarchies of perceived national or religious cultures and civilisations are established up to the point where war becomes nothing but the export of 'higher' values, or cynically speaking, a specific kind of overseas aid. Among British Muslims, the consequences are the tendency towards a retreat into conservative versions of Islam, the loosening of one's ties with British society, and perhaps a turn to radical Islamism – as feared by Ziauddin Sardar's friend in 1989.

This discursive polarisation results from an uneven struggle over concepts. What mainstream discourse calls integration today is, in fact, assimilation. Muslims' understanding of integration is consequently stigmatised as its denial. The British writer and intellectual Tariq Ali, paraphrasing Samuel Huntington, called the present confrontations in international politics "clashes of fundamentalisms".[45] British debates on Muslims and multiculturalism obviously are moves towards such 'clashes of fundamentalisms' on a smaller scale.

For the near future, there are two possible scenarios. Either British Muslim criticisms of, and protests against, Britain's wars are regarded as legitimate acts of active integration (which, according to Tariq Modood, is nothing but the participation in a discursive public sphere[46]) or better, active citizenship – and thus must be heard, understood, and taken into consideration. Or criticisms and protests are interpreted as illegitimate acts, symbolising a refusal to integrate. In this case, they can be ignored. Only the first of these alternatives would offer the chance to reverse the polarisation of public discourse and save the multicultural settlement. The present Labour government's unwillingness to acknowledge any link between Britain's wars and the spread of radical Islamism as well as its track record of implementing mechanisms of control and discipline make the positive scenario, unfortunately, the less likely one.[47]

Notes

1 A shorter German-language version of this article was published in *Blätter für deutsche und internationale Politik*, 4, 2006, 483-91.

2 Ziauddin Sardar: *Desperately Seeking Paradise. Journeys of a Sceptical Muslim*, London, 2004, p. 310.

3 Samuel Huntington: *The Clash of Civilizations and the Remaking of World Order*, New York, 1996.

4 Runnymede Trust: *Islamophobia: a Challenge for Us All*, London, 1997; Runnymede Trust: *Islamophobia: Issues, Challenges and Action*, London, 2004.

5 Floya Anthias & Nira-Yuval Davis: *Racialized Boundaries. 'Race', Gender, Colour, and Class and the Anti-Racist Struggle*, London, 1992, p. 158.

6 Quoted in Anonymous: "Multiculturalism Is Dead, Says Race Chief", *Daily Mail*, 5 April 2004.

7 My focus is on the mainstream press as well as Muslim magazines – in the latter group particularly the two monthly publications *Q-News* and *Muslim News* because they work from a pan-Muslim rather than an ethnically specific perspective.

8 Quoted in Tony Brooks: "Fear Over Attacks on Muslims", *The Daily Express*, 20 September 2001.

9 Quoted in Trevor Kavanagh: "PM Slams Racists for 'Despicable Acts' on Muslims", *The Sun*, 28 September 2001.

10 The *Muslim Council of Britain* was founded to give moderate Muslims in Britain a collective voice. Its membership consisted of about 250 Islamic and Muslim organisations of different sizes. See Madeleine Bunting: "Pronouncing a Fatwa on Extremes", *The Guardian*, 20 November 1997.

11 See Faisal Bodi: "Muslims Are a Multitude, not a Lone Voice", *The Guardian*, 22 October 2001.

12 Quoted in Graeme Wilson: "Moslems Failing to Integrate, Says Hain", *The Daily Mail*, 13 May 2002.

13 Quoted in Steve Doughty: " Muslims 'Must Show Their Hate for Terror'", *The Daily Mail*, 16 November 2004.

14 See Andrew Sparrow: "Britain's Muslims Praised by Brown", *The Daily Telegraph*, 29 March 2005.

15 See Anonymous: "Government Engaging with Muslim Communities", *Muslim News*, August 2005.

16 See also John Solomos & Les Back: *Race, Politics and Social Change*, London 1995, pp.142-3.

17 See Adam Le Bor: "Halfway House of the Hopeful", *The Guardian*, 7 September 1996.

18 See Anonymous: "We Have the Laws. Use Them", *The Sunday Telegraph*, 17 July 2005.

19 See John Rex: "An Afterword on the Situation of British Muslims in a World Context". – In Tahir Abbas (Ed.): *Muslim Britain. Communities Under Pressure*, London 2005, p. 242.
   Migrationwatch UK describes itself as an independent and non-political organisation which intends to inform the British public about immigration numbers and policies without offering any programmatic recommendations. This, however, contradicts Coleman's statements. See <http://www. migrationwatchuk.org – 03 February 2006>.

20 See Polly Toynbee: "We Must Be Free to Criticise Without Being Called Racist", *The Guardian*, 18 August 2004.

21 Quoted in Jack O'Sullivan: "Voices Behind the Veil", *The Guardian*, 24 September 2001.

22 The disturbances started when fascist groups tried to march through city quarters inhabited by relatively high numbers of British Asian people. For an analysis of the reasons and consequences of the uprisings see, Arun Kundnani: "From Oldham to Bradford. The Violence of the Violated", *Race and Class* 43:2, 2001, 23-40.

23 Quoted in Tahir Abbas & Parveen Akhtar: "The New Sociology of British Ethnic and Cultural Relations. The Experience of British South Asian Muslims in the Post-September 11 Climate". – In Holger Henke (Ed.): *Crossing Over. Comparing Recent Migration in the United States and in Europe*, Lanham 2005, p. 134.

24 Quoted in John Kampfner: "British Values Now Come in Many Colours", *The Daily Express*, 10 December 2001.

25 See Anonymous: "Brave Blunkett", *The Sun*, 10 December 2001.

26 Quoted in David Hughes & Rebecca Paveley: "Blunkett Wrong on Asians Speaking English, Says Vaz", *The Daily Mail*, 17 September 2002.

27 *Ibid*.

28 See Anonymous: "Multiculturalism Is Dead, Says Race Chief", *Daily Mail*, 5 April 2004.

29 See Neil Tweedie: "Frightened Whites in Bradford's 'Two World'", *The Daily Telegraph*, 2 November 2001.

30 Anonymous: "Change of Tune", *The Daily Mail*, 5 April 2004.

31 Richard Littlejohn: "Multiculturalism Means Always Having to Say that You Are Sorry", *The Sun*, 9 November 2001.

32 Nicholas Frazer: "Opinions of Difference", *Financial Times Magazine*, 17 April 2004.

33 Patrick O'Flynn: "Blair's Steely Resolve Is Needed More than Ever", *The Daily Express*, 8 July 2005.

34 See Parveen Akhtar: "'(Re)turn to Religion' and Radical Islam". – In Tahir Abbas (Ed.): *Muslim Britain. Communities Under Pressure*, London 2005, p. 164.

35 See Anonymous: "Shared Values", *The Daily Mail*, 13 September 2004.

36 See Anonymous: "Race Relations Disintegrating Societies", *The Guardian*, 16 March 2004.

37 Mohammad Siddique Seddon Seddon: "British Muslims or Muslims in Britain?" *Q-News* 354, March 2004, 33.

38 Quoted in Audrey Gillan *et al.*: "The Big Debate: Young, Muslim and British", *The Guardian*, 30 November 2004.

39 Anonymous: "Government Engaging with Muslim Communities", *Muslim News*, August 2005.

40 See Fuat Nahdi: "Bring Back Real Islam to Our Shores", *The Guardian*, 7 April 2004.

41 Anonymous, August 2005.

42 Michael Mumisa: "The Fatwa 'Supplement' and Why It was a Mistake", *Muslim News*, August 2005.

43 Ahdaf Soueif: "This Torture Started at the Very Top", *The Guardian*, 5 May 2004.

44 See Tariq Modood: "Muslims and the Politics of Multiculturalism in Britain". – In Eric Hershberg & Kevin W. Moore (Eds.): *Critical Views of September 11. Analyses from Around the World*, New York 2002, p.193.

45 Tariq Ali: *The Clash of Fundamentalisms. Crusades, Jihads and Modernity*, London 2002.

46 See Tariq Modood: "Muslims and the Politics of Multiculturalism in Britain". – In: Eric Hershberg, Kevin W. Moore (Eds.): *Critical Views of September 11. Analyses from Around the World*, New York 2002, pp. 193-208.

47 For a critical evaluation of the security measures taken by European governments (among them the British one) over the last years see, Liz Fekete: "Anti-Muslim Racism and the European Security State", *Race & Class* 46:1, 2004, 3-29.

Bibliography

Abbas, Tahir & Parveen Akhtar: "The New Sociology of British Ethnic and Cultural Relations. The Experience of British South Asian Muslims in the Post-September 11 Climate". – In Holger Henke (Ed.): *Crossing Over. Comparing Recent Migration in the United States and in Europe*, Lanham, 2005, pp. 130-146.

Akhtar, Parveen: "'(Re)turn to Religion' and Radical Islam". – In Tahir Abbas (Ed.): *Muslim Britain. Communities Under Pressure*, London, 2005, pp. 164-176.

Ali, Tariq: *The Clash of Fundamentalisms. Crusades, Jihads and Modernity*, London, 2002.

Anthias, Floya & Nira Yuval-Davis: *Racialized Boundaries. 'Race', Gender, Colour; and Class and the Anti-Racist Struggle*, London, 1992.

Fekete, Liz: "Anti-Muslim Racism and the European Security State", *Race & Class* 46:1, 2004, 3-29.

Huntington, Samuel: *The Clash of Civilisations and the Remaking of World Order*, New York, 1996.

Kundnani, Arun: "From Oldham to Bradford. The Violence of the Violated", *Race & Class* 43:2, 2001, 105-110.

Modood, Tariq: "Muslims and the Politics of Multiculturalism in Europe". – In Eric Hershberg & Kevin W. Moore (Eds.): *Critical Views of September 11. Analyses from Around the World*, New York, 2002, pp. 193-208.

Rex, John: "An Afterword on the Situation of British Muslims in a World Context". – In Tahir Abbas (Ed.): *Muslim Britain. Communities Under Pressure*, London, 2005, pp. 235-243.

Runnymede Trust: *Islamophobia: a Challenge for Us All*, London 1997.

---: *Islamophobia: Issues, Challenges and Action*, London 2004.

Sardar, Ziauddin: *Desperately Seeking Paradise. Journeys of a Sceptical Muslim*, London, 2004.

Seddon, M. S.: "British Muslims or Muslims in Britain?", *Q-News* 354, 2004, 31-33.

Solomos, John & Les Back: *Race, Politics and Social Change*, London, 1995.

Contributors' Addresses

Dr. Sebastian Berg, Britische und Amerikanische Kultur- und Länderstudien, Philosophische Fakultät, Technische Universität Chemnitz, Reichenhainer Str. 39, D-09126 Chemnitz.

Daniel Dornhofer, Institut für England- und Amerikastudien, Johann Wolfgang Goethe-Universität, Grüneburgplatz 1, D-60323 Frankfurt am Main.

Prof. Dr. Gabriele Linke, Institut für Anglistik/Amerikanistik, Philosophische Fakultät, Universität Rostock, D-18051 Rostock.

Prof. Dr. Hartmut Möller, Hochschule für Musik und Theater Rostock, Beim St.-Katharinenstift 8, D–18055 Rostock.

Professor Michael Paris, Department of Humanities, University of Central Lancashire, Preston, Lancashire, PR1 2HE, United Kingdom.

Dr. Holger Rossow, Institut für Anglistik/Amerikanistik, Philosophische Fakultät, Universität Rostock, D-18051 Rostock.

Dr. Christian Schmitt-Kilb, Institut für Anglistik/Amerikanistik, Philosophische Fakultät, Universität Rostock, D-18051 Rostock.

Dr. Thomas F. Schneider, Erich Maria Remarque-Friedenszentrum, Markt 6, D-49074 Osnabrück.

Jun.-Prof. Kathleen Starck, FB 7 Anglistik/Amerikanistik, Universität Osnabrück, Neuer Graben 40, D–49069 Osnabrück.

Professor Penny Summerfield, Head of School, School of Arts, Histories and Cultures, University of Manchester, Manchester M13 9PL, United Kingdom.

Dr. Doris Teske, Didaktik der Anglistik, Institut für Anglistik, Universität Leipzig, Beethovenstr. 15, D-04107 Leipzig.